Also by
G. Michael Dobbs

Escape!
How animation broke into the mainstream in the 1990's

For Mary Cassidy —

*Without whom very little in my life
would have been possible.*

15 Minutes With...

40 Years of Interviews

G. Michael Dobbs

To Janet !
a fellow artist !
Mike Dobbs

Bear Manor Media

Published in the USA by:
BearManor Media
PO Box 71426
Albany, Georgia 31708

ISBN: 9781593935924

Printed in the United States of America.

Book design by Mark Masztal of reMARKable Design
Cover illustrations ©2014 by Mark Masztal

Cover illustration key l to r: Ray Bradury, Leslie Glass,
John 'Bowzer' Bowman, Alice Cooper, Lillian Gish, Leonard Nimoy,
Maureen O'Hara, Vincent Price, Don McLean, Buster Crabbe,
'Rowdy' Roddy Piper and Dave Atell.

Acknowledgements

Seldom do journalists want to recognize that their celebrity interviews are mostly made possible through the cooperation of publicists. I gather it's some sort of cold war that has been going on for decades. I will gladly buck the trend and thank all of those who have helped me.

Naturally, I deeply appreciate the time and willingness of every one of the people interviewed for this book. I'm sorry there were many that were not included.

My wife, Mary Cassidy, lent invaluable support and criticism of this project, and the book's wonderful design was the handiwork of designer and illustrator Mark Masztal. He can be reached through www.masztal.com. Hire him for your project.

Lastly, I must thank my parents, now both gone, for their support of their writer son, even though I know my career mystified and worried them both.

Table of Contents

Mixed Bag

The Comedians

G. Michael Dobbs

INTRODUCTION

Perhaps the first question any journalist has when they land an interview is "How much time do I have?"

Unless you represent a major media outlet, the chances are you will have ten to twenty minutes to speak with someone well known. That's not much time and it requires writers not only to prepare to use those few minutes wisely but also to be able to improvise. Many actors will tell you the secret to a performance is listening and reacting. The same holds true to interviewing.

I would guess that ninety-five percent of all reporters working right now haven't had the opportunity of doing what was long considered the gold standard of interviews: those found in the front of Playboy. Those writers traditionally were given lengthy access to their subjects over a period of several meetings and then carefully edited the interview together in such a way to present a well rounded look at a person.

Over the years, being profiled in Playboy became prestigious. Today, a profile in Vanity Fair or a conversation on a morning news show or "Fresh Air," is also considered the height of the interview.

In a professional writing career that started in 1975, I've had one opportunity to do multiple interviews with someone that lasted more than fifteen minutes and that was with William Gaines, the publisher of the much respected EC line of comics in the 1950s and the publisher of MAD magazine.

The opportunities to do intense sit-downs don't come very often if you are a working class journalist.

Most of the time when a reporter has some time with someone famous there is a purpose attached to that interview and invariably that subject has something to sell. A book, television show, a movie, a new record, or a political objective are probably the most common reasons anyone mildly famous would want to speak with a writer.

Otherwise, why submit yourself to something you can't control? Perhaps the only time a celebrity would allow himself or herself to be intensively grilled is if it panders to their vanity. If a major magazine, for instance, selects a particular person for a lengthy profile, there is certainly an unmistakable element of ego buffing.

The key to a good interview is to allow the subject to get his or her plug into the story, but to try to find the time to ask something that makes your few minutes with this person and your story different.

One of my journalism professors, a former Chicago newspaper reporter, said all of the best interviews he conducted were in bars. Somehow that sounded sort of romantic to me when I attended college in the 1970s. That was hardcore – a reporter in a cheap suit getting some elected official to spill the beans through a liberal application of booze with one eye on his watch and the other on his notebook.

The scene has the ring of being from "The Front Page," or my favorite newspaper movie "Five Star Final" – catch it the next time it's on Turner Classic Movies.

I've interviewed hundreds of people. Most were not famous. Some – many of which are in this book – were. Only two of those interviews were conducted in a bar – once with a Penthouse magazine centerfold and once with an exotic dancer who was staging a retro burlesque show.

So much for the romance from the era when reporters wore fedoras with a press pass stuck in the band, drank their Scotch neat, and called into a newspaper to speak with a re-write man.

The fact is, most interviews are done at the convenience and schedule of the subject and the more famous a person is – or the hotter he or she might happen to be at the time – the probability grows that a writer will have to jump through many hoops to get what he or she needs.

If a star has a new movie out and you get on the list to speak with him or her for 10 minutes then you call at the appointed time, ask your questions and say goodbye. You don't meet her at her hotel room when she is in town or at a high-end restaurant for an extended sit-down, if you are a working class writer such as myself.

Instead you work with a publicist in securing the time and you find out if there are restrictions to what you can ask. Sometimes those restrictions are for legal reasons; sometimes it's about ego.

If you are working on a story about an outstanding investigation, the district attorney may speak with you but won't comment – at least on the record – on anything unresolved.

I spent five years as a local radio talk show host and one of my first interviews was with a state senator – later a member of Congress – who told me off the air at the beginning of my program that he wouldn't talk about some particular issue. I acquiesced to his demand, although I hated doing so.

Why? I wanted to preserve my access to him in the future. This is the game you have to play with news sources, many times elected officials. If you embarrass them, they are not going to speak at all with you in the future.

A reporter has to walk a line between doing the story that needs to be done and understanding reality. Some times idealism wins at this game and some times reality wins.

If you decide to bash someone, make sure you don't wound the person. Instead, "kill" him, because if they can hurt you in the future, they will.

With people from show business, violating restrictions might mean a publicist won't cooperate with you in the future or it might result in a celebrity ending the interview much earlier than you hoped. Of course that can also make for a good story.

It's always wise to negotiate about restrictions, to make sure that perhaps some of that forbidden information can be discussed.

With celebrity interviews, I've seldom encountered the problems of someone speaking off the record, as it is usually politicians who want to do that. Essentially, someone speaking off the record wants you to know something, but you cannot attribute any of that material to that person directly. That's when you see phrases such as "according to a source close to the governor" being used, chances are that source was the governor.

Many of the interviews one sees on television are the end result of both negotiations and pre-interviewing. A producer will go over questions or subjects to make sure everyone is happy with the direction of the interview.

Some of the interviews in this book had some restrictions, but there were no pre-arranged questions and answers.

When I was on talk radio in the 1980s, I jumped at the chance of having actress and businesswoman Cassandra Peterson on my show. She is better known as Elvira, Mistress of the Dark. The publicist came on the telephone prior to the live interview and told me that I wasn't interviewing Peterson, but instead Elvira.

The idea of interviewing a character was not what I had in mind. The segment was lame. I stank trying to set up improvised comedy bits.

In 2011, I had the chance to interview Peterson again. This time it went well as I spoke to Peterson and not her alter ego. At the end of the interview, I told her what had happened years before. Peterson, who was a member of the famed comedy troupe The Groundlings, is a friend of Paul Ruebens, better known as Pee-wee Herman.

She said that back in the 1980s she was impressed that Ruebens never broke character even in interviews and she wanted to do that herself. We had a good laugh about it.

Some interviewers believe strongly in doing a minimal amount of research because they believe they are representing an average reader or viewer who is fairly ignorant on the subject. This approach worked well for Larry King, but then he was as famous, if not more, than his subjects. I watched a few interviews conducted by King in which his approach actually wasted time. I wanted him to get on with a meaty question instead of the soft ones he was throwing.

A regular working reporter doesn't have the luxury of assuming an interview subject will be gracious when asked questions that reveal the reporter's ignorance.

I believe in doing research because it has been my experience that if you actually prove to a subject you know something about them, they will favorably respond.

Also doing research may change whatever prejudice or perspective you might have about the subject.

An example of this was when I interviewed Clayton Moore, the actor who played the Lone Ranger in the long-running television series. I made a point of not talking about the Lone Ranger until about mid-way through the interview. I spoke with him about his entry into show business and roles he had that didn't involve wearing a mask.

My reward was Moore saying warmly to me, "You really know some thing about my career."

At the end of the interview, he said "Adios amigo!" I teared up. After all this was a childhood hero of mine. Thank goodness I was on radio.

Being a fan can work in your favor in an interview if you don't fixate on questions that seem obsessive and if you show that you actually do appreciate the person's work and you're not just blowing smoke.

I interviewed actor and director Leonard Nimoy about an exhibit of his photos in a local art gallery. I didn't say a word about "Star Trek," despite being a fan. It wouldn't have made sense within the context of the conversation.

If I'm a fan of someone, I will often admit it as I've learned over the years that it is one way to break the ice and to relieve my own nervousness.

Revealing that you actually like someone's work provides a bit of humanity to a process that can be very repetitive to celebrities. I had the opportunity to speak to actress Maureen O'Hara and told her the truth: I had had a crush on her since I was about twelve and I thought she was a very under-rated actress.

Both are true statements. She looked at me and said she agreed with me – she had been under-rated. The interview went well.

On the other hand, sometimes you meet someone whom you admire and find out the worst. I loved the music of Don McLean, and when I interviewed him the encounter was so negative it put me off listening to his recordings for years.

People frequently make assumptions when speaking with a reporter that they share knowledge on a subject. For me, interviews are about learning and if I do not understand something, I slow things down and make sure I'm keeping up.

When I've not done my homework, I've paid for it. When first interviewing comic Jim Breuer I was under the impression he was still on "Saturday Night Live." That was a mistake and Breuer – whom I've interviewed three times – let me have it in a good-natured way.

Having a list of questions is also invaluable, although one has to go with the flow of the conversation. I had exactly ten minutes with rock legend Alice Cooper and every minute had to count. Cooper was courteous, highly professional, sharp and expected me not to waste his time. I didn't.

If you're a journalist, it's imperative you watch institutions that create news besides city hall. Colleges, museums, and entertainment venues are the local places that bring in the celebrities who can become interview material. I'm always surprised when local media outlets fail to understand three journalistic truths: first, the average person is interested in famous people, and especially interested if they are coming to their area; second, the average person would like to know in advance of a celebrity's appearance; and third, the celebrity is seeking a full venue for his or her appearance and might be willing to do an interview to help sell tickets.

It's amazing how many editors do not understand those three dictums.

How did I get into writing, much less interviewing? When I was a young teen, I became seriously interested in movies – especially horror, science fiction and fantasy – and there was no one at my small town high school who shared my interests.

Listen, getting excited about the new issue of "Famous Monsters of Filmland" was something I learned not to speak about at Granby Junior Senior High School in the somewhat rural town of Granby, Mass. It's little wonder I didn't date until I was a senior.

Through "FM," though, I learned of the world of fanzines – amateur magazines published by geeks like me. Interesting enough, there were no words like "nerd" or "geek" then. We were just fans.

I was thrilled to find fellow fans and decided to publish my own 'zine as a means to communicate, if nothing else. I didn't want to make money. Luckily for me, my father, who was an industrial arts teacher, not only had his own spirit duplicator machine at home – so I had a printing press – but he also taught me how to silk screen.

And so I launched my fanzine "Inertron." The name came from the substance that enabled comic strip hero Buck Rogers to defy gravity in the twenty-fifth century.

My interests undoubtedly mystified my parents, but my dad kept his remarks to a minimum and my mom helped me by being the typist for the magazine.

My 'zine never had more than 100 readers, but it was the reason I became a journalist. I was hooked on writing.

I quickly learned that what drew people to fanzines were interviews with the stars and authors of our type of entertainment. And so, I decided to seek out someone who would draw attention to my little 'zine.

My legs were literally shaking when I called Buster Crabbe in 1972. I sat in the kitchen of our home with a microphone stuck with a suction cup on the receiver asking questions to the first movie star I had the opportunity to interview.

And not just any movie star: it was Flash Gordon.

I had found out that Crabbe lived in Rye, New York, and had written him. He very graciously replied with his telephone number and a time and date to call.

At that time, Crabbe was riding a wave of nostalgia that brought attention again to performers such as Buffalo Bob Smith of "Howdy Doody" fame and Clayton Moore, the Lone Ranger himself.

It was the first time that the childhood heroes of the Baby Boomers saw they had a second or third career as college students rediscovered them.

Clarence Linden "Buster" Crabbe came to prominence in the 1932 Los Angeles Olympics as a gold-medal winning swimmer. His athletic fame was translated into a contract with Paramount Pictures.

Crabbe was a utility player at Paramount. He was handsome and had a great physique, something which was played up in his first starring role as a Tarzan-like hero in "King of the Jungle" in 1933. He was never deemed by Paramount brass, though, as anyone who was "A" film material.

Instead Crabbe found himself as a supporting player or as the lead in program pictures. Perhaps his most prominent role for many people was in the W.C. Fields comedy "You're Telling Me."

His place, though, in cinema history was assured with the success of the three "Flash Gordon" serials in which Crabbe played the comic strip hero. Serials were deemed as entertainment for children and other not so demanding audiences, but the Flash Gordon serials received a prominence that few serials reached.

After his contract with Paramount ran out in 1940, he found a new home at PRC, the lowest of the low budget studios where Crabbe made westerns and jungle adventure films.

In the 1950s, Crabbe made numerous appearances on television and had his own successful series, "Captain Gallant of the Foreign Legion."

Acting took a back seat starting in the 1950s, when Crabbe became involved with several profitable businesses – a swimming camp, an affiliation with a pool company and work as a stockbroker.

Crabbe had made his final film, a comedy titled "The Comeback Trail," in which he played a retired cowboy. He was clearly enthusiastic about the film, which received scant theatrical release and has yet to appear on home video.

He died in 1983.

One thing I learned at the tender age I conducted this interview is just because a statement about an actor or director is made in a book by a film historian that doesn't mean it's true. Crabbe refuted two "facts" that were assigned to him by other writers.

Also in my ignorance, I sort of had an idea that if you worked in a genre of film – such a serials or low budget Westerns – you knew other people who worked in similar films. That wasn't necessarily the case.

BUSTER CRABBE

1972

This interview originally appeared in my fanzine "Inertron" in 1972.

Since you were an Olympic champion I was wondering what your opinions were of this year's Olympics [1972 in Munich, Germany].

Well, I think it was very poorly handled, much to be desired management wise. I certainly didn't agree with taking the Gold Medal away from the youngster Demanche who won the 400 meters, he's the one who had the asthmatic condition with the pill. I think it's inexcusable that two boys were sleeping when they were supposed to be up for the preliminaries and that began with, I feel, the coach's and management's fault, not the athletes.

The basketball was certainly an all fouled-up affair and if I had anything to do with the Montreal Olympics in 1976 I certainly would take a wary eye at what might happen before they spent a lot of money preparing for the 1976 Olympic Games.

There is a new book out entitled "Heroes, Heavies and Sagebrush" that claims your first movie was "Island of Lost Souls" with Charles Laughton. Is that true?

No, I was not in that film at all. My first was "King of the Jungle," a Tarzan-like picture Paramount made and released in 1933. I don't know where that 'Island of Lost Souls' came from.

I was wondering if that had been any rivalry between you and Johnny Weissmuller?

Sure there was.

When you were both Tarzan?

Well, no. I never considered myself a Tarzan. I thought you were talking about the competitive days. You know he's older than I am and I started off as a kid racing him. After the '28 [Olympic] games he retired from swimming and started in the movies in 1930.

Did you make up your own Tarzan yell?

No. The Tarzan yell, which was learned by a lot of kids – the original Tarzan yell, the one Weissmuller did – was the brainwork of my wife's father, a fellow named Tom Held, who was a cutter at MGM. They didn't know what kind of yell they were going to do, and, believe it or not, it turned out to be not one voice. The original Tarzan yell was three – a baritone, a tenor and a hog caller. Then Weissmuller learned it, and every kid in the neighborhood learned the Tarzan call, too. So they used it ever since, but originally it was three voices, three separate voices all melted together.

I know that you worked with W.C. Fields on a picture.

"Oh yes, I worked on two."

Do you have any stories about him?

He was just as he was on the screen. As a matter of fact, this nostalgic thing has been a plus for his films. Box-office-wise his films drew, but he wasn't a big tremendous box office star. I would hazard this: that the Fields pictures are doing better now than when they were first released 30 or 40 years ago.

Do you ever get tired of being recognized as Flash Gordon?

> DEAR MIKE:
> YOUR NOTE ARRIVED TODAY – MANY THANKS –
> I THINK YOUR SUGGESTION OF A TELEPHONE INTERVIEW WOULD BE MOST SATISFACTORY FOR ME BUT LET ME GIVE YOU MY PRESENT SCHEDULE WHICH BRINGS ME BACK SEPT. 22ND
> AM OFF WEST THIS FRIDAY HITTING ARIZONA, CALIFORNIA (BOTH L.A. AND SAN FRANCISCO). WILL VISIT HAWAII – BUSINESS AND VACATION, BACK TO INDIANA STATE UNIVERSITY AND KNOX COLLEGE ON THE LECTURE TOUR I STARTED ABOUT A YEAR AGO AND HOME.
> I THINK IT BEST YOU CALL ME AFTER MY RETURN – MY HOME PHONE 914-967-1224 WHICH I'M SURE YOU WILL KEEP IN CONFIDENCE –
> GOOD LUCK!
> *Buster Crabbe*

Buster Crabbe was truly a nice guy to spend some of his time speaking with a green as grass kid – me.

Well, no. You know, you didn't have the coverage in the old days in the middle '30s and early '40s, you didn't have the coverage you do now with television. Not that many people recognized me. More people recognize me now even though I'm older, as having played Flash Gordon than in the '30s and '40s, I think. They run the things on television and let's say it plays to two million people. A serial that played to two million people might have taken two years to do it.

You were one of the top Western stars. Who were your favorite cowboy stars?

Well, Tom Mix. I used to see him as a kid. I thought he was really tops: Col. Tim McCoy, too. I liked [Wild Bill] Elliot very much in fact. You know, nothing fancy in dress and what not.

I was just reading Jim Harmon and Don Glut's new book, "The Great Serial Heroes," that you were offered the role of Superman first in the serial, which eventually starred Kirk Alyn. Is this true?

No, that's not true.

I heard that you've finished a new movie with Chuck McCann in it.

Well it's a thing called "Comeback Trail," and the deal is that it is supposed to be previewed now. It was made a year and a half ago, but they have been stalling on the cutting. However, I think that it's going to be a very funny Western, a semblance to a Western, take it or leave it – it's in a Western locale.

The plot is about a couple of fellows, Chuck McCann and Bob Staats, who are producers of skin flicks, horrible skin flicks, and they have to do something to make some money because they owe a lot of money.

In checking over the bills they owe, they come across an item of insurance and Chuck wants to know what this $12,000 worth of insurance is about. Bob explains that when you make a film, you've got to insure it in case anything happens, you know, if the negative film is destroyed by fire or some such thing.

The wheels begin to roll and they decide to make a Western film and instead of taking a young fellow whom they could develop into a Western star, they pick an old fellow for a reason.

They're going to make him do all of his own stunts, all his own falls off of horses ad infinitum, hoping to bring on a heart attack and have him drop dead on the set so they can collect the insurance.

They insure the film for $2 million and go about finding the fellow and it turns out to be me.

All during the film we go along telling our story, you see it's a film within a film – you see us actually getting ready to shoot the scenes for the film – it bounces back and they never do succeed in putting me away, so to speak.

That's the story. It's a funny picture, a real funny picture. These fellows are good; they work well together like a Laurel and Hardy team. I think that after the film is shown and I've only seen a couple of days work and some cuts – I've never seen even a rough cut of it – but watching the fellows work together and whatnot, I really think that they have a chance of getting to be a comedy team a la Laurel and Hardy.

Other than your Flash Gordon role, which role is your favorite?

Well, I like the "Captain Gallant of the Foreign Legion" – that was 65 films we made for television in 1954 and '56– because my son was in it. I enjoyed making that series. He was with me all the time and that was kind of fun.

Speaking of that series, some people would condemn it today because its supposed excess of violence would be detrimental to Saturday morning viewers.

Oh that is so very wrong! Take a look at what they have on the screen now! This is tame compared to what's going on now! Look at cowboy pictures that they make now. Look at pictures Clint Eastwood and people like that make! Blood and thunder! This, they looked down upon 25 and 30 years ago. No, we don't even hold a candle to what's going on. Too much violence? That's asinine.

Well, it was bothering me because I was raised on your Foreign Legion show and the old Lone Ranger series.

Sure, they were a lot of fun. If they try tried to shoot you and they weren't successful you shot them, you know, it was one of those things. But violence wise we don't even compare.

Which role have you enjoyed most in life: that of an athlete, movie star or a businessman?

I never really considered myself a movie star. One of the reasons for that is that I never had a top-grade triple-A script and a top-grade triple-A director and producer. I never had the chance to work with a real big director in the business. The result is that I made action pictures, which turned out to be fortunate for me. The Billy the Kid Westerns, all the Westerns I did for Paramount, the serials I made and the other action things stood me in good stead because when television came along they sort of resurrected me, so to speak.

But I always considered myself, when I was a college student and before that, as a fair to middling swimmer and I go for the physical fitness type of thing, That's why I'm involved in the Masters Swimming program now, which is for guys and gals who aren't so young anymore.

I was reading a book by William K. Everson who said that your career, like that of W.C. Fields's Paramount career, was mismanaged by the studio.

I think that they could have really done something with it had they put on their thinking caps and brought me along. They took me dripping wet of out of a swimming pool.

Now don't misunderstand me, I had a year in law school and wasn't a dummy who came out of left field or anything like that. I think with a little bit of grooming and the right kind of coaching, then I might have been able to do something, but that's over the hill now.

I was there a long time at Paramount and I did what I was told – you know body and soul belonging to Paramount Studios. The type of comedy that Fields did, I don't think they appreciated. I think that they could have done a better job promoting him – tours and things. Maybe he turned them down, I don't know, maybe he said the hell with them – "I don't want to go on the road" – but I kind of doubt this because he came off vaudeville back east here. I think the man has a point particularly in regard to W.C. Fields.

Well, he mentioned in the book that they gave you a fairly good starting picture, "King of the Jungle."

King of the Jungle was fine, but it was the "Me Tarzan, you Jane" type of thing. The word got out around the studio that regardless of my background – you know, college and a year of law school – that "he looks fine if you've got a life guard part, you strip him down and put him in a G-string, he's okay, don't give him any dialogue." This is what I had to live down the first two or three years there.

Would you like to do more films after this last one?

Oh yeah, sure, I'd like to work in a movie. Of course, I'd have to be a character [actor] now. I love to play heavies. I had more fun playing the heavy than the lead by far. Love to play the real nasty guy.

Thank you Mr. Crabbe for allowing me to ask you these questions.

No bother at all, Mike.

Interviews for my fanzine that followed, included James Pierce, a college football star in the 1920s who played Tarzan in *Tarzan and the Golden Lion*, among other roles, and the publisher of *MAD magazine*, William Gaines.

I sold a version of the Gaines interview to a local alternative weekly, *The Valley Advocate*, which also bought the first interview I conducted that wasn't a fanboy subject.

Veteran NBC reporter and commentator Edwin Newman was appearing at the Eastern States Exposition promoting his book *Strictly Speaking: Will America be the Death of English?* in 1975. I had heard about it and managed to arrange to speak to him at the sales table. The book was a New

York Times bestseller, and Newman, whom I had grown up watching on television, was a gentleman, which undoubtedly soothed my nerves.

The following is my first paid interviewing gig – speaking to the veteran NBC newsman Edwin Newman about his book, *Strictly Speaking*. He was appearing at the Eastern States Exposition in 1975 to promote his book and I didn't get any set amount of time with him. Instead, I had to ask questions in between interactions with people who wanted his book and autograph.

As the time of the autograph session grew near, the crowds started to grow around the display book and magazine distributor Samuel Black had set up at the Eastern States Exposition. Women fresh from the Old English Lavender stands and the Miracle Juice display now giggled and pointed to the sign that proclaimed television newsman Edwin Newman, author of the best selling book *Strictly Speaking*, would be here.

The display's attendants looked slightly apprehensive when he didn't appear at 1:30 p.m. Newman had a full schedule of interviews with the local press that morning and the delay is understandable. Suddenly, the crowd began to applaud as they spotted the newsman through the crowd. Smiling easily, he sat down at the table in the front of the display and began autographing paperback editions of his book.

Strictly Speaking is an entertaining but effective criticism on the current state of the English language. Newman feels that due to the effects of the combined jargons of the social sciences, government and business, clear precise speech is becoming a thing of the past.

Of course, these jargons have been passed on to the average person by the news media, a fact that Newman neither apologizes for nor ignores. Some of the book's meatiest examples of the change in our language come from the pages of The New York Times and the broadcast media.

Newman makes a strong argument that today's language has gone mad searching for complex ways to say simple things. The language used in the Watergate testimonies and tapes is a language so full of "time frames," "dialogues," and "stone-walling" that it requires an interpreter for the reader to fully understand. However, this type of language is as close as your college course description guide. Educators in the social sciences have invented a new language to describe various situations in our society, and Newman quotes examples of this from a Hampshire College publication.

But before the reader can conclude that this book is another essay on the inferiority of the English spoken by Americans, Newman dedicates an entire chapter to the ways the British have destroyed their language. Newman also doesn't want readers to assume the establishment minions have been the only ones taking the clarity out of speech and writing. The many sportscasters and sports writers in this country have contributed greatly towards less descriptive speech like "pretty good" and Howard Cosell is virtually a one-man language wrecking crew.

The people at the autograph session react in different ways to meeting a man they see frequently on national television. Two middle-aged ladies smile and make the inevitable comment that Newman "looks just like he looks on television," while a grizzled new England farmer strides up to the table and states, "Yes, Mr. Newman, I see you quite often. Keep up the good work," and then walks away. Newman is cordial with all and very patient even with the most obnoxious autograph seeker.

"One effect of writing a book is that your authority is increased, or what is thought to be your authority and you're taken for something of a celebrity, he told me during a slow period. "Now if you're on television with any regularity or prominence, you're something of a celebrity anyway. But writing a book seems to add to that. Especially if you've written a book on a subject of this kind. People think that you're an authority on language. Well I'm not an authority on language; at least I'm not speaking from a professorial point of view. The arguments I make in my book, I try to support, and if I am an authority, it would only be because people have been convinced of what I've written. But they wouldn't be convinced that what I wrote was right simply because I'm an authority."

Some critics of Newman's book said that the English language is going through a period of evolution and the changes that Newman criticizes are part of this evolution.

"Language is always going through an evolution," Newman said. "Some of the phrases we use are becoming outmoded. What I'm writing about is not what I take to be the evolution, of the language, but the decline of the language through a misconception of what eloquence is, a misconception of what expressiveness is, or through a misconception of what useful language is. In other words, while it is true that in any given time a language is evolving. We are also in a period when our language is bloated. It's being distended. It's being ruined by the nonsense that comes out of the pomposity, out of the banality and out of the particular influence of the social sciences. People expend an enormous amount of energy finding new ways to express old ideas, trying to conceal the fact that they have no ideas at all. That's not evolution, that's decline."

If there is such a decline in our language, I asked Newman if there were any way we could fight it.

"I think that any fight of that type would have to begin with the individuals. I don't believe there is any organization set up to do that. I don't think that the country stands the need for another committee. I think that in any case as soon as you have an organization, language goes to pot, goes to pieces. But it seems to me that individuals can affect organizations, particularly organizations of which they're members, by insisting on simple, straight forward, precise language."

Listening to myself blurt out questioned tortured syntax, I realized that I was quite self-conscious speaking with a man who had written a book on the mis-use of the language. I wondered if he found a lot of that now.

"I find a certain amount of that, but what I find much more of is people being amused and making jokes about it and saying, 'Here comes Newman; no one say *viable, hopefully, supportive,* or *endorsive.* Don't say *dialogue.*' People say they're afraid to speak in my presence, but they usually smile when they say that."

The crowd was building up again. Newman leaned over the table and took his ballpoint in hand for the next group of fair-goers who wanted to get a copy of his new autographed book. I wondered how many would take the time to read it.

The only reason a local or regional publication would have a chance at a celebrity is because he or she is coming to town for a purpose. I learned through my five years on local radio as a talk show host that celebrities viewed the electronic medium differently.

During my radio tenure, I discovered I didn't require having a local hook for an actor or writer to be interested in speaking with me. People appearing on television shows were happy to speak to me if their show was in my market. Authors wanted the exposure for their books.

Politicians were, for the most part, overjoyed to get onto radio.

My time on the air was 1982 to 1987, a time when stations still hired local talent and the Fairness Doctrine, which required stations to present both sides of a controversial issue, was still in force. When the Fairness Doctrine was revoked, the rise of syndicated program espousing one political point of view began and stations started getting rid of local hosts, whom they had to pay, and replacing them with syndicated shows that were for free. All the local stations were given time in those shows to sell ads.

Local hosts were supposed to be jacks-of-all-trades, talking about many subjects. Their shows would change from hour to hour, depending upon the guests.

A show also reflected the interests of a host, and as soon as I realized that station management didn't care what I did, I decided to care just about my interests and those of my audience.

If there was someone of note coming into the area, I tried to book him or her to appear either by phone or in person. When I look over the list of people I was able to interview on a 500-watt daytime AM station, I feel a little pride.

The first "celeb" was a personal favorite of mine: music historian Dr. Demento. Soon after, a science fiction convention in town gave me the chance of having actors Barry Morse and Sarah Douglas in the studio. Douglas was dressed in a black leather outfit that closely resembled her costume on the Christopher Reeve "Superman" films. I was a little intimidated, but she and Morse were wonderful.

It's one thing for a journalist to sputter and pause while he or she is asking questions for a newspaper story, but an interview that is broadcast live is quite another matter. You really don't want to sound like an idiot and stumble around. On the other hand, you don't want to ask questions that all sound pre-scripted. The best way was to simply try to have a conversation with the subject.

If your subject is in the studio, you had to balance between speaking with the guest, running the controls and watching the clock. Keeping your finger on the seven-second-delay button was also a good idea if your guest was accepting calls from your listeners.

A partial list of people I interviewed for my radio show, some of whom are in this book, would include two Playboy playmates – Terry Nihen and Debbie Johnson – actors such as James B. Sikking, Lucie Arnez, Richard Crenna, Keye Luke, William Benedict, Virginia Christine, Rick Moranis, Dave Thomas, Antonio Fargas and Mark Metcalf; authors Gerri Hirshey, Sidney Sheldon and Cleveland Amory; directors George Romero and Larry Cohen; abortion rights pioneer Bill Baird; Myra Lewis, the former wife of seminal rocker Jerry Lee Lewis; former Attorney General Eliot Richardson, Sen. George McGovern, Massachusetts Gov. Michael Dukakis, Rev. Ivan Stang of the Church of the Sub-Genius, Mel Taylor of the legendary instrumental guitar group The Ventures, folk artists Tom Rush and Aztec Two-Step, Larry "Bozo the Clown" Harmon, Phil Proctor and Peter Bergman of Firesign Theater, Jack Benny co-star Dennis Day, comedians Lois Bromfield, Emo Philips, Yakov Smirnoff, "Weird" Al Yankovic, and cartoonist B. Kliban.

Two memorable interviews were with Clarence Nash, the voice of Donald Duck and Andriana Caselotti, the voice of Snow White.

I even interviewed Dick Wilson, who was Mr. Whipple, the slightly twisted grocer in love with Charmin toilet paper in several decades of television commercials. He was fun, cracking toilet paper jokes. "It may be toilet paper to you Mike, but it's bread and butter to me," he cracked.

The easiest two hours of my five years on air was with wrestling superstar Bob Backlund. For the life of me I cannot recall how Backlund decided to come on my show. I had interviewed him once at a local match and I thought he was going to slug me when I asked him how did he responded to people who claimed wrestling was fake.

But somehow, Backlund called me and wanted to come on my show on Aug. 14, 1984, ten days after his last match with the WWF and less than a year after he lost his championship title. Backlund was highly critical of Vince McMahon, the owner of the WWF.

The phones simply didn't stop ringing for the two hours with adoring fans.

The next day, I received one of the oddest phone calls in my career. Vince McMahon called me completely unexpectedly and said he had heard I had interviewed Backlund and wanted to know if I was interested in writing for his new wrestling magazine.

I was gob smacked, and I mumbled some ambiguous reply. I was startled by the call – how did he know in the pre-Internet days of the 1980s that I had spoken with Backlund? How did he know I was a writer?

I never followed up on it. Perhaps I should have.

Other great moments were interviews with the first lady of American cinema Lillian Gish, and a personal hero: Vincent Price. Gish had recently re-issued her autobiography, and her publisher wasn't cooperative. Undaunted, I contacted her agent, and Gish agreed to an interview. She was very sharp, and it was a pleasure speaking with her.

Price was appearing at the University of Massachusetts at Amherst with a one-man show titled "The Villain Stills Pursues Me." My wife and I had front row seats for what was a fantastic evening. The next day, Price conducted a press conference, and a fellow writer and I attended it. We asked most of the questions, and Price walked out of the building with us, continuing his remarks.

With some of these interviews, I was able to take some of the conversation and turn it into a written piece that I sold to various publications. My best sale at this time was USA Today, which bought an interview I did with attorney and author Alan Dershowitz who spoke to me about his book *The Best Defense*.

I always advise people to only sell first publication rights and try, if they can, to structure an interview so it can have multiple uses or sales.

The interviews in this book are from the 1980s and then skip forward to 1999. During that gap, the bulk of my free-lance writing time was dedicated to *Animato! The Animation Fan's Magazine,* which I co-owned and edited from 1992 to 1997. Many of those interviews were collected in my book *Escape! How Animation Went Mainstream in the 1990s,* also from BearManor Media.

As the managing editor of a group of weekly newspapers, I use interviews with celebrities as a way to change readers' conceptions about what a community newspaper should cover. People have said to me they didn't expect to see an interview with Leonard Nimoy or Dave Attell or any number of other people in a "small" weekly with 122,000 readers.

That's the power of getting a good interview.

Wrestler Walter "Killer" Kowalski in character at an interview I conducted with him at the former Mountain Park in Holyoke, Massachusetts. I wasn't prepared for this pose!

VINTAGE HOLLYWOOD

VINCENT PRICE

1983

For film fans, especially horror film fans, of my generation, Vincent Price doesn't need much of an introduction. However, I can't make the assumption that people today are aware of his career as much as we greybeards.

The accomplished actor had made a name for himself in featured character parts for more than a decade in Hollywood even before he had become a horror star.

Although from the early 1950s on, Price was probably more associated with appearing in horror films, he was also recognized for a variety of activities. He was a serious and learned art collector and advocate. Sears and Roebuck even hired him to curate a program that allowed people to buy prints of both classical and contemporary art, something he reportedly took very seriously. He was comfortable in the kitchen and wrote cookbooks.

A Yale graduate, he was suave and distinguished and yet tackled his varied career with a sustained gusto. He lent his classically trained voice to a number of narrations. He could switch from movies to television with ease and he could be an evil villain in one and a foil for Red Skelton in another. Some people perhaps have forgotten that Price also had a career on Broadway, as well, including being a member of Orson Welles's Mercury Theater.

In this discussion, he certainly shows his two sides of being cultured and intelligent and down-to-earth. He also showed a bit of his many interests.

When I learned in 1983 he was coming to the nearby University of Massachusetts to present a lecture, I was overjoyed. A quick call to the public relations office literally resulted in two comp tickets for my wife and I in the front row.

Price's presentation was *The Villain Still Pursues Me*, and in it he discussed playing the bad guy on both stage and screen.

Afterwards, he signed a few autographs. The next day he met with students in a class and then conducted an informal press conference attended by myself, fellow writer Stanley Wiater, and several students. I've made my best effort to denote which person asked which question. Some questions have not been assigned.

Price proved to be very good natured and candid, exactly as I had hoped. I was amazed that despite his acclaimed career and his fame, he continued to work as hard as he did. At the time of the interview Price was seventy-two, but he showed few signs of slowing down. His admission of having to re-configure his life in order to be home more with his wife was very touching.

Meeting and speaking with him was an amazing moment in my life as he was certainly one of the performers I admired the most. After the question and answer session, Wiater and I walked out of the UMass Fine Arts Center with him. He chatted with us as if we were all peers. There was no pretense, no "star" behavior.

Years later, I hunted down his address and proposed a book just on his films. He sent me back a note that indicated he was already involved in such a project, which eventually became *The Complete Films of Vincent Price*. Timing is everything in this business, and I wonder what would have happened if I had contacted him a year earlier.

Wiater presented an edited form of this interview in two publications, his book *Dark Visions* (now out of print) and an issue of *Fangoria* magazine. For this book, I went back to the interview tape and added material that has not been presented to the public since I broadcasted it in 1983 over my radio talk show.

***

(Wiater) You co-authored a book with your son called, appropriately enough, "Monsters." It seemed like a work long overdue, since your previous books have been about cooking or art, and not about this aspect of your career that you're best identified with.

(Price) Yes, but it was a very serious book that my son and I did about the things in life and in mythology and religion – in all history of things that are larger than life – "the monster." Chaos. The Leviathan. These things that were there right from the beginning of folklore and mythology and that had to be overcome by man. The kind of subliminal fears that people have of things larger than life. The dinosaur, King Kong – they're very obvious ones, but it was really a much deeper book than that. I think the publishers – who finally went out of business– were very sloppy in their handling of it. They wanted it to be a kind of facetious book, to be about movie monsters and everything else. Well, there have been dozens of those, and we didn't want to write another one. It got very good notices, but it wasn't the kind of book the publishers wanted, so they didn't push it.

Why so few films in the past decade? The ones you made in the early 1970s, such as "Theater of Blood" and the two Dr. Phibes movies are considered among your best.

I was sent some scripts. But the last ones I did make, the ones I really enjoyed like "Theater of Blood, which I think is a marvelous movie, or the Dr. Phibes films, were send-ups. So everything that was sent to me after that were exactly the same story. Done in a different way or with a different plot, maybe, but significantly the same story. Or they were overly violent. Since I'm active in other areas, I didn't really need them – so I didn't do them.

You said earlier that today's films are simply no longer suspenseful.

I think they've lost a sense of humor. And I really think that humor – and I don't mean "funny" or "send-ups" – I just mean they have to have a basic sense of humor. But some of these films are really terrible. They are violent; they have no writing in them at all! They're just a series of technical acts of violence. And I know how they're done, so they don't take me in. [laughs.] But one I saw the other night on television with Charles Durning, *The Night of the Scarecrow,* I think it was called and it was marvelous! I was terrified. I was on the edge of my seat. Yet it was simple; there was very little violence in it at all. It was just this wonderful suspense film, with a kind of sly humor.

What are your thoughts on the belief that some critics have where horror films can carry over to inspire acts of horror in real life?

I think there is some of that. I don't think there can be any question about it, but it depends on what you mean by seeing a horror picture. My definition of a "horror picture" is *Taxi Driver.* Which I think is one of the most terrifying pictures I ever saw. Or *Marathon Man*– they were really frightening pictures to me. Well, *Taxi Driver* was the inspiration for that little fellow who took a potshot at President Reagan. And sometimes I think they do have an influence, but no more influence than the front page of the newspaper. These were valid films, but I think there was too much of it; we got down to a point where we had no humor at all. Everything was so serious, you know? And so boring! There is fun in life.

You must get a lot of offers for projects still, especially from young people just starting out. Do you ever take on any of these offers?

Oh, yeah! I do a lot of them, too. A bunch of kids came up from San Diego one time, with a young Japanese-American boy who was a brilliant photographer. And he showed me some stills he had done of a film called "Annabelle Lee." It was very simple, but it was so beautiful! He asked me if I would do the narration for it, because they then thought that with a "name" attached to it, the film would get some attention. And they did. They got right up to the Academy Awards with it! [Laughs.] But it was fun to do, just fun to do! I think that a person who has been in the business so long is there to be used. I love doing it.

But it has to be something very special to pique your interest?

Well, I've been in the business nearly 50 years now, and I try not to accept things that aren't a challenge. I mean I won't do another mystery show or another horror show unless it really is witty. And fun. And scary. And everything is right, or I don't want to do it. I don't want any part of it. I just did this summer, Gilbert and Sullivan's "Rudigore." And it was marvelous! My God, the challenge of doing it with an all-English cast, doing Gilbert and Sullivan in England! It was really wonderful. I've never worked so hard in my life. I was a basket case at the end of it, but it was worth it.

(Dobbs) So was this the reasoning behind your most recent feature film, "House of the Long Shadows," the project contained all the desired elements?

Yes, I thought it was a reversion, going back to the old fashioned kind of show. I don't know how it turned out; I hear it's not being too well cut, but I don't know. I haven't seen it.

(student) On the PBS series "Mystery," which you host, there is animated material designed by artist Edward Gorey. Would you like to do a film in that low-keyed kind of style?

Dear Michael
    Good of you to write and to
want to do a biog — sadly I'm already
committed to one —
        Thanks for the offer & interest
                Sincerely
                Vincent Price

An easy rejection of my book proposal from Vincent Price.

Yeah, I really would. I think mainly because when I was at Yale we had a cartoonist who had gone to Yale just before I did and he was now in the New Yorker. It was Peter Arno and he really a very funny man. There's a big revival now of Peter Arno. That kind of Charles Addams humor is terribly funny. I don't think we've really caught it on the screen.

I really want to do what I want to do. Being in that class today was exciting, such a challenge. How can get out of them? How much can you give them? It's a tremendous challenge because it's all off the top of your head. I never do it the same way twice because they never are the same questions.

I love Gorey, but there's a funny thing in the reasoning of those introductions [of *Mystery*] – the British do not make their television to fit our time pattern. Some of them are 23 minutes, 26 minutes. When they get through making it that's the end of it and they put it on television. In London, a show will go off the air at 16 minutes before 9 and the next show will go on five after 9. They don't think anything about that because the BBC isn't commercial.

It's a funny thing. There a certain place in the stories that we do that you have to pad. There's no question about it. You have to explain why this happened, why that happened, there's some of them that go on too long but there is nothing we can do, so they got Gorey to come in and do some of the animation, which I love.

(Wiater) Have you ever heard this quote from Roger Corman about your work? "The keynote of his art lies, I believe, in his uncanny ability to embody and project the effects of mental aberration. He is rightly noted for his speaking voice, and suave, polished presence through which he can convey eerie gradations of a sinister motivating force."

My God, did he say that? [Laughs.] I couldn't agree with him more! That's pretty pretentious isn't it?

Of course you use your voice, you know, you use it for the effect you're going to get. Of course, it could also be a very funny voice. As I was saying about this tape of a Jack Benny show I was hysterically funny in it and I was really amazed because it was all situation and it was Jack Benny. Jack Benny was the kind of comedian who was so generous that he would give you three-quarters of his lines if he thought they were funnier from you, but it always ended up being the The Jack Benny Show [laughs] you know, because he was that kind of generous man. Some of them aren't.

(Wiater) Your villains, especially in the Edgar Allan Poe adaptations, were always both terribly cruel, yet terribly tragic figures.

That's what I tried to explain last night: "that there but for the grace of

STARE INTO THIS FACE

.....COUNT IF YOU CAN THE ORGIES OF EVIL!

SHUDDER... at the blood-stained dance of the Red Death!

TREMBLE... to the hideous tortures of the catacombs of Kali!

GASP... at the sacrifice of the innocent virgin to the vengeance of BAAL!

VINCENT PRICE STARRING IN

EDGAR ALLAN POE'S IMMORTAL MASTERPIECE OF THE MACABRE

THE MASQUE OF THE RED DEATH

in PATHÉCOLOR

from *American International*

The classic ad design for one of Price's best Edgar Allen Poe films.

God go I." The most interesting of the villains are the ones who have been made villains through circumstance.

Like Roderick Usher in "House of Usher?"

Yes, like Roderick Usher. If you lived in that house, you'd be very strange, wouldn't you?

(student) What do you think of the recent radio series, the "CBS Mystery Theater" with host E. G. Marshall? Is dramatic radio still a viable medium?

Yes, it depends an awful lot on the writing. The only thing I have against the E. G. Marshall ones was that they are a little old-fashioned. They were sort of consciously old-fashioned, as if, here we are kiddies and we're listening to an old medium. Radio is not an old medium. It's a very present medium. I do a series in London called *The Price of Fear* for World Service on BBC, and the listening audience is a 100 million people, which ain't bad! [Laughs.] These stories are written by the very best writers in England, and the actors are unbelievable. I was sent two tapes before I left London, and they are incredible ... All the top actors of England do these stories. And I've been the host, the connection between them.

(student) What did you think of the recent television adaptation of "Nicholas Nickleby?"

Gosh, I found it difficult. I know you're not meant to – I should be very highbrow. [Affecting a posh accent] I adore it my darling. I just adored it. [raising his voice with a growl] I was sound asleep about three-quarters the way through because it looked to me like a photographed stage play.

(student) How about "Romeo and Juliet?" That was adapted for television?

Now they were staged, they were adapted for television. I didn't feel *Nicholas Nickleby* was adapted for television it was just a photographed stage play. And I wish I had seen it in the theater because I think it was terribly exciting.

But when they go in on a close-up you know, and just arbitrarily and you can see everything around it. It was not staged as a television show – not to me it wasn't. I wish I'd seen it in the theater because I hear it was marvelous.

(student) Do you see the Price family becoming another acting family like John Carradine and his sons, who are all actors?

Oh my God, I haven't got that many kids! [laughs] No, John is really extraordinary – all of his kids have done so well. Very talented. You know they were all very separated from John for along time and yet there was a very warm relationship with the dad – marital difficulties.

My daughter loves theater, but I don't know if she's going to do it or not. It's up to her.

My son is a writer. But they are all doing things they like to do. He's a poet and a very good poet. He's been published all over the world. The money you make from poetry; let me tell you, you'd starve to death in the first three weeks. I asked him one time, "Doesn't it bother you?" And he said, "I'm the richest man I know." And he is. He lives his life the way he wants to live it and he'll do everything to be able to keep at the poetry thing, the writing thing. He edits a magazine now that's a very successful little magazine. But it's just constant work. He works harder than anyone I know, for less pay. But he's happy.

I think that's one of the things we're all going to have to get used to: the world is not going to be as affluent as it was ever again. I can't see how it can be. Too many people with automation. I saw a thing the other night with robots doing the engines. Well they do it so much better than people. You just worry to death about it because this was a great big plug for automation and the use of Japanese techniques. Nobody mentioned the fact it put about 7,000 men out of work.

Somewhere we have to come to some conclusion about this. It's difficult.

(Dobbs) You've been a champion for Native American artwork in the past. Are you still concerned about it?

I'm still concerned about it, but I haven't been on that board for 10 years. I ended up being the chairman of the Indian Arts Task Force in the Department of the Interior. Our job was not the preservation of Indian art but the inspiration of Indian art because the Indians were giving it up because they could get a better job in Albuquerque filling a gas tank or sweeping a factory than they could making jewelry.

Our job then was to find the markets and in many cases re-teach some of the young people the crafts that had been handed down to them because they had forgotten. I think it worked. It really worked. I was on the air every five minutes talking about it.

Indian art and craft has really come into its own now. Of course the Japanese made them too. We found, for instance, in the National parks they were selling handmade American Indian jewelry made in Japan. On the back it would say "made in Japan" and you couldn't believe the National Parks were selling it. It was unbelievable, unbelievable.

So we got laws passed. That was our job. We got laws passed in about seven states that they had to explain it; state that this was real hand-made American Indian jewelry and this was junk. [laughs] They didn't have to label it junk, but they had to label it what it was.

(student) Would you be interested in helping to fund an experimental theater like they have in London?

Me start it? Oh Gosh I've joined everything. I'm a joiner. [groans] I belonged to the Mercury Theater and Orson [Welles] blew that. It didn't last the minute it became successful.

I joined another theater company, the Playhouse Theater Company with Laurette Taylor, and we had one success and that was the end of that.

And I joined three national theater companies, none of which lasted. Two of them were people who absconded with the money.

It's a tough country to work in that way. It really is. There are 15 groups in California who've tried it. There's no one made it yet.

(student) Do you find the British are more accepting to new ideas in theater?

Yup. Yup. And our theater has been tremendously influential over there. You see the thing is, it's a country with almost a 1,000 years of audience education. And it's incredible. The English go to the theater the way they drink tea. It's part of the necessity of life. With us, it's a luxury, and unfortunately now monetarily it's become a luxury in England, too. I used to go when I was a student in London. I was living on $100 a week, including the tuition and everything, and I saw every play. I could go to a play for a quarter. You can't do that in London now. It's 8 pounds, 10 pounds, 30 pounds for a big hit show. It's terrible. It's like New York.

(student) I've heard it's easier to get actors in England.

When I did *Theater of Blood*, we had Michael Horden, who had just been made a knight, he's one of the great Shakespearean actors. We had Harry Andrews, who's considered the greatest supporting Shakespearean actor in the business, we had Jack Hawkins – every single person in that company was a huge star. They came out from plays they were doing in the West End, only about an hour's drive to the movie studio. They did their day's work, and the movie was worked around them. I was the star of the picture, and I would have to stay late to do all the fill-in scenes so that so-and-so could go back and do his play in the National Theatre! Which is bloody well right, you know? It's more important that I should have them working with me, than to do a little extra work for the privilege of having them. Diana Rigg. My wife, [Coral Browne] incredible people! Twelve of the greatest actors in England.

(Wiater) What did you think of Diana Rigg? She's become a cult figure because of the 1960s television series "The Avengers."

I loved her. She's marvelous. She's just opening in *Heartbreak House* with Rex Harrison, which would be fun to see.

(Dobbs) Mr. Price you obviously are a huge talent and you're intellectual so why have you appeared in films that are beneath your talent? Is it a pragmatic attitude that you are an actor and have to work, like in a the film "Dr. Goldfoot and the Bikini Machine?"

Dr. Goldfoot and the Bikini Machine (1965) was one of the funniest scripts I ever read in my life. It was a musical. They cut out all the music. They shot the numbers, because it was Frankie Avalon and myself, you know, and it was a very funny picture and a very funny idea. They [the producers] destroyed it. They got so terrified of it that they destroyed it. And you have no control over that, at all.

I did a film one time called *Up in Central Park* (1948) with Deanna Durbin, who was the greatest star in the business at that time. And they cut out all the music and it's a musical comedy! Suddenly you've got a musical comedy without music! It had Dick Haymes and they had no [musical] scenes in it. *Close as Pages in a Book,* one of the biggest hit songs of all time and they cut it out. Now, I didn't say, "Cut it out!" It was unbelievable.

The film was based on the successful Broadway musical by Herbert Fields, Dorothy Fields and Sigmund Romberg.

Sometimes you do dogs. [pauses] I did one in Italy once – mainly because I wanted to go to Italy, to tell you the truth – and also it was not a bad script. But, they lost the soundtrack. They had never kept a complete script. There were seven people in it: two of them spoke Taiwanese, two of them spoke German. I spoke English, and the rest of them spoke Italian. So they had to get lip-readers to look at the scenes to find out what the hell we were supposed to be saying! Because they lost the soundtrack and the script. Now, what do you do about that?

(Dobbs) I guess another problem is working on a film that never gets a proper release.

That's right.

For example, I wanted to see a film you did with Peter Cushing called "Madhouse" which never played here in Western Massachusetts.

It's now just coming out in England, almost ten years later. Don't ask.

Is that particularly disappointing to you?

Sometimes. Sometimes. It's sometimes terribly disappointing. You can never tell. It is a business. It should be an art form, but it really a business.

I've seen some of the biggest stars in the business like the Roy Scheider and Meryl Streep story [*Still of the Night* 1982], which everyone thought was going to be one of the huge successes of all time. It was a dog. They didn't make a dog. Something went wrong. They released it wrong. They released it at the wrong time. Something went wrong with it.

About five of the pictures this year that everyone thought were going to be big, big successes and they didn't make a dime.

"Annie" for example.

Well I thought *Annie* was the dullest musical I ever saw in my life. I thought if one more kid sings that Goddamn song I'll kill myself. *Tomorrow, tomorrow!* [wailing out of key]. Oh!

But why did they make it into a movie in the first place? It's got to be duller as a movie than it was as a theater play.

(student) There have been several 3-D movies in the past few years. Do you think they will have a future?

I don't really think so. The one that's made the most money of them all was *House of Wax,* which made millions of dollars, and still does every time they rerelease it. And people take their kiddies to see something they're never going to see again because you might already wear glasses, and then you've got to wear 3-D glasses on your glasses. The funniest thing about making *House of Wax* was the director was a man with one eye; so he never saw it [the 3-D effect]. You have to have two eyes going very well to be able to see 3-D, and he had one glass eye. [laughs] He never saw a thing! I loved that.

(Dobbs) Your co-stars in "Night of Long shadows" were Peter Cushing, Christopher Lee, and John Carradine. Could you tell us what it was like working with all of them?

It was the first time we'd been in a picture together, and we've all done pictures together – except not the four of us. It was very much fun, because I enjoy those men, and they enjoy me, and we're great friends. So that's jolly.

(student) Of all the legendary horror stars you've worked with over the years, who was your favorite?

[Pause] I think Boris [Karloff]. He had a marvelous sense of humor, and he always struck me as very funny, because there was that funny sort of lisp he had. And that strange complexion, which was green, he was a funny man. He was always very sinister, but at the same time he struck me as very hysterically funny, so I adored working with him. I loved him as a person, too.

(Wiater) Then do you see yourself as representing the end of an era in terms of horror stars? There doesn't seem to be any "son of Boris" or "son of Vincent Price" around to carry on the tradition of great screen villains.

Oh, I think there are! Bruce Dern, for instance, is a marvelous heavy; I really hate him! Oh God, can he be mean and nasty! He could be wonderful in this kind of picture if he ever wanted to make one.

(student) Are there any roles in horror films today being played by younger actors that you would love to play?

No, not necessarily.

(student) Are there any other roles you've wanted to play but haven't?

Oh, I suppose so. King Lear. As I've said, we've always got Shakespeare. But the English do it so much better than we do. We are not good at it. We're self-conscious at Shakespeare. The English – it happens. It's wonderful.

(Wiater) Is there anything besides acting that you're most proud of in your career?

That I've done everything. I've done musical work. I do a lot of symphony work, I do a lot of poetry reading and records of poetry. I do college lecturing, which is very much a part of my life. I do a lot of different things. I know it makes people highly suspicious because we're a nation of specializers. But I couldn't care less; that's the way I wanted to live my life and the way I have.

There's nothing that sticks out?

I think it's been a whole to me. I found that the cookbook that I wrote really has been a marvelous introduction to another world, that I wouldn't ever have had, had I not written that book. A book I wrote on American art has given me an entré to places I would never have had, had I not written that book. I'm a very lucky fellow. But I worked for it – very hard.

(Dobbs) Any chance of an autobiography? "Vincent Price by Vincent Price?"

No! [laughs] Everybody's written one. You know, anybody can write anything they want to about you. Somebody did a thing called *Vincent Price Unmasked.* I don't know what it's about; nobody asked me about it at all. They can write anything they want about you. I wrote an autobiography, [*I Like What I Know,* 1959] but it was not what I've done, but what I've seen, and that to me was a much more interesting way of doing it. I would like to write one, but not just about movies.

Unless you've slept with Shelly Winters, what do you have to write about? And who wants to sleep with Shelly Winters? Lot of people did, but I don't think any more.

(student) Is there a focus on one thing in your career now?

I'm trying to figure out a way because of a certain thing that happened in my family – illness, my wife – I'm going to have to work in a different way. Yet I cannot say I'm going to retire and consequently I'm trying to figure out how I can fill my time and not be as actively out of her life as I have been.

[Price had married actress Coral Browne in 1974 after they had worked together on the film "Theatre of Blood." Browne died in 1991 from breast cancer.]

We've been together an awful lot but there have been points where people become jealous of your activity. How am I going to do it? I'm not a fellow who is very good at sitting at home. I've never had a vacation in my life because after I've got sand in both ears, that was it – that was the end of the beaches. To hell with it. I'm really a very active fellow and my idea of a month in the country is 42nd Street and Broadway. I love to walk through the towns and villages and right back to the city.

I'm trying to figure out how I can be so busy, but stay home a little bit more. I think I can do it. [pause] Thank you all.

LILLIAN GISH

1984

I had learned that nothing is gained by not posing the question if someone is available for an interview and sometimes that query has to be posed to different people.

Screen legend Lillian Gish had released new edition of her autobiography *The Movies, Mr. Griffith and Me* in paperback. I thought it would be a marvelous opportunity to speak to someone whose career had almost spanned the length of motion picture history on my radio show.

So, I called the publisher and spoke to the publicist assigned to the book. "No, Miss Gish would not be interested" was the answer. I called the Screen Actor's Guild, which at that time had a service that allowed a person to get the name and telephone number of a member's agent. I contacted her agent, who quickly replied in the affirmative.

When I was interviewing her, I realized that some of her answers were a tad rambling, but she always got to her point. I sent her the following print edition, which ran in a local arts newspaper. I have scanned her thank you letter, which appears at the end of this piece – unicorn stationary!

I contacted her by letter twice more and she always responded quickly.

She died in 1993 at the age of ninety-nine. If you've not seen her movies – she did some great work in sound pictures as well – then I suggest checking out *Way Down East,* (1920) *The Wind,* (1928) and her last film *The Whales of August.*

***

Gish has been experiencing a revival lately, at an age (estimated between eighty-seven and ninety) when most take a well-deserved breather. This year, her 1969 autobiography (*The Movies, Mr. Griffith and Me,* Prentice Hall, $9.95) was reissued, and she was honored as the second woman to receive the American Film Institute's lifetime achievement award. She participated in the re-release of two of her greatest silent films, *Broken Blossoms* and *The Wind* (the first a Griffith production) and maintained a busy schedule of appearances on television and film. Her new movie, *Hambone and Hillie,* has been released by New World Pictures.

Never married, Gish says she is married to her career. It has been a highly successful union. Perhaps the greatest actress of the silent era, Gish appeared in most of the best-regarded D.W. Griffith features and later helped produce such classics as *The Wind.* She spoke in a telephone interview from her home in New York.

Beginning her career as an actress at the age of five, Gish entered films when Griffith offered to double the salary she was receiving from legendary theatrical producer David Belasco. Early in her movie career, she relearned many of the techniques of acting.

"I was playing a very good part, and I thought I was overacting and when I saw it, I asked Mr. Griffith why it didn't come across on the screen.

One of Gish's collaboration with director D.W. Griffith was "Way Down East," (1920), which she recalled was a harrowing experience.

"He said, 'Well, you know, the camera opens and shuts, opens and shuts which means only half of what you do is up there. You have to make up for that, but you must not be caught acting. If you're caught acting they don't believe you.'"

"Well, the only way I could learn was by hanging a mirror on the side of the camera so I could see my face, so that I wouldn't make faces, so I would tell the story with my face, with my eyes and thought, because the camera is psychic, according to what John Barrymore said.

"We never had stand-ins, or any of the things they have now. You did whatever was in the part. In *Way Down East*, I was lying on the ice. I was out in the blizzard until my eyelashes got icicles, and I couldn't keep my eyes open. You had to do whatever the character did. You had to be it. You couldn't act it. There's no school like the camera, and no one can teach you to act except the human race. You study the human race. Watch them, how they act, how they react.

"Whenever I had to act a death scene, such as a character with tuberculosis, I'd go with a priest to a county hospital. We would go to the ward with the tubercular women, and I would tell them what I was there for, and instead of being hurt or insulted, they would be so delighted they could help in some way. They would tell me how they coughed, how their throats looked, how their faces were, what they did when they were dying. And that's how I learned to do whatever it was I did."

Gish recalled her experience of acting in a film to try to help convince the American public to aid France in World War One. When they weren't in production, Griffith would tell Gish and her sister, Dorothy, to visit the hospitals in London where the wounded were treated.

"We were made by Griffith to go to Waterloo Station or Victoria Station and watch people when they said goodbye to their loved ones or when they were down there to meet them without their arms, legs or sometimes in wooden boxes.

"And that's how we learned. He said, 'You know nothing about life. This is your chance to learn, God willing you'd never have such another chance.'

Besides using techniques that anticipated the Method school, Gish also took dance, voice and fencing lessons to gain mastery over her body.

One aspect of today's movie business that astounds Gish is the lack of rehearsal time for the actor.

"It's a wonder to me they are as good as they are. We, in the nine years

I was with D.W. Griffith, never saw anything in writing. There was no such thing as a script. You went into a room, he called out the plot, and you went through it over and over until you got so sick of it. You had to find the character, and he had the plot in his mind."

It was Griffith that Gish initially set to write about when she began her autobiography.

"The idea for the book was originally from Reader's Digest. They approached me to do a book about Griffith, and I said, 'I'm not up to that. I won't do justice to the man because I've never written a book. I can't spell; I only had five months of schooling.' And they said, 'We'll help you.'

"And they sent a young man up here for about a year, asking questions, and helping me. They're like an octopus ... they can get any information from any part of the world. And the films [of Griffith's] were around the world.

"This was the man [Griffith] who gave film its form and grammar, and we use it to this day. We haven't changed it. The only one who has added to the dimension has been Walt Disney with his animated films. But other than that, I know of no one who has added anything.

"Well anyway, I went to Switzerland because I knew if I stayed at home, I'd use any excuse not to write. And I took my pencils and paper to a hotel above Monteux where no one spoke English. I would get up early in the morning, at 8, with my pencils and paper and I would write until 12. I'd get dressed and go get lunch and go into the mountains and think of what I should say and write the next day. I didn't take a dictionary.

"I didn't take any notes. I wrote out of my own head and memory and imagination.

"I came back after three months and gave it to them. They said, 'This is fine, but it's all about D.W. Griffith.' And I said, 'I thought that's what you wanted.' And they said, 'No. You can't write about him without writing about your sister and yourself. Now you go back and write a book about the two of you. And put it together and we'll have what we want.'

"Well, I went back the next summer and wrote about us. They said, 'That's fine and now you can put it together.' That was the third summer, and I found I needed a secretary to type it. And I called [Charles] Chaplin, who lived in Vevy, not far from Monteux, and I've known him for years. He was in Ireland ... His housekeeper said, 'If Mr. Chaplin were here, I know he'd let me do it.'

"Well, she did. I came back, I gave it to them, and they said, 'It's wonderful but it's a little long, now you'll have to shorten it.'"

Finding herself bored with the book, Gish put it aside while she was busy with television, theater and film projects. After several years, Prentice-Hall approached her about the project, and after some editing, published the book in 1969. Gish was especially proud that foreign editions in Arabic, Burmese and other languages were released.

She attributes the worldwide interest in the book to the fact that she was writing about an international language: film. And Gish firmly believes that the silent film was the best way to tell a story that could transcend national borders, a view shared by Griffith.

She recalled that in 1921, Griffith produced a sound film entitled *Dream Street.*

"Griffith looked at the film with the talk and the singing, and said, 'Why, I'm committing suicide with this. Only 5 percent of the world speaks English. Why should I lose 95 percent of my audience?' And he took it back to the studio and took all the sound out of it and turned it into a silent film. And silent films as I have found out, having been in the early ones, made the world all the same. Wherever you go in the world today and I've been around the world three times within the last eight years, everything looks like America ... same tall buildings, they all dress like we do. It [film] made the world one."

Gish is an ardent champion for a return to the use of silent film. The recent successes of the French silent, *Napoleon,* and *Broken Blossoms* and *The Wind* in Great Britain support her belief.

"I'm working and I think it [the return of silent films] will be successful, and I hope that when I go, someone will take it up and bring great music and silent films back," she said.

Gish thought *Gandhi* would have made an excellent silent, and hopes for a day when the artists and poets of the world can use silent film as their medium.

While so many people are dazzled by the ever-improving technology of film today, Gish believes the medium in still in its "babyhood crawling around on the floor."

She said, "Their [film's] future is yet to come. Help with it, and make it the universal language."

She added, "Griffith told us, you know, that we shouldn't make fun of film. We called them 'flickers.' He said, 'Don't you ever let me hear you use that word again. Don't you know you're working in something that was predicted in the Bible? There was to be a universal language for all men to understand, and that would bring about the end of war and the millennium. You think of that the next time you face a camera.' Well, you tell youngsters, 12, 13, 14, 15 years old that and they take it very seriously, and we did."

In 1986, I did a series of interviews with character actors during my tenure as a radio talk show host over at WREB in Holyoke, Mass. An acquaintance of mine had set me up with a series of actors and I was able to speak to people who had long careers in movies and who had played in both big pictures and small. To a person they were a delight to talk with and I only wish I could have had more time with each of them.

VIRGINIA CHRISTINE

1986

Virginia Christine is one of the legions of character actors who were never achieved huge fame, but worked steadily in a stream of movies that ranged from *The Mummy's Curse* to *High Noon* to *Judgment at Nuremberg*.

She became a favorite of producer and director Stanley Kramer, who also used her in his films *Cyrano de Bergerac* and *Guess Who's Coming to Dinner?*

It's interesting that Christine took the route in Hollywood that she did. Strikingly beautiful, she could have been a leading lady in the 1940s, but she took secondary and character parts. This move extended her career.

For twenty-one years she was the commercial spokeswoman for Folger's Coffee playing the Swedish accented "Mrs. Olsen," a lucrative assignment for her that might have blinded people to the fine work she did in a wide variety of film roles.

When I interviewed her in the mid-1980s, she was still acting.

Married to fellow actor Fritz Feld for more than 50 years, she passed away in 1996.

***

How did you get into acting?

I've never done anything else in my entire life. I sang in funeral homes to put myself through college. But I always wanted to be an actress since I was nine years old. I was fortunate when I married my husband because he helped me professionally a good deal ... when I met my husband who is a professional actor and older than I, he said, "Read for me" and I did and he said, "I don't know how good you are because you're a bag of tricks," which is the usual thing young performers resort to. [laughs]

We were married and I fell into my own trap I thought I could use him for all the advice I could get ... Fritzie, my husband said, "I will help you if you promise not to sign any contracts until I say that you are ready," which I did.

We were married just last week on Nov. 10 for 45 years.

Who says those Hollywood marriages doesn't last, right?

Right! [laughs] He helped me considerably with coaches, fencing and dancing lessons and finally put on a production of Ibsen's *Hedda Gabler*. And I had offers from two studios, Warner Brothers and Fox, and that's how I started. That's a long answer to a short question.

You did what became a controversial picture toward the beginning of your career, Mission to Moscow. [The film depicted the career of the second ambassador sent to Russia following the Communist revolution and was reportedly shot by Warner Brothers at the request of President Franklin D. Roosevelt as part of the war effort. After the war the film was criticized for its depiction of Josef Stalin and Russian communism.]

Right, I considered myself to be fortunate to be in that. It was not a large part, but it was a very controversial film in that it was the first thing that showed anything pro-Russian. It was a good film, a good picture.

I know that many of our listeners who are horror film fans will be excited to learn the attractive brunette who was in The Mummy's Curse in 1944 was actually the attractive blonde I'm talking to.

Oh, I knew you would come to that Mike. [laughs] It's strange because that was a B-picture. It was made at the Universal lot and no one thought anything of those things. They were related to second-class citizenship among films and that one turned out to be a classic. I got more attention from *The Mummy's Curse* than any other film in my career.

You went through quite an ordeal on that picture.

It was a tremendous ordeal. It was horrifying. Once I was cast for the picture I had to go to the make-up artist who created all of the [make-ups] for the Frankenstein monster. He was a master really.

Jack Pierce.

Jack Pierce. Right you have it. And Jack had to okay me, my bone structure so he could mummify me [laughs] and he said yes.

And we shot the whole picture and Jack kept coming on the set. He loved to toot his own horn and would tell me, 'Don't worry about what I'm going to use on you Virginia. It's something new, but don't worry about it.'

So I began to worry. On the last days of the film, when they shot the scene when I came out of the dirt on the back lot – it wasn't nice clean dirt on the set, it was on the back lot that still exists at Universal. The night before, I was a nervous wreck, so my husband called Jack and said, "What are you putting on Virginia? She's a wreck." He said, "Nothing but Denver mud pack," don't worry.' [laughs].

So he liked to put on a good show, too.

I came into the make-up department, I think about 4:30 in the morning, and worked five and half hours on me just filling in the cotton on the curves [of my face] and then putting a mudpack on that to make the mouth wizened. And the eyes are sunken and so forth. Finally a very normal thing happened, you know, I had to go to the bathroom and they had to do my arms too. So I had to be taken like a baby and my sense of humor was very close to the surface and if I laughed I would crack the mask on my face that had been dried and we would have to start all over.

Then I got very hungry. They finally parted my lips a little bit and gave me a malted milk.

I walked into that back lot and they had dug a grave right in the soil. I laid down in the thing and began to think about all of the creepy crawlies that were in the earth. Then they covered my body with burnt cork that photographs just like soil. They covered the face and rolled the camera and said action and I had to come out as the mummy.

You don't expect such a long answer did you?

Well a lot of people think motion picture work is glamorous and I think you told them how unglamorous it could be.

Well it got more unglamorous. I had to walk into the back lot lake, which is full of frogs and probably malaria, and algae and all kinds of slimy things.

How was Lon Chaney Jr. to work with?

He was a very nice guy; he had his tendency to drink a bit. They had a costume made for him with a zipper up the back and that was his permanent mummy costume … anyway we muddled through that one and we survived it. Everything was fine except for the last day [laughs].

You did seven pictures for Stanley Kramer. How did you become involved with him?

With Mr. Kramer, I believe I started with *High Noon*. And then he was just very good to me. I coached Olivia DeHavilland with her Swedish accent in *Not a Stranger* with [Frank] Sinatra and Robert Mitchum. It had a very good cast, but it didn't do well.

Stanley has been very good to me.

Have you ever been upset that you have played small roles in movies and not the leading roles?

I was the leading lady in several pictures when I started out and my love in life told me the character parts are much more interesting. You act longer and I just always navigated toward characters parts and enjoyed them more than playing an ingénue or a leading lady when I was very young. There's more meat to the roles.

Character actors I've interviewed say they have a longer career because they are able to use their age as another fact of their character parts.

Right. And that doesn't happen to leading ladies, although I must say I'm very happy to see a return of some of our best actresses, you know like Anne Baxter, Jane Wyman and Dorothy Maguire. There are several actresses who have come back from retirement from the screen and it's so nice to see that familiar face again.

They were leading ladies and now they've gracefully gone into character work. Character people have been at it since the beginning. They are character types. I just enjoyed it more.

I have to ask you about the role for which you're best known, that of "Mrs. Olsen" in the Folgers Coffee commercials. Did it affect the rest of your acting career?

I was with Folgers for 21 years. I came of age with the company. I had played a lot of Swedish and foreign roles, always, the casting director called me and said, 'I want to make a test.' I really did not want to do the first commercial. You know we looked down our noses a little bit. We were snobby – not any more, of course.

I had a very happy relationship with them for 21 years.

In putting a crimp on the rest of the acting, it certainly has done that. I don't know. Some performers say it hasn't bothered them, but the longevity and the identification of this character seem to have been very strong and now I have to go to work again and try to get rid of that image.

Do you think that television has replaced the low budget films as the training ground for actors these days?

Probably, particularly the soap operas because I remember doing serials. That means 13 episodes that ran every Saturday afternoon in theaters in the early 1940s and that was a training ground for actors. It was a tremendous training ground because the script was as thick as the Los Angeles phone book and we had pages and pages and pages of dialogue. It took six weeks to shoot those. It was many hours to film.

Today I admire so much the soap opera actors because they are shown scripts they have to learn overnight. It's very good training, gaining confidence doing those kinds of shows.

The television films shows, I don't know if they are as good a training ground or not. When you shoot it, if it isn't right, you can shoot it again. That's isn't true for most of the soaps they like to go straight through.

The same thing went for the B-pictures, you know. You do it and get in the can [laughs.]

I followed that conversation with one with her husband Fritz Feld, a man whose name might not be familiar to some movie fans but whose many appearances even in small roles were indeed memorable, thanks at least in part to a mannerism he developed of slapping his hand over his mouth to make a loud popping noise.

He was one of the busiest character actors in Hollywood and appeared in hundreds of films, television shows and commercials over his long career. He acted up until 1989 and passed away in 1993.

FRITZ FELD.

I've seen you in so many movies and you've always been a delight.

Thank you. Thank you very much. You've just been talking to my beautiful wife who is much more interesting than I am.

How did you get started?

I was born in Germany and my father was a printer. He wanted me to be a printer, too… He made a mistake. He built a puppet theater – a very large box for my brother who was a designer and myself. We put on a lot of shows for kids. That started it.

Then a relative of mine was an actress who connected with the theater somehow and finally I went all by myself to the acting school of Max Reinhardt, but I didn't pass, he said, "We can't use you. You're lisping."

My father was delighted. He said, "It serves you right. Now you're going to be a printer."

But he saw himself I was very sad. So, six months later I went to the same acting school with his permission, and I passed with flying colors, and I was the first in the acting school of Max Reinhart for two years.

Then I became an actor in Max Reinhardt's plays and finally working to become the fifth and fourth and third and second and the first assistant of Max Reinhart who was a giant of the theater.

How did you make the transition from theater to silent film?

I played in the Deutsches Theater, which was the dramatic theater of Germany. I played character parts and they asked me to play in pictures. I played mostly old, old men, 75 years old, and I was only 19 or 20 and did very well.

I played in some very prominent pictures, one was *The Golem* which went to America and a matter of fact was shown in the museum. We found out that everyone in the picture including the extras was dead for me. I am a rare museum piece.

"The Golem" is a very important German silent fantasy film.

And another one was *Christian Wahnschaffe,* [I played] another old man. As a young man I was to play Romeo. I started immediately to recognize that I wasn't a good looking Romeo type and had a small stature, so I immediately played hunchbacks, witches and I had a complete freedom in my profession. There was only one other Ernst Lubitsch. He was an actor and director at the Reinhardt Theater. When he went to America I filled his parts, very grotesque parts. Because grotesque parts are rare, I made a success.

How did you get to this country?

Well, being the first assistant of Professor Max Reinhardt – he got an offer to produce *The Miracle* in America and he wouldn't take me. When I asked him he said, "You are with the girls. You always make fantastic goo-goo eyes at all the girls and I'm putting on a very important play, a very holy play in America. America wouldn't allow such a person to flirt with the girls, so I can't take you."

I was heartbroken because I was his first assistant. Then a man by the name of Ana Nillson who was his chief musician and went to America with Reinhardt, said, "My God, Fritz, you have talent. You must come to America naturally."

So he arranged a meeting with the go-between Reinhardt and the producers in America. So I went for $60 a week, which was millions of marks because of the inflation at the time. I got a contract to go to America and I went in 1923 to New York.

When I came to New York ... I immediately jumped in and helped organize the masses, which was 750 people on stage, the biggest show in America.

You worked with Emil Jannings in "The Last Command" (1928) directed by Josef Von Sternberg.

A very funny thing happened. During the movie one night in a big mass scene, Emil Jannings put me in his room and said, "Fritz, I know you have been the first assistant of Reinhardt. Von Sternberg is an excellent director, but he doesn't know anything about controlling masses. I want you take over the whole direction of the picture."

[I said] "Mr. Jannings I can't do that. I was broke and I asked Von Sternberg to give me a job and he gave me a job. That would be horrifying [for me to do that]."

[Jannings said] "You fool! You God damn fool I make you the director."

Anyway, I directed the scenes for Sternberg, but I didn't stab him in the back directing the entire picture.

You left acting for a while and directed.

That's right. I always wanted to direct all my life. Strangely enough, when I was ready to direct I got a job playing a director in a picture. I played about seven directors in pictures and, finally, I said I had enough, I don't want to. Ernest Lubitsch, who was chief of the Paramount Studio, asked me to become an editorial assistant and strangely enough he didn't want to be head of the studio, he wanted to direct himself.

So, he said, "Fritz, I'm leaving you and I'm going to ask for you to become an actor again."

So instead of being free to direct I had to act again because he wanted me to act in *I Met Him in Paris* with Claudette Colbert and I played my first comedy part.

Was that your first comedy role?

No, on stage I played comedy but in pictures I mostly played heavies. In silent pictures I played heavies with guns. This was the first hotel clerk... I had went to different agents and I asked would you help me, I'm playing a big part – [Their answer was] "You're too little, and I don't think you can play comedy."

Well the picture came out. I got the best write-ups and all the agents came and said we want to present you and I said, "The hell with you, I don't want you anymore."

I saw a movie called "Lancer Spy" (1937) with George Sanders with you in a good part recently.

People ask what was your best part. Well, I say every part I play is like a pregnant woman having a baby: every one is different and liked. But I must say that *Lancer Spy* is one of the best because I was the assistant of George Sanders. It was George Sanders's first picture, and I coached him to become a German, although he was an Englishman, playing an English spy.

You've made 425 movies?

That's correct – for Hollywood.

That's a tremendous amount of work.

Well, I enjoy it. I enjoy my profession. I never had one moment of sadness that I am an actor or a director or a writer. And I never did anything else connected to the entertainment profession acting writing, directing, coaching, publicity man and talent scout.

You acted on one of the Marx Brothers films, "At the Circus" (1939).

Yes, that was the only one I couldn't get along with.

Are you speaking about Groucho?

Yes, he was strange. He was a very difficult man. Although I played a lovely part, unfortunately the very best moment of the picture they cut out for television.

[*Feld played an orchestra conductor who hasn't realized the floating platform on which he and his musicians are playing has been cut and drifted into the theater. At the end of the musical segment, Feld's character takes a bow and falls into the ocean.]*

Does that editing irritate you?

Yes, we running into the same situation in coloring films. When they sold films to television they cut them to one hour. It was horrifying to take masterpieces and cut them but nothing could be done.

Now we're in the same situation coloring pictures. They take tremendous pictures taken by great photographers in blacks and white and color them.

I see that you did a film at RKO with Lupe Velez ["Mexican Spitfire's Baby, 1941], who was one of Hollywood's great characters.

She and Carole Lombard swore like troopers, but they were such charming ladies you never minded it.

You also performed in a little horror film that is difficult to see today, "Cat Man of Paris" (1946).

We called for fun Republic Picture, "Repulsive Pictures." Anyway we played there and Mr. Yates who was the chief of the studio, which made mostly western pictures, tried a movie called *I've Always Loved You,* (1946) a million dollar picture. He attempted to do this picture and a very funny thing happened in it.

The star of the picture is a musician [a concert pianist played by Catherine McLeod] who is in a school with different pupils and [the teacher] walks around correcting them playing the piano; saying "You have bad fingering." It was all played by [Arthur] Rubenstein, pre-recorded and he wasn't told to play badly so he played beautifully.

So when the man says, "bad fingering," it is ridiculous. It was the most beautiful music.

Anyway, after the picture is finished, I was on the same lot and I had to do the picture you just mentioned.

Naturally, I had to ask Feld how he developed his popping noise and mannerism, which he did without asking.

I call myself a creative actor. In other words I just don't do what's written. I'm creative because I invent things and the producers know it. I played a waiter called "Fritz" in an Eddie Cantor picture [*If You Knew Susie,* 1948]. Eddie would say, "Fritz! Champagne!" And I said, "Champagne!" and popped, and they all laughed.

So I thought – do you remember Hugh Herbert [a popular comic actor who punctuated lines with "woo, woo, woo"] – I thought this would be a good idea to keep this as a trademark. And today people wait whenever I play a part [say] "Where is he going to put the pop?"

So the "pop" became stronger than the word, and my wife and I travel a lot, so now, for instance, in Africa all the kids are popping. When we go to a restaurant they go, "There is the pop man." It is very funny how all of this caught on.

Over your long career how has the industry changed?

Unfortunately, tremendously. I'm the only one in Hollywood who predicts it will come back, but right now it has been destroyed completely. Each studio had some great men … as producers and the head of studios they knew what the public wanted and they built a tremendous organization where actors were trained and all that is gone now.

FRANK COGHLAN, Jr.

2009

Frank Coghlan had a long and varied career in show business starting at the age of three in silent films, progressing as a teen and young adult. He appeared in a large number of films before entering the Navy and training as an aviator in World War II. After his 23-year career in the military, he returned to acting. His best-known role is that of Billy Batson in the 1941 serial *The Adventures of Captain Marvel,* certainly the role that introduced him to me.

Coghlan died in 2009.

***

I first asked him about his entry into motion pictures.

In the year 1919 at the age of three I made my first movies [laughs] and I went off the set crying.

Do you remember the title?

Yes, it was *To Please one Woman* starring Clara Kimball Young. I got the magnificent sum of $3 for the day's work.

Were your parent's show people? Is that how you gravitated to the movies at such an early age?

Actually not. My folks moved out here from New Haven Conn. For the reasons of health for my father's mother, who was an invalid. We settled in a place then called Edendale, now it's on the Glendale freeway. At that time that's where many of the studios were centered – Max Sennett's and a few others. My dad did work as an extra in a few pictures until he relocated into a steady job, and I guess, as a result of that people saw me around the studios. At the age of three I had bobbed hair, looked like Jackie Coogan, I guess. He had just done *The Kid* with Charlie Chaplin. So people asked my mother, "Why don't you get the little boy into movies?" And she said, "Oh no. I wouldn't do that."

But finally, my dad wasn't doing too well in his new job, so my mother did take me around to this one studio and I got this first job... she took me around to the other studios and pretty soon I was working pretty steady. In the next four years I put my father through college. [laughs]
Usually it's the other way around.

Yes, I put him through chiropractic college and he became a chiropractor as a result of my film earnings.

You were initially billed in movies as "Junior Coghlan."

Yes, I was Frank Coghlan Jr. and at home I was called Junior. That was the name I went by at first. I used that name clear up to high school age at which time my agent thought it was time to get rid of the junior. He tacked it on the end so people would remember and for a few years I was Frank Coughlin Jr. Now I just go by Frank Coghlan.

You were in many silent films and one of them was called "Square Shoulders (1929)."

That was the final silent film that I made and the last film I made under a five-year contract I had for C.B. DeMille [the legendary producer and director]. It co-starred Louis Wolheim, who was an excellent character actor of the era. He was sort of an Ernie Borgnine type. In fact they both played the same part in different versions of *All Quiet on the Western Front*.

I played a boy, a little orphan kid as usual. My father [played by] Louis Wolheim discovered me and actually stole money from a bank and left it in a trust fund for me to go through a military school. I was about 12 years old and had my first leading lady, the lovely young Anita Louise who was then 11.

The film had a touching conclusion with your character laying a bugle on his father's grave.

Yes, he had been a bugler in World War I and taught me to play the bugle. After I got into this military school, he got a job as a stable hand. I knew him but I didn't know he was my father. So when he did pass away I blew *Taps* over his grave with the bugle he taught me to play. [My character] never realized he was my father.

How did your contract with Cecil B. DeMille come about?

In 1925, Cecil B. DeMille was casting for one of his big pictures called *The Road to Yesterday* and I was recommended to him by Marshall Neilan who was a real fine director of the era and for whom I had made three movies.

DeMille tested me for this small part in it and I got the part, went on location to the Grand Canyon with William Boyd and Vera Reynolds and

Joseph Schildkraut. Rode it out for five years there. I was the kid on the DeMille lot. Jackie Cooper was the kid at MGM. [Jackie] Coogan was out of the business and soon Shirley Temple was the kid at 20th Century Fox and Rooney later at MGM.

All the studios had their kid and I was C.B. DeMille's kid. I remember a picture of me when I was 10 years old with shaggy hair with a sad look on my face and DeMille was supposed to have said, "Junior Coghlan is the perfect homeless waif."

So there! [laughs]

Just for your information. DeMille sold his Studio to Pathé a few years later and later then RKO/Pathé and then just RKO. The contract, though, was signed by C.B. DeMille.

The popular vision of C.B. DeMille is that of an autocratic man in rising jodhpurs with a megaphone. Was that an accurate picture? Did he actually use a megaphone on his sets?

Yes. Most of his films were the big epics with crowds. He had to be heard. He used a megaphone like Rudy Vallee sang through. In later years [he used] a hand-held public address microphone. He was a very autocratic, demanding director when he had big crowds, but when he was in intimate scenes of just a few of us he was actually a very tender likable fatherly man.

Were you worried about sound coming to motion pictures and its effect on your career?

I guess so because I was only 12 turning 13 and that's a period when the kid's voices aren't very good. They're changing. Strangely enough *Square Shoulders* was made silent, but then they re-shot the final few minutes of it with sound. It was difficult in those days because camera noise had to be masked off. They had the camera in a little room all by itself. Microphones were hidden all over the place in flowerpots and over your head – not the single mic on a boom like they have today.

I would say I had a very young – I still do – light voice, but it was only a year later when I made my first all talkie. I played "Sam" in *Penrod and Sam* at Warner Brothers. I survived all right. I wasn't out of work for a long time.

In "Public Enemy" you played the James Cagney character as a boy.

"That's right. I played Jimmy Cagney as a boy and Frankie Darro played Eddie Woods as a boy. There's about a 12 minute sequence at the beginning of the film where it shows the degeneration of these kids from petty crooks to out and out gangster and how we were led astray by a couple of guys at the pool hall.

Strangely enough when that film shows on television, it's a good way to cut 12 minutes from it if they want to squeeze it into two hours. Something that first prologue doesn't show.

You're right I did play Jimmy Cagney as a boy and it led to a marvelous friendship between the Cagney family and us. He was a marvelous man.

I have to ask you about one of my favorite kid actors Frankie Darro.

Oh Frank was a real character. He was raised in a circus atmosphere by his parents. He was a marvelous acrobat. By the age of four he could do great tricks. He was a little on the coarser side than some of the other kids that were around the studios, but he was a marvelous guy. We worked in lots of films together.

He was a great rider and I became a pretty good rider and we played jockeys quite often. In fact, in *Charlie Chan at the Racetrack,* he played the crooked cheating jockey and I played the crippled jockey trying to make a comeback and filled in his shoes and won the big race as a result.

Frank was a real good guy. He was a fine athlete, great hockey player – used to skate like the wind. He was just an all-around good guy.

During the 1930s were you under contract to any studio or were you a freelancer?

When my contract with C.B. DeMille ended at end of 1929, the beginning of 1930, I then became a freelancer and was and still am to this day. Always under contract to the picture you were making, with the exception of a series of comedies I made for two years called *The Frolics of Youth.* There I was under contract year by year as we made those comedies.

Although you were very busy during the 1930s, you are probably best known for your role as Billy Batson in the 1940 serial "The Adventures of Captain Marvel." How did that role come about?

I believe I was handpicked for it as I was one of the best-known young actors available at the time. I kind of looked like the cartoon character Billy Batson. I don't recall competing with a whole bunch of other actors for the part. I think I was pre-selected for it.

At the time it just seemed to be another job, but it has now become the classic of the action serials and I guess I'm best remembered for that part, even though I made others that I thought were more inducing of stardom than that.

Tom Tyler and I co-starred in it you might say. When I go to conventions, it's all *Captain Marvel* they all seem to remember.

I have to ask you about my favorite western star Tom Tyler. I know, though, you didn't have much contact with him in the production because you're playing the same person.

Well, with the exception of when I said, "Shazam," and the puff of smoke would go up. Tom would have to step into the same footsteps and repeat the world "Shazam" and he was there.

Frank Coghlan graciously signed this still for me featuring him and Nigel De Brulier from "The Adventures of Captain Marvel."

He would then go about dispensing the villains and I could go off and read, but in many cases report to the second unit and continue working on other scenes.

But yes, Tom and I were never in a scene together with the exception of the dissolve of the "Shazam."

Did you get to know him at all?

Tom had been a friend of my family for years. It just so happened my family, my mother and father were great friends with another couple and Tom was their best friend. My parents and Tom used to go out to dinners and parties together. I wasn't as buddy-buddy with him as my parents because he was older than I am. Yes, I had known Tom through the years, admired him. He was an Olympic Games weight lifter [Tyler was actually an AAU weightlifting champion], a very powerful man. But with it all, he was a modest mild mannered gentleman. Of course, when we spent 12 weeks on a picture together we were very friendly.

Tom was a good actor. His westerns seem to be the best known, but he played some good important parts.

After you shot "Adventures of Captain Marvel," you went into the Navy.

Yes, we shot *Captain Marvel* the very first few months of 1940. I kept working on other films, but I entered the Navy in December 1942. I went through flight training and became a Naval aviator and I stayed on active duty for 23 years. I retired in 1965 and I resumed acting again.

How was that transition for you?

During the 23 years I was on active duty, though an aviator the Navy made very good use of my film experience. Between 1952 and 1954 I was in the Pentagon in the Office of Information in charge of the Navy's motion picture program and the producers came back to me for script approval, and to arrange for locations. During that time I set up *The Caine Mutiny*, *The Bridge at To Ko Ri*, and the final film was *Mr. Roberts*. I did many others in between but those are the three outstanding ones.

And then the final years of my active duty I was in charge of the Navy's Hollywood office and there I was on the sets all the time giving technical advice and consulting with the writers and directors. It was a marvelous job for me and the studios liked it too. They knew they had a Navy officer who could see both sides of a script.

It kept your hand in the business?

Yes, it did. When I returned I still knew all these people on a first name basis and it was quite easy for me to return to acting.

I know you do a fair amount of television work, including being the commercial spokesman for Curtis Mathes television sets.

Right. For five and half years. Those were wonderful. I don't know if they showed them in Massachusetts or not. They were in 43 states.

We saw them up here. I kept thinking to myself, "That guy looks familiar and that voice is familiar," and then hit it hit me, it must be the guy who was in "Captain Marvel."

And at the end of each one [commercial] I would say, "Curtis Mathes, the most expensive television in America. And darn well worth it."

What do you think of motion pictures today?

I must say that on the average I don't like them as well. I think the movies we made in the '30s in most cases were clean and uncomplicated and you could take the whole family to see them. Now, of course, they are still some great films being made, the Robert Redfords and Paul Newmans and all that, but golly there are other films, these murder things, hacksaw-type murders, I wouldn't want to take my grandchildren to see them, I can tell you that.

It is disappointing that with all of the movies today that we talk about a low- budget film being $10 million. In the 1920s and '30s if someone had suggested spending $10 million they would have been taken out and shot by the studio chiefs.

You know, all of Mickey Rooney's *Andy Hardy* films were made for a quarter of a million dollars apiece. There was no spending more because the number of people who came to see each one, so why spend another $10 when they didn't have to? A quarter of a million – you couldn't make a one-reel comedy for that today.

I imagine the producers at Republic studios were very cost conscious there.

They were, but they didn't waste a nickel, either. They knew what was happening every minute. They made a good product and they made it as economically as they possibly could.

WILLIAM "Billy" BENEDICT

William "Billy" Benedict's greatest recognition by the public probably came from his long-running participation in the *Bowery Boys* series as "Whitey," but Benedict had quite a career besides those comedies. He appeared in Westerns, serials, B-movies and big budgeted films as well chalking up hundreds of credits in not just movies, but television series as well. According to the Internet Movie Database, he had almost 300 appearances in films and television shows – not quite at Fritz Feld's output but damn close.

When I spoke with him he was still very active primarily making commercials, which he described as "quick and you can make a buck." He died in 1999.

***

How did you get started in motion pictures?

Well I go back to 1934 when I came to California with my older sister. We settled here. Originally I had been a dancer. The dancing business was rather sparse so I began to hit the casting offices around. I happened to be in the right place at the right time and got a part with Edward Everett Horton called *$10 Raise* at the old Fox Studio on Western Avenue and Hollywood.

From there you became a very busy character actor, which you are to this day.

Yes, I think that I am.

Were you nervous breaking into pictures?

I must say I was a little apprehensive to say the least, but I got off to a good start because the people that I was involved in with the first picture, which was directed by George Marshall, a delightful man, and we became very good friends and also Edward Everett Horton, with whom I also became very good friends.

And everybody involved in the making of the picture from top to bottom were very kind and very helpful to me. All in all I got off to a good start.

Did you get offered a contract or did you work as an independent?

Before the picture was finished, they put me under contract – a seven-year contract as they called it in those days with six-month options for the first year and yearly options with an increase in salary. So I was at Fox for almost two years. During the time I was under contract, most of my time was spent on loan to other studios.

What are some of the films in which you appeared at that time?

The first picture I had a big role in was *College Scandal* (1935) at Paramount. Then I did *Witness Chair* (1936) at RKO. I went to Universal and did *Three Kids and a Queen* (1935) with May Robson, Henry Armetta, Herman Bing, Frankie Darro, and Charlotte Henry who was the original Alice [in *Alice in Wonderland* (1933)] and a young man who played a crippled boy who went on to become a big producer in television Bill Burrud.

You received quite an education in acting by going to different studios and playing in a variety of films. Did you ever take acting lessons?

When I was in school I took a lot of drama. As I say I was very fortunate. I had a lot of help. I was rather observant. When you work with someone like Edward Everett Horton and you observe what this man does if you don't have some of it rub off you're a complete idiot believe me. He was a fine talent and a beautiful man and very helpful to me … There were some great directors who were extremely helpful.

How did you get involved in The East Side Kids/Bowery Boys series?

That's an interesting story. When I began freelancing – I don't remember the exact date, probably around 1937 or so – there was a man who had been an assistant director at Fox named Sam Katzman. Sam went out on his own and began making pictures of state rights release. That meant he made a picture put it under his arms get on a plane or a train and go to a city and make a deal with some theater owner and run the picture.

So, Sam called my agent and said he had a part for me in a picture and asked would I do it. Well, my agent said, "Do you know Sam?" and I said, "Yes, I know Sam. He's a nice man."

[My agent said] "Well Sam wants to use you in a picture. He can't pay you enough to amount to anything, but if you want to have some fun why don't you do it?"

So I went to see Sam and the film was to be directed by a man I knew by the name of Robert Hill, Bob Hill, who had been a director at Universal.

I did the show, if I'm not mistaken the first one I did for Katzman was a boxing picture *Flying Fists*, (1937) with Herman Brix [an Olympic star who later changed his name to Bruce Bennett and had much success at Warner Brothers].

We ran into some weather problems and Sam's operation used a slight story and lots of stock footage, a very, very short budget, and a three-or four-day shooting schedule. We ran into some weather and we couldn't shoot. Sam was in a bind and wanted to know if I could give him an extra day without any pay. I wound up doing that.

One thing led to another I did another picture for him. Sam didn't forget so when he started doing the East Side Kids I would see him in the Hollywood post office and he said, "Come on down and see me I'm doing a series of pictures and I'd like to use you."

I did go down to see Sam and he threw a script across the desk and told me to pick out what I liked to play. I said, "You're never going to pay my salary Sam." [He replied,] "Try me. What's your agent's phone number?" I gave him the number; he called and paid my salary, which surprised a lot of people.

When I first started working for Sam, I was not a member of the East Side kids gang but after I did three pictures I became a regular member. Then Sam and Leo [Gorcey], the star of the series] couldn't get together contract wise and it wound up that Jan Grippo became the producer and I signed up with them and worked with them up until 1951.

[In 1945, Grippo and Gorcey split from Katzman and produced a new title for the series, "The Bowery Boys," which gave Gorcey a 40 percent ownership of the property.]

The films were a favorite with audiences when they were first produced and then found new generations of fans on television. What do you think was the secret of their success?

Simplicity. The stories may not have been the greatest in the world but you had a bunch of kids and a lot of young people could identify with them. We got into a lot of trouble. Right won out, the good guys won always. Looking back in retrospect, in fact I just watched one last Saturday morning – they're running them here now – and they were rather funny to say the least. I think as new generations of young people come along they find them very entertaining as do the older people. I don't say it's a phenomenal thing. It just happened to be dog-gone good entertainment made at a price during that particular period, it fitted the bill and Monogram and Allied Artists a lot of money, a lot of money.

What was it like to work with Leo Gorcey and Huntz Hall?

[laughs] It could be mad at times, but however they were very talented we worked hard, had a lot of fun and I think we came up with something.

Was Gorcey half the tough guy off screen as he was on screen?

No I think he might have liked to have been. Leo had an act that worked very well in pictures. Occasionally off screen he played the same part. He was an extremely talented man and a dog-gone good businessman as far as investments go.

Can you tell me something about the serial "The Adventures of Captain Marvel?"

Now you're talking about one of my favorites. In fact last evening I spoke with our mutual friend Frank Coghlan.

How did you find yourself at Republic Pictures doing that serial?

Someone asked for me on that particular show, but the deal was made through an agent. We went to work, Frank doing "Billy Batson" and I doing "Whitey," and what fun we had believe me. It has become a classic in its own right.

Those were days we would leave Republic studios at about five o'clock in the morning and take the stretch – big sedans they had actually stretched them out – and we would wind our way to Iverson's Ranch which had been used location-wise for a long time and we would go about our business chasing down whatever we were chasing at the time.

We put in long hours but we had a lot of fun.

Was there a big difference working between Monogram and Republic?

At that time, they were pretty much on the same par because they made pictures for a price. In other words, their budgets were low on the totem pole. They were comparable I think in the method they went about making their motion pictures ... the big difference [between them and the larger studios] was the amount of money they had to spend and the length of time of the shooting schedule.

I know many of your scenes in the Captain Marvel series were with Frank Coghlan. Did you get to know the star of the film, Tom Tyler?

Oh yes, Nice man, quiet, a hard-working individual. He took his work very seriously and did a good job – did an excellent job.

Did you perform in many Westerns?

Of yes, the first Western I did was at RKO with George O'Brien. What a delightful man. We became very good friends. I did some shows with Gene Autry and Roy Rogers.

Of all of your films that you did what are some that gave you the opportunity of showing off your talents?

Well, number one the first picture that I did *$10 Raise,* another picture called *The Witness Chair* (1936) with Ann Harding at RKO, *Libeled Lady* (1936) with Spencer Tracy, Myrna Loy and Jean Harlow and Bill Powell. *Great cast!*

Oh tell me! And a great story and *The Oxbow Incident* (1943) that has become another classic directed by a wonderful man William Wellman. He was a great director and a great writer. That's a start anyway.

KEYE LUKE

Keye Luke's films are the perfect example of the career of a character actor. Luke worked with everyone, at studios large and small and in films that were classic, while other forgettable.

He is best remembered for performances that bookended his career: Charlie Chan's number one son and Master Po in the television series *Kung Fu*. Luke, though, turns up in many films and television series and his last appearance was in 1990 at age eighty-six in Woody Allen's film *Alice*. He died the next year.

Luke was "discovered" through his artwork for movie publicity items and remained an artist throughout his life. Like other Asian performers, he had to cope with typecasting. He was an Asian actor who worked in an environment in which white actors were cast more in Asian roles than Asians were.

***

How did you get started in acting?

I was doing some advertising artwork for *Flying Down to Rio*, the picture that starred Fred Astaire and Ginger Rogers for the first time. And the producer Lou Brock liked my work and we became very friendly and he said, "I'm going to make a sequel and it's going to be called *Home to Shanghai* and it's going to have Anna May Wong in it and I want you to play her love interest."

So I said, "Lou, I'm an artist." And he said, "Oh, you've been around. You know what's it all about. Put you in a couple of shorts to get experience and let's go."

That's how it got started. My publicity friends took it up and gave me a lot of publicity and first thing I knew I was an actor [laughs].

Your first big role was in a Greta Garbo movie, "The Painted Veil" (1934).

That came after a couple of shorts I did for experience, I went into the Garbo picture. My former advertising boss was at MGM and he called me out here and I took my drawing out because I thought he wanted to me to do some artwork. Instead of that he handed me a script and said read page so and so and page so and so [and asked,] "How would like to play that part?"

Well, I said, "Gee that looks good." And he said, "Okay let's go down to the casting office." We went to the casting office and he said, "Wait here."

I sat in the reception room and I heard him in this loud big voice – he was a circus barker at one point – "Out of China's 400 million, gentlemen, I give you China's greatest actor." [Laughs], which was amazing. That's real Hollywood.

There was dead silence. He went out through another door and I poked my head in the room and they saw me and they laughed, "Get out of here you bum!" They knew me because of my artwork you see and I knew them, all of these casting directors.

One of them said, "Come on back, take a test. If you're good, you'll get the part."

I took the test. I got the part. So that's how I got into the Garbo picture.

Did you have the opportunity of speaking with Garbo at all? Was she accessible to her supporting cast?

Yes, she was very reserved but she did talk and she was very gracious. We talked about world conditions and this that and the other thing – very profound subjects [laughs].

Before we talk about the Charlie Chan series, I'd like to speak with you about "The Good Earth" (1937).

Oh yes, well that was one of the greatest pictures ever made in Hollywood and I'm certainly grateful and fortunate I was in it. I played the part of the oldest son who went to college and came back home just in time with is knowledge of agronomy to save the crops from the crickets.

Many people today have forgotten the star of the film Paul Muni.

Yes, Paul Muni was one of the greatest actors who ever lived, one of the most conscientious and painstaking. He was absolutely100 percent zeroed into what he was doing all the time.

Did he do a lot of research in order to create the illusion of being Chinese?

One thing about Paul was that his features lent themselves to an Oriental makeup and he didn't look like the beautiful profiles you associated with Hollywood's leading men. I thought visually with his makeup he was very convincing as Chinese and of course he studied the part thoroughly as he did every part he ever played and he played some magnificent parts, the important men of history. This Chinese peasant was one of those characters he conceived of on a universal scale. He sought it not just as an individual in China but also as man for the world, as a man would be in any part of the world under those conditions.

How did you become involved with the Charlie Chan series?

The whole thing came about when I was in Seattle. I was very high brow [laughs]. I was reading Shakespeare. My brother was reading the Saturday Evening Post. One day he said to me, "Hey Keye, this Charlie Chan is some detective in this Saturday Evening Post." I said," I'm not going to read that. That's low brow stuff." [Laughs]

When I came down to Hollywood, I wound up doing advertising artwork for the Charlie Chan pictures at Fox and that of course led to my eventually going into them when my advertising boss of mine at Fox said, "Now that you've turned

Keye Luke

actor due to all the publicity come on out here and see what you can do."

So I went out and saw him, Gabe York, and he took me down to the casting office [and was told] "Too bad you didn't come yesterday. Had a marvelous part for you. The part of a Japanese spy blowing up the Panama Canal, but I had to give it to someone else. But go down to Western Avenue."

You see Fox was in two parts then. One part was up in Beverly Hills and the other was down in Hollywood at Sunset and Western Avenue – the old Fox Studios and that's where the Chans were made.

We went down there and the casting director whom I knew said, "We're going to put the number one son in the Charlie Chan pictures for the first time. No reason why you shouldn't play it." He called the author [screenwriter] whom I knew who said he would put in a great part for me. He did and after the preview they signed me to do the series.

What was Warner Oland like to work with?

Warner was an actor of the old school. He was taught to cast aside his own personality and create a character the audience can believe. With his natural Oriental looks, he came by that naturally, he was Swedish you see. He approached it from the standpoint of a Chinese Mandarin scholar. That was why he gave such a convincing portrayal. He was courteous, kind. He saw through everything. No one ever out-foxed him … everyone looked up at him. Everyone consulted him.

Many good actors worked in the Chan series and I think "Charlie Chan at the Opera" was one of the finest.

I think it was the finest. It was my favorite. *Charlie Chan at the Opera* with Boris Karloff. For the music Oscar Levant wrote the original music for the opera sequences and many, many others were in it – Bill Demarest, Margaret Irving. You see, all the actors in Hollywood, all the supporting actors wanted to get into the Chan pictures because they were marvelous showcases. That is why we were always able to get the finest supporting cast.

Were they fun films to make?

Yes, they were marvelous films to make because everyone thought we were making the best detective stories in Hollywood. We were proud of the work and we were absolutely wrapped up in it to give the best possible performance.

One thing that has absolutely fascinated me is that you worked everywhere from MGM to Monogram. I caught you the other day in a movie with Frankie Darro, "The Gang's All Here." (1941)

We did a series of youth pictures and they were very popular. Frankie Darro was a superb little actor.

Were there many differences in working at a studio like Monogram as opposed to MGM?

Well, let's just say there was a difference in resources – put it that way. But was far as making pictures, the spirit was the same and the attitude was the same. You felt a little richer at MGM than you were at Monogram.

Many people remember you as well as "Master Po" on the television series "Kung Fu."

That was my favorite role. That was the role I was most happy to play and most happy to get. Where could you possibly find a situation where you find a Chinese actor who can give forth with the philosophical sayings of the old masters, the old philosophers? Amazing that it should happen in Hollywood.

Do you think it's been difficult for you to get those serious roles because you are Chinese?

They have seemed to come my way. I am Chinese and I would say there is always difficulty for any actor getting a part, but I've been very, very lucky. I've done what I think have been some very satisfying parts.

Did it every bother you or any other Asian actors that non-Asian were being cast in Asian roles?

There were no Oriental actors who had the talent or the box office attraction, you see. You must remember that films are made for a white audience and Oriental players are necessarily supporting players. Once in a while there's a fine part and I've done some of those, but generally they are just simply supporting parts.

Now, of course, the situation is changed, There are many fine Asian actors who are qualified to play the finest parts you can give.

You recently appeared in "Gremlins" (1985) playing the ancient and mysterious merchant who had the little creature.

That was a very marvelous engagement. Everyone connected to the picture had such fun with it. We didn't try to take it to seriously, that was evident in the picture There was an element of fun and humor running through the whole thing. That character I played was not a new character to me, still it has certain elements about it that were unusual, especially in the last part when I gave the folks a lecture on how they're ruining the environment and don't appreciate the gifts of nature.

You had the opportunity of working with one of my favorite actors in your career, Peter Lorre.

Oh, Peter Lorre, God bless him. He was marvelous. He was marvelous. We had such fun together. I did two pictures with him and I was also in pictures we were both in. I did two pictures in which he was the star and we had so much fun. We talked about the old days when he started out in Vienna as a comedian. He said, "For heaven's sakes, I did the picture *M* and now I can't even get a comic role."

You were in his first American film "Mad Love" (1935), in which you played his assistant.

[In the movie] We were camped out at the French prisons and we grabbed the bodies of all the guillotined prisoners and took them back to our laboratory and try to put heads and bodies together and bring back life [laughs].

And you were in a film in which he played Mr. Moto and you played Lee Chan. ("Mr. Moto's Gamble" 1938)

The picture we were doing with Warner Oland had to be suspended because Oland was ill, so they took the film we already had shot with Oland and turned it over deftly, very cleverly into the picture with Peter Lorre.

Who was the best Chan of the men associated with that role: Warner Oland, Sidney Toler or Roland Winters?

By all means Warner Oland. Visually he was the most effective and artistically he was the most effective. His attitude and interpretation of the role was so masterful. You see most people thought he spoke pidgin English because of his haltering style of delivery. The reason he did that was that he was acting in Chinese, thinking in Chinese and transferring his thoughts into English, which was not his natural tongue. So naturally he fumbled a little.

That made a marvelous effect.

You were in both "Green Hornet" serials (1940, 1941).

Yes I was the original Kato. With a karate chop I felled many a big man in those pictures [laughs].

Kato was the brains in "The Green Hornet." He came up with the car and the gas gun.

Let's just say he was a big help. [laughs]

You've had a long career and I've spoken to other veterans of the "golden era" of Hollywood who have spoken of the differences in the film business today and then.

There are technical advances of course. The special effects boys are simply geniuses at what they do today. We didn't have that in the old days.

Our pictures were made to entertain and that's what we tried to do: to make the best possible entertainment.

Today, I know they still make entertainment but also try to astonish you with these effects. I'm not saying these are not good, but it's different. For the actor, it's still the same thing: he has to know his words. He has to project. He has to convince the audience that he is that particular character he's playing. And that doesn't change. The money might change, the rulers of the studio, the directors, etc. [may change]. But for the actor his job is still the same.

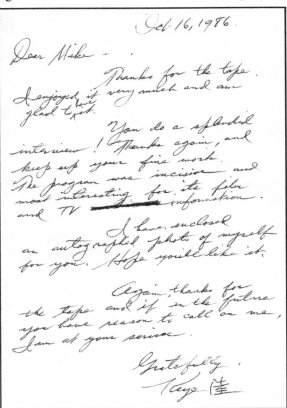

The note I received from Keye Luke. It's always fulfilling to know that an interview went well.

DICK WILSON

One role can change an actor's life and that was certainly the case with Dick Wilson. He was a busy character actor who had appeared in movies and television when he won a part in a television commercial in 1965. That role was a definitely odd: a grocery store manager with a fetish for soft toilet paper. "Mr. Whipple" was the spokesman for Charmin toilet paper for more than 500 commercial over decades. Wilson kept working on television although millions of Americans recognized him for just one thing.

Wilson had no regrets about his most significant role and said with a flourish, "I loom large in lavatories."

He acted until 1989 and died in 2007.

***

How did you get started in show business?

I was in vaudeville for over 20 years. From there to radio, Broadway, motion pictures, television.

You've done it all!

And I spent one season in the circus. [laughs] I love to watch the circus but it's a hard life, that's all I have to say.

Did you come from a show business family?

My father used to be the interlocutor for the Moncastle Minstrels in England, which was many, many years ago. You hear all the wonder stories about that and you say, "Boy I want to be part of that."

I've heard that you have a good story about you and Clark Gable.

Oh! One day I was coming out of MGM, and Louis B., Mayer would not let you thumb your way from the front of the studio. He thought it was very demeaning and if you did you never worked there again.

One time I came out of the gate and it was raining and I had my suit on. And when I say my suit I mean my one suit. I came out and a car came up with curtains on the side, the old touring cars. A voice said to me, "Are you going to Hollywood?" and I said, "Yes I am. I'm going near Grauman's Chinese Theater."

"I'm going to the Hollywood Hotel. It's close to that, one block."

"Marvelous," I said and I got in and I looked and it's Clark Gable. As soon as I got in he said, "Is this your first day on the picture?" I said, "[nervous sputtering sounds]." I couldn't answer the man.

Everything he asked me I had a rotten answer for him. It was terrible. When I got out of the car I said, "Mr. Gable I'm not really as stupid as this, but I have to go home and explain to my mother that Clark Gable picked me up and took me home. The following morning at 7 o'clock there will be two people with white coats and a van waiting for me to get up so they can take me away."

He said, "Are you going to work tomorrow? I'll pick you up."

I said, "No. I'm not going to work tomorrow I only had one day on the picture, but I tell you what: pick me up anyway, but give me enough time to get a whole bunch of people to watch it. You can drive me two blocks and I'll get out and walk home.

And he laughed and thought it was funny. He was a wonderful man.

I couldn't dig up a filmography of you. Could you tell us some of the films you worked on?

I have to work backwards: *Incredible Shrinking Woman* with Lily Tomlin, *World's Greatest Athlete*, *Shakiest Gun in the West* with Don Knotts, *One Man's Way*. Oh let me see. I should have had my biography out here – I have it all written down. I've done 38 pictures.

Were you ever under contact or were you always a freelancer?

At Repulsive, I mean Republic Pictures, which we all call "Repulsive Pictures."

It was not fun working there. It was one of the smaller studios. I was under contract for the great sum of $75 a week. You were in as many as four movies a day. You would go from one stage to another and they would say, "You're an Arab, go to wardrobe," and the next one they'd say, "You're a seaman, Go get a sailor suit."

And they'd give you what to say when you went over, maybe three or four lines, maybe one, you never knew.

There are now people who love their westerns and serials and their reputation has taken on a new light.

It's different now. It's defunct. No one can ask questions of the boss or bosses.

Did you do Westerns there?

Sure I did, a whole bunch of Westerns. I did *The Hanging Tree*.

Did you work with Roy Rogers or Gene Autry?

Yes, I worked with Rogers on the series. I was always the bad guy and I played the head of the bad guys in this thing. One of my henchmen was a fellow you might know named Robert Mitchum.

I wonder what happened to me, but I know what happened to him [laughs].

So how did you wind up on the Charmin commercials?

It was very easy. I was a co-producer of a show in Las Vegas and my agent called me. I thought that was very strange as I had him listed with missing persons!

He said, "How do you feel about toilet paper?" This was at 9 o'clock in the morning. I said, " I think everybody should use it."

He said, "How would like to do a commercial for toilet paper?" I said, "What do they pay: paper or money?"

He said, "It's an audition." I said, "How do you audition toilet paper?" He said, "It's a screen test. Would you go down there and see them?"

So I went to Los Angeles the following morning and we shot the stuff. Put it on films and shipped it to New York, and we did our first commercial the following Thursday, for toilet paper mind you, in Flushing, Long Island, at Max's Market. [Actually Flushing is part of Queens in New York City.]

When we first start we shot them in little grocery stores and when we went to California we shot them in Korean grocery stories for years.

Did you ever mind the jokes made about your character and the commercials?

When they're talking about you at least you're in the public eye and I worked for Proctor & Gamble and when I was mentioned they loved it and that was okay with me. That means you're doing your job properly.

How many years did you do that?

I'm in my 23rd year.

I understand from reading about other commercial actors it can be a lucrative living.

I don't like the kind of pictures they're making today and if I took my clothes off the first four rows would throw up, so I do want to do those kind of pictures. I'm very happy.

I always tell people, "I deal with the toilet. I don't necessarily have to make the pictures that belong in the toilet." I'm very happy with what I am right now.

Do you feel more comfortable with comedy than you do with drama?

Yes, I've always been a comic, always. Except for my sojourn with Republic where in every picture I was a bad guy.

I've seen you pop up in many sit-coms over the years.

I was the running drunk in *Bewitched* for nine years. I was "Col. Gruber" on *Hogan's Heroes* for four years. On *McHale's Navy* I was "Dino Barone." I did a lot of in and out stuff.

I was "Maxie the cab driver" on Lee Marvin's *M Squad*. I did a lot of in and out stuff.

People have said that if you worked at Republic or Monogram on low budget pictures that prepared you for television.

Yes, nobody would believe you that you did an entire picture in 10 days. They could shoot a picture in 10 days and have it ready for release in 21 days. That seems impossible but that's true. Music dubbed and the whole thing.

And television is a lot like that.

Exactly. I was a one-take wonder. They used to hire me because I could do it in one take. They used to say, "What is your motivation?" I'd say, "Money. I'm an actor."

What are some of the difference between the ways movies are made today and the 1940s and '50s.

The speed. I was walking down the street one day, and I was with a friends, and I wanted to show off. I wanted to call my agent: I had a new one. He said, "Where have you been? You're going to Honolulu this afternoon." I said "Holy mackerel."

I got my suitcase packed. I went to 20th [Century Fox]. They put me on the bus. We went to Honolulu. The next day I came out on the beach and the director said to me, "Who are you?' I said, "I'm Dick Wilson. I play the crook."

He said, "We don't get to you until we get back to L.A. Where did you get the ticket?"

"Your secretary."

So I stayed there 12 weeks in Honolulu. I worked 20 minutes in Honolulu. I came back worked another eight weeks in Hollywood and if you can find me in the picture you get a gold doubloon.

What was the movie?

The Wake of the Red Witch (1948). They took the time in those times. Today they don't take the time. I don't understand why they don't when it's so important.

JAMES LYDON

James Lydon was best known as "Jimmy" and was one of the most prominent child stars of the late 1930s and into the 1940s. He rose to fame as the movie embodiment of *Henry Aldrich*. He played the lead character of the popular radio comedy based on the life and of an average American teenage boy. Lydon starred the role in nine movies, which he told me had a negative impact on his career because of typecasting.

He did overcome that image and appeared in such films as *Life with Father* with William Powell and the film noir outing *Strange Illusion.*

Affable, but candid, Lydon didn't pull any punches about what he thought of being a star as a child and teen. Unlike other child stars, Lydon made the transition to adult roles and also to the other side of the camera.

He said show business is a "business of blind dumb luck and I've had my share of it."

***

How did you get started in show business?

That's a long story that would take more than this morning, Mike. I was a child actor on Broadway in New York. I come from a very, very large Irish American family. I have eight brothers and sisters. We lived in New York City during the Depression and you know what that was like or maybe you're too young to remember, I don't know [chuckles]

It was imperative we make a living. We had a nasty habit of eating you see. I fell into the theater only because it paid $45 a week, which in those days in the 1930s during the Depression was a fortune.

So I began as a stage actor in New York and since Paramount Studios owned a huge sound stage on Long Island I began to make shorts and things there. Finally, I made a feature for Paramount in New York in the 1930s and went under contract to a director who was very disappointed with Hollywood after many, many years of working out here and made his feature there.

When I went under contract to him, he suddenly ran out of money and he couldn't pay me anymore. He sold my contract to RKO, a studio out here in California and I came out here in my teens.

One of your RKO features was "Little Men" with George Bancroft, who at one time was one of the top box office attractions in the movie business. He had a reputation for being an egotist and I was wondering what it was like to work with him since child actors are known to steal scenes even from veteran performers.

Ah, but they don't know they are doing it, you see. [chuckles] George Bancroft as I remember and these are only my opinions, mind you. Bancroft was a very difficult man. I don't think he ever really made the adjustment that so many people had to make from being a big star – and he was – to a kind of also-ran over-the-hill character man.

He was an irascible gentleman. He was a good actor, a little heavy handed, but a good actor. But I found him not pleasant. Jack Oakie, on the other hand, Kay Francis and the other people were just marvelous – so was the director. But Mr. Bancroft was a little difficult, let's put it that way.

And besides it wasn't his picture. It was Kay Francis's and mine. [chuckles] I don't think that made him happy either, you see.

What was it like to be a child and teen actor? So many of your peers, such as Mickey Rooney, Jackie Cooper, and Judy Garland, have come away with a degree of bitterness. Looking back, do you feel you have missed out on something?

My thoughts are very mixed on that Mike. I resented terribly working all through my childhood and into adulthood when my eight other brothers and sisters were allowed to do anything they wanted.

You see, I was in the middle of my family. I have four older brothers and a brother and a sister and a brother and a sister who were younger. I was in the middle of these nine children. Unfortunately, my mother made no distinction between any of us. My mother is still alive, by the way, she's 92 and lives in Albany, N.Y.

When all of my brothers and sisters were out playing baseball and all the things kid do, I was in New York doing radio or theater and then in California making motion pictures. And so I really was robbed of a childhood. My mother couldn't help me because of circumstances and then because of the added circumstances that I was lucky and made a lot of money.

And so I couldn't stop working. My thoughts going back on it, I always wanted to go to college and I never could go for the most ridiculous of reasons. I wanted to be an architect. Most of my friends outside of the business today are architects. But I could not stop making all that money to take four years to go to college. Besides I did not have what people outside of my industry would call a normal schooling. We had just what the law required out here [California]. In New York, we got whatever we could scramble together as far as what an education goes.

And so consequently, looking back on it, I'm glad today. Because I love my industry very much, I'm glad that I had to go through that. But I have two daughters, both now grown-up and married and when they were little children, very early on they were told and made to understand that if they wanted to get into this business, there was no way, even to approach the motion picture industry or the theater or anything else, until they had a college diploma in hand.

Then if they really wanted to I would reluctantly help them. Does that give you an idea of how I felt? [laughs]

Pretty clear, pretty clear.

It's not any kind of life you would imagine and some of the people you mentioned like Rooney, Garland, and Cooper were all good friends of mine and those alive are still good friends of mine today. I watched those very talented young people grow up and almost to a person be terribly warped and some of them destroyed, in the case of Garland, by being a child, in a child's body with a child's mind and expected to act and react like an adult. It was no way to raise a child in my opinion.

The money was absolutely necessary at least to me and my family and I'm sure for the others, but all the other things that came with it were terribly unfair.

Even today I'm a director and a producer mostly now, I kind of wince when I have to cast a child or work with a child as a director or that sort. I just know what is going to happen to them in certain cases. It does not make me happy, but we use what we have to use. If we need a chair, we go and get one. If we need a locomotive, we get one. If we need a child actor, we get one.

The role for which you are best known is "Henry Aldrich."

Unfortunately it was.

Why do you say "unfortunately?"

Well, again, it's a difficult thing to say to people who have not been in this industry – how one could resent and resent very deeply a series like the Aldrich series it ran for years and years on the screen all over the world.

Because they only see the so-called glamour in such a thing or the notoriety. Everywhere you go people are asking for autographs or whatever – all the exterior things that don't mean anything to us. We're there to make a living and in some of our cases a very good living.

It's only a living, a way to make a living for us. In my case, I was a dramatic actor in New York, apparently a fairly decent one and started in films making straight dramas. Suddenly I was put into a comedy series by the studio I was under contract to and the thing hits the public eye and that's the only thing I'm allowed to do. I'm not allowed to make anything other than those.

The stigma attached to it after a number of years making this series was so strong that it took the next three or four years and in some cases even longer to break that image and go on and do a number of things that I had been trained to do.

Looking back on that series I do have some fond memories, the people we made them with, the director who directed all of them, now dead; the woman who played my mother who eventually became my mother-in-law because I married her daughter – and still married some 34 years later. Those things were accidents and maybe pluses, but those are the only pluses I can think of except, for making the money quite frankly.

One of your films after the "Aldrich" series was "Life with Father" (1947). You were able to work with one of my favorite actors, William Powell.

A wonderful, wonderful gentleman. He's gone now. [I also worked in that film with] Elizabeth Taylor, a lovely lady, a lovely lady. She was a child. I think she was 15. I looked 16 or 17 but I was 23. [laughs]

It was marvelously produced by Warners and it was directed by their premiere director Mike Curtiz. And Mike was an interesting man.

I've heard so many stories about Curtiz being a monster on the set.

I didn't find him so and most people really didn't. Those people who worked for him a short time, such as one day or three or four days found him exactly what he was. Mike was a Hungarian and he had been a wrestler as a young man and he spoke very fractured and broken English. Mike was a very artistic, marvelous director, but he had such trouble with the English language, such trouble communicating to the cast and the crew that he would break off into tantrums of screaming and hollering.

But once you got used to that sort of thing and you understood his impatience rand his violent outbursts he was a most wonderful man. We used to laugh at him. Mike would stand in the middle of the set and scream and holler. He would also wind up his tirades by saying, [adopting an accent] "Who gets the big dough? You or me?" And everybody would laugh and Mike didn't mind. He was just letting off steam because he couldn't communicate.

I found him wonderful and delightful and a great director.

You just mentioned playing a 16-year-old at age 23. Was the adjustment difficult for you to get adult roles?

Yes, I would say so – difficult because I never looked my present age until I got into my fifties. For instance I spent about 15 years playing high school kids in films.

The other thing was I really truthfully – not saying I enjoyed being in front of a camera, making the money, the notoriety, no, I never cared about that – [didn't want to act], but my bent was to make films, not to be in them.

The adjustment from being a child actor to being a teenager to being an adult was not as hard for me as it was for my contemporaries because I wanted to be behind the camera and not in front. I did whatever my studio told me to do and my studios were many: RKO at first, then Paramount, then Columbia, then Warner Brothers. In those days of the studio system you did what you were told. Certain actors groused about it, but I never did. I was always in the cutting rooms or the dubbing rooms or whatever learning how to make film so one day I could do what I wanted to do and that was director film. I do now. I also teach it and that's very gratifying and wonderful.

I used my time at a studio when other people didn't. In those days, Paramount, for instance, to show you how our work schedule would be like, I made three films a year at Paramount. We shot 21 days on each film six days a week in those days. That's approximately three weeks work, three times a year. Well, that's not a great deal of time really for the money they paid you. Most actors under contract in that situation would spend it doing whatever. There's very little outside of our industry that interests actors.

They were many times depressed, uncertain about the future. I went into the studio every day and I was the only kid on the lot, so every one let me into the cutting rooms, dubbing stages, the scoring stages [voice rising in volume for emphasis] and I had a wonderful time. It was a great learning experience because our business is not one you can really learn out of a book – I don't think there are any books – but there are some good [college] courses, I teach one occasionally. The only way to learn our business is to do it, to see it done and then there is no mystery.

And so that's what I did with my time when other actors were always off balance with the great long waits in-between films even though they were being paid.

Among your credits is being the associate producer on "The Learning Tree."

That's right. That was Gordon Parks, our first black director and producer. It was a marvelous experience for Warner brothers, again.

I've had great deal of good fortune to be connected – in the producing end – with some of the most memorable television series of our era and some features. For Universal I was part of the producing team for *McHale's Navy, Wagon Train, Alfred Hitchcock Hour*. For Warner Brothers, *77 Sunset Strip*. *Mr. Roberts* for 20th Century Fox. I supervised the first year of *M.A.S.H.* and then did my own shows for them in the producing end, *Anna and the King* with Yul Brynner.

For features, I produced seven features for Warner Brothers with some of the leading actors today such as Jimmy Caan, Robert Duvall in *Count Down*. I made Bob Altman's first film.

It's been a marvelous experience and I've had a wonderful time. I think my life now is very, very rewarding. As I say I do now all the things I always wanted to do: produce, I have my own company, I direct occasionally and I teach at UCLA in the extension courses. I teach production and pre-production of motion pictures. I do not teach acting. I don't think anyone can teach acting.

Would you consider going back to acting?

I do all the time. I make commercials in front of the camera and behind the camera. I'll do a *Simon and Simon* once in a while or whatever comes along. I'm not about to quit and retire. This is the only thing I know. It's been the only thing I've known for 48 years. I'll be, in 1987, a professional for 50 years.

MAUREEN O'HARA

The only reason I was able to sit down with legendary film star Maureen O'Hara is that I had built up good will with a number of people in Holyoke, Massachusetts, the location of the radio station where I worked in the 1980s.

O'Hara's film roles include the now iconic *Miracle on 34th St.,* the 1939 version of *The Hunchback of Notre Dame, How Green was My Valley,* the original *Parent Trap, The Quiet Man* and many more.

Holyoke, one of the very first planned industrial cities in the country, is home of the second largest St. Patrick's Day celebration in the nation and part of the annual event is saluting a prominent Irish-American with the John F. Kennedy Award.

I was lucky enough to be the only journalist invited to a luncheon of a reunion of these award winners and O'Hara came back to Holyoke for that event.

I sat across from her and next to former Postmaster General and National Basketball Commissioner Larry O'Brien and his wife. I'm sure some of the people wondered why I was there. I certainly hadn't won a Kennedy Award and I'm not even Irish!

Later on, I was able to interview several of them for my talk show. Face to face interviews are always easier in that body language and facial expression can help you determine how the interview is going. Is the person comfortable? Open to questions? Does he or she want to get the hell out? With a telephone interview these issues are more difficult to assess.

The flip side is that an interviewer has to be more on his or her game as well. In my case I was speaking to a woman on whom I had had a crush since I watched her films on television as a kid.

She was friendly and plain spoken, answering questions directly. That helped since I was quite nervous sitting next to one of the screen's greatest ladies.

As of this writing, she is 93. She last acted in 2000.

***

You're definitely one of the under-praised actresses in American cinema and you've worked with everybody who is anybody – John Wayne, Charles Laughton, Jimmy Stewart. Of all of the films that you did which are the ones that meant the most to you?

Well, I made 55 all together and it's very difficult to say which ones please you the most when you saw them and which ones you had the most fun making and the most wonderful people to be with. I think without doubt *The Quiet Man* was one that was such a marvelous film and one that all of my friends were in it, including my two brothers. It was a family film. Everyone in the picture was related in some way.

I made 55, and out of the 55 I think there were only five I really wasn't proud of. When you say I wasn't praised for my performance, you know something I agree with you. But then when you think back on it I have a letter from John Ford to me in which he said – I can't use his language because some of it was kind of strong – that I was the best so and so and so and so actress in Hollywood.

When you have a letter like that from such a great director like John Ford and when someone like John Wayne thought the same thing and someone like Henry Fonda thought the same thing and someone like Vincent Price said the same thing on television as John Wayne said it, well if those people praised me, thought I was wonderful and always wanted to work with me again, I think that's praise enough for me.

I was signed to work in films from the theater by such a great actor as Charles Laughton. I was the only person he signed in his life. I must say, won't you agree, to have the respect of those people is very, very precious indeed and I'm very proud of it.

And I think I'm a darn good actress! I really do.

You know something I've done everything. I've done comedy, gay flippant comedy like in *The Parent Trap*. I've done bawdy comedy like in *The Quiet Man*. I've done drama like *The Long Grey Line* and *Sentimental Journey*. And I've done all of those adventure things in the desert you know. You had to climb up on a camel and say the most outrageous dialogue and make it sound acceptable and sensible. And the Westerns. I've done stunts. I've been a lady and I've been a rough lady. I think I'm pretty good myself.

[At the time of the interview O'Hara had retired from acting. She took a break from 1973 to 1991.] Obviously you take pride in your work. Why aren't you acting now? Is it that you've not received good scripts?

One of the major [television] shows – I won't say which one – called to ask if I would do five episodes. And now you're going to learn that I'm a very vain human being. I said, "No. I would never be part of somebody else's show. It has to be my show and I have to be number one."

I've been number one all my life and I could never accept being number two or any other number.

And now you've learned the terrible secret of my terrible vanity.

A number of your contemporaries in Hollywood have written books about their lives and careers. Are you going to write one?

Well truthfully I would love to write the story of my life. I shouldn't say that our lives, my family. I'm part of a very big Irish family. I love them, I'm very proud of them. We had the most magnificent grandparents, mother and father.

I would, yes, like to write a book from the day I was born through to the time I came to Hollywood. And from Hollywood to now, or perhaps my heartbreak when my husband died, but it would be a book that would be very sentimental and very warm and very wonderful and I don't know if publishers would want that kind of book, because they publish the other kind.

I love to gossip. I'm Irish. And sure it's fun to gossip and chitchat about the people I've worked with. But there are many stories, yes they're interesting, yes they're wonderful, but I don't believe I have the right to put any of those stories in print. Because I'm always cognizant of the fact that one day I have to stand before God and answer for it and what if He said to me "Why did you put that in print? Why did you tell someone's secret?"

What would I answer? So I don't believe I have a right to write a book other than the kind I would like to write and perhaps I should just leave it as a heritage for my children and my grandchildren. And if someone wants to publish it, if somebody wants to read about a mad Irish family, wonderful.

She did write her autobiography *"Tis Herself"* in 2005.

CLAYTON MOORE

1987

For me as kid, there was no television hero more compelling that The Lone Ranger. I watched the show religiously and so when I had scheduled an interview with Clayton Moore I have to admit I had some trepidation. Would I think is my childhood idol was worthy of all of my fond memories?

For anyone who does this kind of work, there are certainly times you speak to someone whom you admire and there are few things as crushing for an interviewer to discover the celebrity you like is a bit of a jerk.

I'm happy to say that was not the case with Moore.

Some actors when closely identified with a particular role feel trapped or typecast, but not Moore, who spent the majority of his career as an actor as The Lone Ranger.

He spent years laboring as a stunt man, appearing in bit roles and switching from playing a hero and a heel, but found a calling portraying the radio hero who became true American mythology.

Moore started playing the Lone Ranger in 1949 and did so essentially until he passed away in 1999. Although a reported wage dispute took him off the series for a year, the public demanded his return.

Moore had received some odd press over the years as some people claimed he identified too much with his role – some went as far as saying he thought he was the Lone Ranger. There was no evidence of this when we spoke. He clearly had a sense of humor about himself.

I interviewed Moore when I had a talk show on WREB in Holyoke, Massachusetts. At the time, the station was receiving a newsletter that carried the names and phone numbers of various people who wanted to be interviewed to promote a new book, movie or television show. At the time, Moore was riding pretty high again with his appearances as The Lone Ranger.

He had recently been allowed to actually appear in his Lone Ranger costume after a five-year prohibition. The Wrather Corporation, owners of the Lone Ranger property, had gone to court to strip him of that ability as they were planning a new Lone Ranger film. Moore made appearances wearing sunglasses (which landed him in a television commercial for Corning sunglasses) and the public certainly sided with him, especially after the film was a dud.

Clayton Moore was seen as Buffalo Bill in this 1952 B-Western *Buffalo Bill in Tomahawk Territory.*

New episodes of Moore's show had ceased production in 1956 (although new shows continued to appear on air until 1957), they were rerun into the 1980s and were still on the air in some markets when I spoke to him. His two feature films as the Ranger were also popular.

I had called the number in the newsletter to set up the interview and was surprised when Moore's distinctive voice was on the line. Initially he wanted to know how I got his number and I told him. He wasn't very happy. But as soon as I explained, he was fine and said he hadn't expected the newsletter to have printed the information so soon.

He was going on a tour of appearances and asked to me call him back in several weeks. I did and he quickly set up a time to talk live on the air. He expressed thanks to all of the fans who had supported him through his fight to retain the right to appear as the Lone Ranger.

How did you get the role of the Lone Ranger?

Well, Mike I was awarded the role back in 1949 along with "Tonto," Jay Silverheels.

Was there a large field of actors with whom you were competing?

Yes there were a large group of actors up for the role and I'm very happy to say that old Kemo Sabe was awarded the role.

Actually the TV show stopped shooting in 1956, but we released a feature picture of the Lone Ranger called *The Lost City of Gold* in 1957 and then I made a tour of the United States and over in Europe with the feature picture *The Lost City of Gold.*

Would you like to get in front of the camera again?

Yes, I would like to do another feature picture of the Lone Ranger before I ride up to the big ranch in the sky, but I don't know if that will ever happen. However, the TV series was a lot of enjoyable work, but it was difficult. We made three pictures [half-hour episodes] a week – one every two days.

That was a tremendous schedule. What kind of preparations did you have to do as an actor to learn your lines and block scenes out?

Overnight! The writers would write 15 shows and we'd go out and shoot 15 shows straight. We'd mix them all up. We never shot them in continuity. So the names, of the places and the bad guy's names, the Indian tribes and the Indian chiefs all had to be [memorized] overnight. Even the characterizations that I did [the Lone Ranger would frequently appear in disguise to gather information]. It was not an easy job, but it was a very rewarding job in many ways.

Prior to you being cast as the Lone Ranger, you were very active in motion pictures in both features and serials. You would play a hero in one and a villain in another. Did you enjoy that switching back and forth?

Frankly I did because I am an actor and as actors we like to play different roles. My favorite is the good guy in the white hat, of course.

You were under contract to producer Edward Small and appeared in the swashbuckler, "The Son of Monte Cristo." Did you enjoy that kind of role?

Hey, you did your homework!

First of all I was under contract at Warner Brothers as a bit player. Prior to Warner Brothers, though, and in between Warners and Metro-Goldwyn-Mayer, where I was under contract, I did stunts, I did bit parts, I did my own fights, my own horse riding. All the difficult stunts I did myself.

Then I was under contract to Edward Small and then to Republic Studio and then to The Lone Ranger show.

Speaking of stunt work, I read you that had appeared in a circus aerial act.

Yes, I performed in a flying trapeze act for a good many years.

Was that good experience for your stunt work?

Yes, it gave me the ability to fly through the air off of horses [laughs] onto the ground, doing fights and a number of different things we have to do in the stunt business.

What was working with Jay Silverheels like?

He was the finest man I ever worked with – perfect gentlemen, great sense of humor, [he was a] very, very dear friend.

When "The Lone Ranger" was originally on television, there were a lot of westerns, for both children and adults, but now the genre is in disfavor.

We're in a cycle right now that the westerns are now coming back. In the next year, year and half, you'll see a lot of westerns. I can't guarantee it. But I think you'll see westerns on television and feature films.

The kids have the space age and that's very important. They're pioneers just like we were.

You mentioned the characterizations you had on "The Lone Ranger." I remember the Lone Ranger would head into town disguised as an old prospector. Was that something you welcomed, to get from beneath the mask?

Of course my favorite is the mask, the costume, the silver bullet, but I did enjoy doing characterization. I think I did six or seven of them. There was the old timer, a cantankerous Army sergeant, a Swede, an Irishman, an Italian character, a real elderly doctor. They were a lot of fun to do. I enjoyed it.

***

Although Moore never did appear as the Ranger in another film, he and Jay Silverheels did make several very funny and memorable commercials – several for humorist Stan Freberg.

All of his *Lone Ranger* television shows have recently been released in a single set.

FILM MAKERS

I've had a love affair with motion pictures since I was in junior high school. Ever since then I gravitated toward any opportunity to speak with someone who has made films: actors, directors, producers and technicians.

RICK MORANIS & DAVE THOMAS

1983

For me there have been four comedy groups that have made a difference in my life: The Marx Brothers, Monty Python, The Firesign Theater and "SCTV." They share the fact that all of them seamlessly wove together low comedy, physical humor, satire and social commentary in a very distinctive manner.

Speaking with Rick Moranis and Dave Thomas in 1983 has been, to date, my only opportunity to talk with any of the SCTV cast and I only got the interview because the pair were going to major cities publicizing their movie *Strange Brew*. I was able to speak to them while they were in Boston.

"SCTV" proved to be the launch pad for many popular characters; the public especially loved the McKenzie Brothers, created by Moranis and Thomas. The beer-swilling brothers hosted their purely Canadian program *The Great White North* on the series and their slacker humor was a huge hit.

***

Rick Moranis: Basically, we took a step from the McKenzie Brothers on the television show to make a smooth and quick transition from the type of program that everyone was used to seeing them in and pulled them out of the real word and made them three-dimensional, kind of explain their characters a little bit. We also tried to blend fast paced comedy with a real strong adventure story. All I'd really like to tell you is that it's set in a brewery. There's no reason to be secretive, it's my own personal opinion. I love to not know anything about a movie when I go to see it and often movies are wrecked for me when people start telling me individual scenes and jokes and all kinds of stuff from it.

Basically the guys go to the brewery with the mouse in the bottle, the old gag we did on television, to try to get free beer and they wind up getting caught up in this plot by an evil brewmeister. Beyond that it's hopefully a lot of good laughs.

Was this your first feature film?

Moranis: Yes it was. Dave had a small part in *Stripes,* but on the bigger scale we wrote this for ourselves and wound up directing it together. It was a pretty big undertaking relative to television.

Was it intimidating to have Max Von Sydow as your co-star?

Moranis: In the beginning there was. Working with someone like that is a little bit intimidating. But he was such a nice man, that after the third or fourth day he was also like a friend. He came up to me and said, "If there's anything you want me to do, just feel free to ask, just suggest."

And we became pretty close during the shooting and his performance speaks for itself. He's terrific in the film.

How did Doug and Bob come about?

Moranis: In Canada, There are some laws called Canadian Content laws. These were designed years ago by the government in an effort to sort of insure some kind of Canadian identity, cultural identity in the arts. For years we were dominated culturally by international product, especially American product. We all grew up watching American television and watching American films and listening to rock groups from England and the States and now Australia.

I never thought there was anything wrong with that. Canada is a big country but there's not that many people there and the ones who are really good at what they do wind up doing it and the others are like anybody else working in the same competitive arena.

Well, the government came along and instituted these Canadian Content rules to subsidize the arts and promote Canadian culture. By the time it had its effect on SCTV, we were asked to do two minutes of extra programming that were uniquely Canadian to fill up time that was otherwise occupied by commercials on the half hour show. In Canada it runs on the public network and there were no commercials.

So we said, "What do you want us to do with these two minutes? We're all Canadians, we're working in Canada, we're selling this product abroad. Do you want us to sit in front of map of Canada and drink beer and fry back bacon? Wear parkas and talk like we're from way up north?"

And they said, "Yeah that would be fine."

So we started doing that. I don't know what it was. It was just two of us. I don't know what got people excited about the McKenzies. We enjoyed doing them because we improvised the material all the time. They're nice guys. They were just fun to do.

We did them on the TV show. They became popular. We did them on the album. After the album sold well, we were approached by a number of studios in California so we did this picture.

Were Canadians offended by the McKenzies as being an example of Canadian culture?

No one was really offended. In some circles, people resented the fact that we had taken this satirical shot at the government legislation. But intellectually, I think these people realized that we were right. The government should have stayed out of that and we wound up having a laugh on all of them. Just like in the United States there are all kinds of regional cultures, the South is different than the East and the West is different than the South. In Canada there are all kinds of strong regional cultures, too. If you try to find one overall cultural identity you're fooling yourself.

That's why we came up with the McKenzies and this now has rapidly become one of the newer images Americans have of Canadians. We sort of laugh at it and a lot of people are laughing with us in Canada. They think it's funny, too.

"SCTV" was hailed as one of the best programs to hit television, won a bunch of Emmys but had a terrible time slot and was not properly promoted by the network. How frustrating was that for you?

Moranis: Well, we enjoyed a great deal of freedom creatively because of the time slot. If you're doing your show in prime time, there are an exponential number of executives who impose their creative beliefs on your programming.

We had the opportunity of doing a show we could really control, which was great for us and one of the things that led to all the accolades that you described. I was happy the show was cancelled before it went bad.

At this point Dave Thomas joined the interview. I asked him if he felt that "SCTV" had been wasted in the late nighttime slot NBC had given it.

Thomas: I suppose so. If had been on an hour earlier on a Friday night it would have received a wider audience. But after a while we just became used to it. We had been underdogs in syndication, then we became underdogs on network TV. Now I think it's ridiculous and ironic they would cancel the show when it received seven Emmy nominations.

Do you think the show's intelligence actually worked against it?

Moranis: It was the kind of show that if you weren't a long time follower of it, you didn't understand a lot of the inside stuff. That was a mistake that we made. There was so much pressure on us to write material – we often amused ourselves. And we were often very inside our own scenarios, our own jokes.

Thomas: Personally I prefer being kind of unreachable by the audience because you're being too intelligent rather than reachable because you're being too stupid, given the choice of the two. I don't think either is ideal but given the choice of the two I wouldn't change a thing.

Moranis: And that's what we tried to do with this movie, something we tried to do with the album – combine the two. We didn't want to alienate anybody by doing something that was just subtle, satirical material. We wanted to do as many cheap jokes as we could and as many clever jokes as we could. I think the McKenzies could facilitate that for us. Unlike "SCTV," this movie is not about show business, it's about a complete fictional reality. We just tried to pepper it with as many different styles of comedy as we could.

Thomas: Plus the McKenzies' audience, I believe, are different than the "SCTV" audience. Although people watched "SCTV" saw the McKenzies, when we did the album we found there was much more of blue-collar, beer drinking crowd out there who likes the McKenzie Brothers who couldn't give two hoots about "SCTV."

Moranis: I'm sure you can understand that. The station aired the album and it must have reached from that station alone more people than the show reached on that terrible timeslot we were on.

Are you two going to remain as a writing and performing team? Are there more television or film projects being planned?

Moranis: Well, there are all of those things right now. The thing we are going to do is wait and see the reaction to this thing. If this does well, we may do sequel or do another picture together. There are lots of things we want to do together and there are lots of things we want to do apart. So everything's up in the air right now. We're having a good time. It was really fun to do this movie and we're on the road right now promoting it. We just hope folks like it. We've got a couple more movies in us.

***

Moranis and Thomas revived the McKenzie Brothers for two animated series, in 2003 and 2009.

BRIAN GRAZER

1984

Today many film fans recognize Brian Grazer as one of the film industry's most successful producers. He has been nominated for an Academy Award four times to date and won the best Picture Oscar for *A Beautiful Mind* in 2001. Among his films are *The Da Vinci Code* (2006), *Cinderella Man* (2005) and *Bowfinger* (1999). At this writing, The Internet Movie Database reports 10 film and TV projects that list Grazer as a producer or executive producer.

Splash was his fourth film as a producer and he was responsible for the film's story. It was his second collaboration with director Ron Howard with whom he has had a long and profitable relationship.

Grazer was doing publicity rounds for *Splash,* which is how I was able to snag him for a radio interview. *Splash* was a huge success both critically and at the box office. I spoke to him before I had the opportunity of seeing the film.

***

So what is "Splash" all about?

What *Splash* is all about is a romantic comedy about a man, an average guy, a guy who has never really had love in his life like many of us, searching for the unrequited love. He ends up finding a girl who is very pure and very sensitive, but later learns she is a mermaid. That basically what it is, a romantic comedy about a man who falls in love with a mermaid, but he does not know that until towards the end of the movie.

I saw an article in Esquire about the making of this film and I take it has been a project of yours for quite a number of years now.

It's been a dream of mine for a long time. About six years ago I was single and much like Allen Bauer, [the character played by Tom Hanks] the lead in the movie. I was just a guy living in Los Angeles, a single guy that really wanted to have a meaningful relationship with a girl but instead was going out with all these girls who had to have a red Jaguar or a Ferrari or some kind of fancy thing in order for them to like you.

So I started wondering if there was a girl out there who was pure and innocent and wonderful. I started fantasizing on the freeway about what it was a mermaid, a girl who was entirely from another civilization, who wasn't polluted from what a very urban society can create.

I thought it would be great if I could fall in love with a mermaid and from that I wrote a 10-page story. I submitted it to United Artists and said, "It's basically a story I'd like to make, turn it into a movie and be a producer of." They said fine and I went and hired Bruce Jay Friedman, a rather renowned New York playwright. That's basically how the idea began.

It stayed at United Artists for six changes of management over the period of roughly three and half years. Every time the management changed they had a new set of notes or new ideas they would like time to incorporate into the script, so consequently it was very tough to get it into the stage where anyone wanted to say let's make this movie because every time I'd get the notes, the new ideas, a new boss would come in and say, "I want this or that."

Eventually there was a president of the studio named Paula Weinstein and I said to her, "It doesn't look like you people at United Artists want to make it. Why don't you please give it to me and I'll take a shot at it someplace else." She was very generous and said, "Go ahead."

I went to The Ladd Company and met with Alan Ladd [Jr.]. That's a company that finances independently but distributes through Warner Brothers. At that time I was just finishing producing *Night Shift* and he said, "Fine. We'll continue to develop it. We'll get it to the stage where you really want to do it." And I said, "How about [director] Ron Howard?" and everyone said "Great."

Between Ron Howard, myself and the new writers, who were the writers of *Night Shift*, we turned it into a script that we were all very, very happy with. At that time, about a year later, he [Ladd] put it into turn-around basically because Ray Stark who is a very famous producer had a project that was very similar to it. [The other film] was with Warren Beatty and Herb Ross was the director. Robert Towne had written the script. So it was real star-oriented piece of material and it seemed at the outset that Ray Stark was going to beat our mermaid movie and no one really wanted to come in second.

Ron and I were basically out on the street, running around to studio to studio saying, "Hey, listen we can beat that project. We can do it faster and cheaper and we have a pretty funny script. We think the script has got a lot of romance and a lot of heart to it as well. Give us a shot."

We got down to three different studios. One of them was Touchstone or Disney. We then evaluated whom we wanted to go with and it was Touchstone because they were more in sync creatively to what we wanted to do. We then made the movie.

It took about seven years to make the movie.

This film had some challenging logistics with locations in New York City and the Caribbean with underwater scenes.

We shot about a month in the Bahamas. It was very difficult. Underwater shooting isn't something people do very often, so consequently no one has come up with any advanced ways of doing it. There's no real sophisticated ways. There are only a few hours when you can shoot, roughly between 10 a.m. and 2 p.m. So you're really spending a lot of time preparing and getting ready to go 35 feet beneath the sea.

From 10 a.m. to 2 p.m. you're using the sunlight, the optimal sunlight to do your shooting down there. You have to be very, very well prepared because the actors do just a fragment of scene before they run out of breath. They do what's known as "buddy-breathing." They go from regulator to regulator so they can breathe underwater. It would take forever if they did the fragment of the scene and came to the surface.

So consequently, the actors are underwater seven to eight hours a day. It's a very long, very hard process. It's very dangerous. It's complex.

When I speak to people about movies they understand what a screenwriter and a director do, but are confused about the role of a producer.

There are all kinds of producers. But the bottom line is the producer gets the money somehow. He somehow gets the money to make the movie. That's basically what a producer does.

Now there's all sort of ways to get money. You can be either related to money (laughs). You can find just a sum of money like through Wall Street or you can do it more conventionally through studios. You get the studio upper management to agree to make your movie. Usually, that's done by having a really great idea or a really great idea and a great script or having a star director involved or star actors. It's about acquiring leverage in order to get the money.

Splash got made without stars. It got made on the idea and the script and Ron Howard and me I guess.

With a cast including Tom Hanks, John Candy and Eugene Levy was it a funny set?

It was real funny. We had a lot of fun on this set. The three of those guys got along real well. They made a lot of jokes about each other and it was a real positive environment in which to work.

GEORGE ROMERO

1985

Romero has done something that few people in popular culture have done: he has created a mythos that has been adopted and used by other writers, directors and artists. Prior to his 1968 film *Night of the Living Dead,* (which he wrote with John Russo) the zombie was not a very popular character in horror movies or fiction.

Historically, zombies were either live people under a spell of drugs or animated corpses doing the bidding of someone else. Romero and Russo re-defined the zombie. It was now a person infected and killed by an unknown virus, but has lived on, in a manner of speaking, "living" to feed on people and therefore spreading the virus.

The re-imagining of a zombie was so successful that I doubt many people associate the word with its historic meaning and Caribbean origin. Anyone who does a zombie movie today owes a thank you – and probably a check – to Romero.

With his subsequent *Dead* movies, Romero showed that he was more than just a guy trying to gross out his audiences. He also was a satirist who used the zombie character to help produce films with social significance.

Romero was no one trick pony. He has made other films – horror and not – that have drawn positive attention from audiences and critics. Working largely outside of the conventional studio system, Romero has been one of the most successful independent filmmakers of the last 45 years.

His last film was in 2009, *Survival of the Dead,* and since then he has been credited as producer on five movies

I spoke to him in 1985 when he was promoting *Day of the Dead,* his third zombie movie.

***

I've not been able to see "Day of the Dead" since it's not been released here as yet. I've read some reviews though and some critics don't seem to like this film as much as its predecessor "Dawn of the Dead."

Most of the criticism I read about this film seems to hold that it's too talky. That's the only clue that I have. The *Dawn of the Dead* fans or some them anyways just wanted more action. This film does have a little more talking than *Dawn of the Dead* had. It's a little darker film. While it has some humor, and I think it has a good bit of humor, it's not as outrageous as *Dawn of the Dead* was. It's not as flip. So maybe that's the reason for it.

You've cast African-American actors and female actors in leading roles in many of your films. Critics have seen this as a social statement from you. Is this something you're consciously doing?

Well, sure (laughs). I don't think it's that much of statement. It's just something I've done repeatedly. Maybe I'm more in a position to do that than a studio would be. I don't have the same kind of pressure. I don't have worry about the same demographics or anything with the films.

I don't have the pressure on from the beginning. I don't have someone sitting there saying, "Well the lead has to be a white male." The usual pressure that go on structuring a cast for a movie. So it's something I've decided to do and I'm in a position to do it.

Back in 1968 when "Night of the Living Dead" came out, did you ever anticipate it would become the international hit it became?

No we never anticipated that at all. We felt lucky that we finished the movie and had someone out there showing it (laughs). It made most of its money in the first year of its release but it didn't get attention at that time.

It got noticed in Paris and Rex Reed wrote about it a couple of years later. It had this afterlife. It came back from the dead (laughs). It became a cult film and got a wider release then.

It was something none of us ever anticipated. I had already made two more pictures that were not nearly as successful and when *Night of the Living Dead* started to get critical attention it did a lot to revitalize my career.

Did you hit it rich with the success of "Night of the Living Dead?"

No, the company that produced *Night of the Living Dead* wound up in a legal action with the distributor and it was awarded $3 million. The picture only returned about $1 million to the company that produced it and that had to be cut up among the investors, it got cut up in a lot of different directions.

I've noticed many different editions of the film in video stores and was surprised by that. Is it in the public domain?

No, it's not in the public domain. There are pirate tapes out there and there's nothing really can be done to stop them because there's not enough income left in the movie to pay the legal costs of fighting the pirates.

What happened again, when the original distributor released *Night of the Living Dead,* our title was *Night of the Flesh Eaters* and we couldn't use that because there was a movie called *The Flesh Eaters.* The distributor changed the title to *Night of the Living Dead.* In the process of doing that they didn't put a copyright notice on the film. It was just a clerical error. As a result there were a lot of people who believed the film did not have a copyright. It took people five or six years to discover that.

A couple of distributors picked up the movie and started to show it. There was very little that could be done. It costs a great deal of money to mount a legal defense for something like that and you don't always win your costs back.

Around 1980, Image 10 petitioned, with the help of my company Laurel Entertainment, petitioned the government for a ruling on the copyright and they did get a copyright clearance from the federal copyright office, but there wasn't anything that could be done.

"Night of the Living Dead" changed the themes and the style of the horror film in a profound way. If nothing else, you're a historical figure important to film.

It's very hard to think of yourself that way. *Night of the Living Dead* was a shocking film. It was intended to be shocking. I just thought it went an extra inch. I didn't think it was that extreme at the time and I still don't.

The zombie films, all three of them are Grand Guignol and they stay within the gothic tradition of horror. They're fantasy films.

I don't think that modern horror films owe very much to *Night of the Living Dead* or to any of the gothic predecessors to the modern horror film. I think that probably *Psycho,* if you really wanted to trace it back, was the grand-father of the modern horror film; in that it took a realistic situation and a real character who was just mad and made the character into a monster.

Scary movies prior to *Psycho* almost exclusively dealt with the super-natural and with fantasy of some kind. *Psycho* was the first really important film that made a human in a realistic situation the monster, if you will.

There were other gothic kinds of thrillers where the threat was human such as *Wait until Dark.* Those had scary moments but they weren't really clas-sified as horror films. *Psycho* was the first horror film that used a monster movie format and all of the traditional gothic trappings and built them around a human monster.

It was the granddaddy of the modern horror films. Most of the modern horror films take their lead from that. Of course, *Halloween,* which was a very well made film, made a lot of money at the box office and became, at least it was touted as the most successful independent horror film ever and that too was not a monster movie. It dealt with a human lunatic as the monster. That gave birth to the rash of slasher movies that the public identified as the modern horror film.

What are some of the challenges for the independent producer today?

The problem is always raising money to make the movie (laughs). And being an independent today doesn't mean as much as it used to mean. Most of the people that work in Hollywood are in fact independent. There are very few people who are working under studio contracts any more.

To be my kind of independent which is to choose not to live in New York or Los Angeles and to make movies in Pennsylvania or somewhere in the middle of the country, in the past was sort of a unique approach to doing it. But now even studios deals are being structured so they can be made somewhere in the middle of country. Part of that is an attempt to escape the high cost of union production. And some of it is probably aesthetic choice to get a different look to the films and use the rest of the country as a backdrop.

Really what I've been doing is no longer quite as unique. I think that my partner and I were able to set up a company to do that and Richard Rubenstein was able to take that company public and has been reasonably successful in setting up an active and ongoing small independent production. If there was anything unique in what we have done it was probably that.

That's been gratifying. Personally speaking I was always tenacious. I just wanted to make movies. I've always managed to find a way to continue to make them without having to go and join a fraternity if you will of one kind or another. I think I can support my own sort of conceit that I am able to do more films closer to my own feelings and aesthetics without as much interference as I might have in the system.

However over the last six years, since 1980 I've made a couple of bigger budget films – *Knightriders* and *Creepshow*– that brought a lot the same pressures that I would have in a studio situation. We're going to go on and do *Pet Sematary* now which also is a bigger budget film and involves a major studio. That too will probably have a lot of pressure come along with it.

We've been able to get to that point and I've been able to put bread on the table by staying out in the middle of the country.

Do you fear being typecast as a director of horror and suspense films?

It just automatically happens. No one is going to think of me if someone gets a script in for something like *Ordinary People.* Well I'm not going to be the guy that they call to see if I'm free to direct it. That's just the way that it goes.

Directors are cast just like actors. I don't mind it because I love the genre that I'm working in. Also I've been lucky enough to make films that are not horror films. None of those have been big hits, so maybe one of these days if I get to do one that is a hit then people will call me up for a different kind of film.

It's just as simple as that, but that's something you accept going in. I never expected it to be any different and that's just the way it runs.

***

Romero did not direct an adaptation of Stephen King's novel *Pet Sematary.* Director Mary Lambert brought it to the screen in 1989.

ABBY MANN

1985

When I interviewed Abby Mann I did not have the opportunity of speaking with this acclaimed screenwriter about his many praised scripts, including *Judgment at Nuremberg*, for which he won an Academy Award.

Instead the time was designated for the firestorm of publicity that had erupted over Mann's television mini-series on the serial murders of children in Atlanta and the resulting trial of Wayne Williams, who, despite the questions surrounding the trial, is still incarcerated.

***

Mann, who died in 2008, had an interesting career as a writer, working on very serious dramatic films as well as episodic television. He stayed active until three years before his passing.

It was not long ago that millions of Americans wore ribbons of green and black and prayed another day would pass without the discovery of another young victim. The grisly string of child disappearances and murders in Atlanta, between 1979 and 1981 ended with the Wayne Williams conviction in two connected killings; the rest of the cases were closed.

The controversy – and for some, the fear and grief – has started all over again, thanks to the CBS miniseries, The Atlanta Child Murders. I spoke last week to the program's screenwriter, whose script suggests that Wayne Williams was railroaded into jail for crimes he may not have committed.

Abby Mann is no sensationalist hack. His screenplays include *Judgment at Nuremberg, Ship of Fools* and *A Child is Waiting*. He wrote the highly acclaimed television film, which served as the basis for the *Kojak* detective series.

Although his previous efforts may have received critical honors, including an Academy Award for *Judgment at Nuremburg,* Mann is facing harsh criticism and a possible lawsuit from the city of Atlanta for his portrayal of Williams's trial and the motivations of the city officials.

"I challenged the prosecution of the Atlanta murder trial to come to Harvard, the seat of law, to discuss the issues of the Atlanta child murders and they did not come," Mann said. "And I still challenge them."

Mann contends that dangerous precedents were set in the Williams case, precedents which could impair the civil rights of all Americans. Mann believes this television production and the accompanying controversy are giving him a forum from which to discuss elements that he said are destroying our legal system.

Mann is not an easy person to interview on this subject. This is his third interview recently on the film, and he runs through his charges by rote. He assumes the interviewer knows as much as he does about the case and reels off details that sometimes make little sense until he is pressed for clarification. He is passionate, though, about the production, and he seems aching for a showdown with Atlanta officials. Several times he repeated his challenge for an examination of the case at Harvard, and his voice frequently rises in volume to stress his points.

Mann has specified several alleged violations of Williams' rights, and therefore our own. He does not accept the validity of the fiber and bloodstain evidence entered by the prosecution, evidence that was key to Williams's conviction. He will not allow the use of a rope and a pair of gloves found in Williams's car as indications of his guilt. He also disagrees with several key procedural sequences in the trial.

And he cannot let go of the haunting fact that Williams was convicted of only two crimes. The rest of the cases are officially closed, but are technically unsolved.

Officials of Atlanta's government, police force and district attorney's office have rejected Mann's criticisms and have mounted their own public relations efforts to counter the author's many media appearances. But Mann holds to his belief that the key evidence is faulty. For example: "On the issue of bloodstains ... a criminal lawyer knows that any bloodstain a laboratory types could be put into one of seven categories. Now, the random type could fit any thousands of people, with some types more rare than others. What bloodstains showed was not important to this case. The probability of two blood stains matching two subjects from any 30 dead bodies selected from across the land, the probability was great," Mann said.

But is Wayne Williams innocent? Mann has no idea.

"I'm saying that this furor and this attempt to try to cast these kinds of things is as unfair as what was done in the trial. What I'm saying is that these procedures that were done in that case were allowed to continue ... the introduction of uncharged crimes which a defendant has to defend and a prosecution does not have to prove, and, quoting them, 'fibers are as important as fingerprints'... if that is allowed to continue our judicial system will be destroyed.

"I don't know whether Wayne Williams is innocent or guilty, but this is beyond that. This upsets your freedom, this upsets my freedom and anyone's freedom," Mann concluded.

Mann's five-hour film was screened for city officials in Atlanta, and what they saw prompted the City Council to authorize a possible suit against CBS. Although no suit has yet been announced, CBS has reacted to the criticism by adding a preface described in the press as a disclaimer: "The following presentation is not a documentary but a drama based on certain facts surrounding the murder and disappearance of children in Atlanta between 1979 and 1981. Some of the characters are fictionalized for dramatic purposes."

Mann became involved in the production when he was approached by the film's producers. At first he was hesitant because he did not want to write a docu-drama, which he says are "too often used carelessly."

"I don't think a replica of events, a photocopy of what has happened, should be done, because when one does that, one appeals to prurient interests," Mann said.

A curious remark about black homosexuals that an unnamed Atlanta official made to Mann caused him to send a friend to observe the trial. The friend then urged Mann to come to Atlanta where he read the trial transcripts and sat in on the rest of the trial.

Mann was impressed by what he says was the near-hysterical tone of the reporters covering the trial and their refusal to consider the prosecution's case objectively. A conversation with one of the victim's mothers, who realized that no one would stand trial for the murder of her child, convinced him to take on the project. Williams was convicted for the killings of a 21-year-old and a 26-year-old. Within 48 hours, the rest of the child murder cases were officially closed.

Although he has been roundly criticized for his script's conclusions, Mann insists that he "bent over backwards" to show both sides of this case. He said his objectivity as a writer had been developed for *Judgment* and the *Kojak* television movie, *The Marcus-Nelson Murders*.

A suit does not bother Mann, who believes litigation will not color the truthfulness of his project.

"If they want to sue, that is their privilege. This is a free country; there are courts. I have no comment other than that," Mann said.

He concluded, "What I'd like the American people to do is to watch it and judge for themselves. And I'd like to have them keep this in mind ... every word from the transcript of the trial is true, I have not changed a comma of it."

LARRY COHEN

1985

Larry Cohen is perhaps one of the most under-rated independent filmmakers of the 1970s, '80s and '90s. Starting his career as a screenwriter for television, Cohen moved into directing with *Bone* in 1972.

His films have proven to be always interesting, even the misfires such as *Wicked Stepmother,* (1989) which was Bette Davis's last movie. *The Stuff,* (1985) *Q,* (1982) *It's Alive,* (1974) *God Told Me To,* (1976) *The Ambulance,* (1990) are all effective examples of how good ideas with a properly allocated budget can create a very enjoyable motion picture.

I met Cohen at a really odd event: a thoroughly fabricated awards show for *Rod Serling's Twilight Zone Magazine* in 1985. The publicists for the magazine, to which I eventually contributed two stories, thought having an award show could drum up some media attention. I went to it with my friend and author Stanley Wiater and Cohen was at the cocktail reception. I struck up a conversation and was able to secure an interview. A journalist is always looking for the next interview and story.

Cohen's last outing as a director was in 2006 when he helmed an episode of *Masters of Horror* and he has been busy as a screenwriter.

***

Tell us a little about your new movie "The Stuff."
A fast food called *The Stuff,* which is very much like tofutti or other ice cream substitute and becomes a major part of the American life, one of the most popular fast foods in America. It's sold in supermarkets and franchises all over the country.

Of course the ice cream industry becomes terrified this will put them out of business so they hire an industrial spy, played by Michael Moriarty, who infiltrates the company and tries to discover how the Stuff is manufactured and of course he comes upon the horrible secret: the Stuff isn't manufactured at all. It's actually a living substance.

It's a take-off on the fast food industry. It's played with suspense, special effects, a great deal of fun and entertainment for all audiences.

You received some very good reviews for your last movie "Q, The Winged Serpent," which also had elements of social commentary, humor and horror. Is that a combination you strive for in your films?

That's what I do and it seems to work. Audiences seem to have a good time. We don't do camp. We don't do the kind of affectionate tributes to old movies, borrow scenes form other people's pictures and do satires on other people's old films. We try to do something new and original ourselves – come up with a brand new type of concept and make the picture with the maximum amount of entertainment value.

The idea is to shock the audience into scaring them but also make them laugh and have a good time. It's more like an amusement park experience where you have a thrill and then a laugh and everyone comes out of the theater feeling really good. It's entertainment and of course that's what has been successful for me before and I keep on doing it.

There are a lot people critical of the graphic violence in today's horror film. How do you view its use?

I find it unpleasant to see people being butchered on the screen. What has happened is the technology has gone so far now you can create models of people and animated models of human beings and you can blow them up and destroy them, kill them and slash them. It looks very realistic on the screen.

Some have gone into the practice of making pictures more and more explicit in this kind of violence. I just find it's gone too far.

A *Friday the 13th* picture, which is successful of course, there is an audience for this kind of film, they kill 13 people in every picture in every imaginable kind of way.

I guess this isn't anything new because if you remember one of the most popular theaters in France for hundreds of years was the Grand Guignol. The Grand Guignol specialized in presenting very graphic horror and they did it with special effect that the audiences wondered, "How did they do that? It looked so real."

So, the Grand Guignol has been going on for centuries and has always been part of the entertainment of France and I guess what he have here is a Grand Guignol cycle of motion pictures.

Everybody goes to see what they enjoy. I personally like a picture with more entertainment value and less horror.

How difficult is it being an independent producer these days?

It's not difficult because there are studios that finance your picture for you. Being an independent producer doesn't means you make the picture yourself. It means you get the financing from the major studios, be it Warner Brothers or Filmways or in this particular picture (*The Stuff*) New World productions. They let me go out and make the film. You don't make it out of their offices. You're not there in their suite of offices. You're in your own office someplace making your picture and going off on location.

Basically, it's easier to be an independent than to be on the studio lot because you have more freedom. People are not around to ask you questions and make suggestions. You have the autonomy of independence.

But basically, that's all it means. I guess you have to take more responsibility for what you're doing because the studio isn't there to pay all the bills. They pay you for the picture when it's delivered. You can't make the picture for more money than you've been given, if you're professional about things and know what you're doing from the start.

Independents, such as you, seemingly have problems with theatrical distribution – of getting a movie in theaters across the country. Has that been a problem for you?

Some of them have more problems than others. Pictures that are hits such as *It's Alive* and *Q* seem to play everywhere. Pictures that are marginal have become a situation in that the expense of advertising in newspapers and television is so high it makes releasing the picture in certain areas prohibitive. You can't possibly get back the money you're spending for the advertising.

Now there are alternative markets for pictures like cassettes and cable television, pictures go in that direction so they get seen by the audiences anyway. So it really doesn't concern me that much of the pictures aren't seen on television, or on cable or on cassette or in a theater. The main thing is my picture gets to the audience. That it makes money. So what's the difference where it plays? As long as it makes money for me and the company that financed it. That's all we're looking for.

Sometimes it becomes evident the theatrical play of the picture is not going to become profitable after all the expenses are paid. You might play it in theaters just for window dressing, but in the long run it's not going to get you any revenue. The main revenue for some pictures is going to come from the cassette sale, the cable sale, and the syndicated and network television sales.

So, the picture gets seen and that's what important. Of course I'd rather have a nice theatrical play because it means your picture is getting a big launching and when it comes to the other marketplaces like cable, people have heard about it from the original theatrical run.

But many times I think the original theatrical run of a picture now is like the hardcover run of a book. They don't expect to make any money on the hardcover they expect to make all the money on the paperback. In the movie business, the paperback is the cable and the cassette and the television. That's the paperback.

I'm looking at your biography and I have to admit I've not heard of two of your movies, "Perfect Strangers," and "Special Effects."

Those movies are coming out in the fall after the big glut of summer movies is finished. They will be released by New Line Cinema and they're both suspense stories and they're both made back to back. I kind of made one picture, kept the same crew and made the second picture, so they were made like one long picture. They are very complex suspense stories. They are not horror pictures, but mystery and suspense. They were made in New York City.

The first one, *Perfect Strangers* stars Ann Carlisle, the leading lady of a picture called *Liquid Sky*, which has been playing for three year in New York in one theater. She's a very talented actress.

The second picture stars an actress named Zoe Tamerlis [now known as Zoe Lund] who had a picture called *Ms. 45*, which became a cult hit around the country and Europe.

So I made these two pictures and they are underground film stars, these people. I was living in New York and hanging out with this New York underground of filmmaking. I was a Hollywood filmmaker living in New York on location and I got caught up in this scene of New York people and thought I would film these pictures on New York City.

They are both quite classy pictures and the video cassettes will be coming out from Embassy Home Video and New Line will be putting the pictures into theaters.

Do you have any artistic rules that govern the movies you make?

No, I write my own scripts. When you write your own scripts it's your idea from the inception. You write a few scripts and the one that you like the best is the one you want to spend six months of your life making a film.

Because it's very hard work making a picture. It's like factory labor. You're on the feet 12, 14 hours a day maybe longer. It's physical labor at locations under unpleasant conditions. You have to really like something a lot if you're going to film it because it's not as simple as staying at home and typing a script. Being a writer is very creative work and comfortable in its own way. We're not subjected to physical pain when you're making a movie.

You've seemed to specialize in fantastic films that are suspenseful. Is there a reason for that?

I don't know I really couldn't tell you. As I say you write what comes to you. Everybody has their own style and some people write westerns, some people write stories of sex and romance and other people write mysteries. I can't imagine why an old lady like Agatha Christie was writing all of these mystery stories [laughs].

We have no idea why some of these things come to us. But I've been writing science fiction and thrillers all of my life. That's what I do.

I had a series that was on TV 10 or 12 years ago called *The Invaders* on ABC and that was my first foray into science fiction. Of course now I've just found out ABC is bringing it back; they're having a two-hour movie made for the network called *The Return of the Invaders* and that will be a spin-off for a new nighttime series.

So it's nice to find out that something I created 12, 14, 15 years ago is coming on the air again.

ALEX GORDON

1986

I met film fan, producer and archivist Alex Gordon and through Alex I met his brother Richard, also a film producer with whom I became good friends. Alex and Richard were among the first film fans who actually became producers and who carried with them their own boyhood interests in film into their adult careers.

Alex started a practice that directors Joe Dante and Quentin Tarantino have adopted: casting favorite actors from their youth in their films. Alex hired Westerns stars he loved, character actors that were semi-retired and even brought back Russian actress Anna Sten, who had a short and tumultuous career in the 1930s, to the big screen in his film *Runaway Daughters* (1956).

Alex's career included working with the now infamous director Edward Wood, who was actually Alex's roommate for a time.

I would see Alex annually at the Cinefest in Syracuse, N.Y., where he would regularly bring 16 mm prints of films from the 1930s and '40s from his own collection to share with fellow film fans. These shows were heaven for someone like me as they allowed me to see movies that I could only read about, if that. The highlight of the convention was always a dinner with Alex and Richard.

After producing 18 films, Alex worked as an archivist at 20th Century Fox and then for his boyhood idol Gene Autry. Although Alex's dedication to Autry was deep, truth be told, he also loved the westerns of Buck Jones. Alex died in 2003.

Gordon: When I was a kid in school the first two movies that I saw were *For the Service* (1936) with Buck Jones who was one the greatest western stars of the early days and *Guns and Guitars* (1936) with Gene Autry, the first musical Western I ever saw. This got me very excited about Westerns. In 1939, when Gene Autry came to England for a personal appearance tour, he made appearances at several theaters to promote his pictures and sang to audiences. I saw him and met him in person for the first time.

As a result of this, I formed the British Gene Autry Fan Club, which had 5,000 members and had a quarterly magazine called *The Westerner* with news about Gene Autry and other Western stars.

That was quite an undertaking.

Yeah, it was a lot of fun. The American Gene Autry Fan Club had about 100,000 members and they were a much bigger organization, but we were growing rapidly when unfortunately, you know World War II broke out in England in September 1939. In 1942 I was called up in the British Army and I had to suspend the club for the duration at that time.

I had to get out one more copy of the magazine because the subscribers were entitled to it. I was with the 11th Armored Division in an out of the way place camouflaged in England and the mail was censored because so if spies intercepted it they wouldn't get any information that would be of use to the enemy. So when I told them I had to get out 5,000 copies in the mail of "the Westerner" magazine they said that was impossible because they didn't have the manpower to read and censor 5,000 pieces of mail.

So I told them all they'd have to do is read one 12-page issue because the others are exactly the same, but they said no, that was no good they would have to look at all of them.

So I went to the chaplain, which was the first thing you always did when you had a complaint, and then I had to go through channels … until I ended up believe or not with the major general who was commander of the 11th Armor Division. None of them would understand. When I go to the major general he understood perfectly and he was a big Gene Autry fan and understood those magazines should go out. He assigned two sergeants to help me get those out. The last issue of *The Westerner* did go out in April of 1942.

What made Gene Autry to be your favorite? There was such a wide assortment of Western stars – Tim McCoy, Hoot Gibson, Tom Tyler, etc.

As kids we were always interested in Westerns and when Gene Autry came into movies in 1934 he revolutionized the Western field. The first movie star was a cowboy star, Bronco Billy Anderson who created the first continuing cowboy hero in pictures, *Bronco Billy*. Then there was William S. Hart making very authentic looking Westerns and Tom Mix and his flamboyant Westerns. Then, as you say, Buck Jones, Tim McCoy, and lot of others came along.

In 1934, Gene Autry revolutionized the field completely by making musical Westerns, not just singing a song in Western, which had been done by Ken Maynard and a couple of others once in a while. The whole formula of the Western changed. It was a combination of cleverly combining action and song and trading on a popular song ... and the plots were completely different than any of the plots that had been used before because the Westerns were modern Westerns. They sometimes had airplanes and cars and things like that.

Yet they combined the action of the old Western and they all dealt with problems of farmers and ranchers that are still prevalent today, like conservation, foot and mouth disease of cattle, floods, drought, things like that.

So it was a very unusual combination of Western action, songs, and problems of farmers, ranchers and cattlemen and this formula clicked so well that by 1939 Gene Autry was not only, since he had been since 1937 the number one Western star in the exhibitor's polls, but believe or not he was number four of all box office stars according to Motion Picture Herald, which was the Bible of exhibitors and the industry. Only Clark Gable, Shirley Temple, and Abbot & Costello were ahead of him in box office draw. He continued in the top ten in 1940 and 1942 until 1942 he went to war and he was off the screen until 1946.

So it was a phenomena, it is difficult for audiences today to realize the tremendous draw of the Gene Autry films. At the time there was a system called block booking on which a company could book their annual output of pictures, 40 or 45 pictures, in a block. So all the exhibitors who wanted to play the eight Gene Autry pictures had to play all the other Republic pictures, which consisted of Westerns and pictures starring Vera Hruba Ralston, which didn't make any money but they had to book them in order to get the Autry movies. [Ralston, a Czech skating star was the protégée and later wife of Republic Studio head Herbert Yates. She became a joke of sorts in Hollywood, although the crews at Republic loved her reportedly because of her kindness and lack of ego.]

After the war, Alex and Richard immigrated to the United States and Alex re-introduced himself to Autry, who hired him as his advance publicity man for his touring shows. Alex did this work, but it was seasonal, as Autry toured in the spring and winter, making films during the summer. He decided to stay in Los Angeles in 1952 to get into the film business as he had done publicity for companies in London, England and New York City.

When I came out here, I had become friendly with several stars including Bela Lugosi, the horror star. My brother and I had arranged for a British tour for Lugosi reviving *Dracula,* his famous role and also for a movie over there, *Vampire over London.* I had written a script for Lugosi called *The Atomic Monster.*

So when I came out here I tried to set this up as a production and it eventually became a real schlock movie called *Bride of the Monster*.

Directed by Ed Wood.

Yes, Edward D. Wood Jr. with whom I was involved with for a while. In fact I roomed with him. That is now considered one of the worst films of all time, like his other film *Plan Nine from Outer Space*.

What was Bela Lugosi really like?

I knew Lugosi from 1947 to the time he died, and Ed Wood and I were about the only ones who saw him in those last years ... Lugosi was a delightful person, a really cultured man, Hungarian and in Hungary he had played Shakespeare. He fled the Communists and came to American in the 1920s where he was first on the stage and then got into movies.

After *Dracula,* he was typed in horror films. He played many other pictures too, but he is remembered for his horror films. He was a very courteous gentlemanly man with a terrific sense of humor.

Around the time Eddie Wood got involved with him, he was quite elderly and not at all well. He was down on his luck and he needed money. He would do anything to make a picture and get some money, but it never stopped him from being very kind, a very nice person. He was not at all difficult. He was a much better actor than he was given credit for. If you see him as "Ygor" in the later *Frankenstein* films, although it is another horror character it is completely unlike Dracula and it shows his ability.

Anyway we were very friendly with Lugosi and I kept in touch with Gene Autry and we tried to put together a film for Lugosi with a lawyer named Sam Arkoff who was very interested in getting into production. Without going into a big deal, this led to the formation of a company called American Releasing, which later became American International Pictures.

Sam Arkoff and his partner James Nicholson, Roger Corman, the famous independent producer and I were actually the start of American International and I produced 13 low budget pictures like *She Creature* (1956), *Voodoo Woman* (1957), *Runaway Daughters* (1956), *Jet Attack* (1958), *Shake, Rattle and Rock!* (1956) and so on.

What was it like working in the low budget field in the 1950s?

It was extremely interesting because there was suddenly a market for low budget exploitation pictures. Some of the major companies were virtually out of business, like RKO, which had been taken over by Howard Hughes and weren't doing anything. Republic Pictures were getting heavily into television and were making a few bigger type of pictures. None of the big companies were making B pictures anymore. The drive-in theaters, which were very strong at the time, needed product, double-bill product. Nicholson, Arkoff's partner, had worked for Jack Broder's Realart Pictures which had reissued all of the old Universal pictures releasing them on double horror bills like *Frankenstein* and *Dracula*.

Nicholson had the idea of making combinations for the drive-in and Roger Corman had made a picture called *The Fast and Furious* with John Ireland and Dorothy Malone. They used that picture to attract the financing by selling it to independent state's rights distributors territorially throughout the United States. They got enough advances, totaling $60,000, to make the next picture.

Our pictures in those days were made in six days and 10 days and the budgets were between $60,000 and $90,000, but they were black-and-white at first, so you can imagine how low budget those pictures were.

The great difference at American International between Roger Corman and myself was this: Roger Corman wanted to get his actors and crews as cheaply as possible and with that in mind he gave newcomers a chance as you probably know he started out people like Francis Coppola, Robert DeNiro, Jack Nicholson, in his pictures primarily because they would work for scale.

I was different. I always wanted to use old-timers in my pictures because I had enjoyed them as a kid and I wanted to talk to them about their old movies. So, my pictures were jam-packed with names such as Chester Morris, Richard Arlen, Bela Lugosi, even silent days players like Jack Muhall ... I wanted people who had been in major company pictures and had names ... I always thought my time in Hollywood should have been the 1930s. I came much too late (laughs).

That was the difference between us.

Your film "Requiem for a Gunfighter" (1965) was a reunion of Western stars.

Yes, that was coming full circle. In 1958, I got through at American International and moved over to Allied Artists and did a picture called *Atomic Submarine* (1959) and then to Columbia where I did *The Underwater City* (1962) and then for Embassy, which at that time was Joseph E. Levine, I did these two Westerns *The Bounty Killer* (1965) and *Requiem for a Gunfighter*. I tried to round up all the stars identified with Westerns who were still alive: Dan Duryea, Richard Arlen, Buster Crabbe, Fuzzy Knight, Johnny Mack Brown, Bob Steele, Tim McCoy, even Bronco Billy Anderson in his last screen role coming full circle from starting in 1903 to this 1964 appearance.

When [Bronco Billy] came into Paramount from the Motion Picture Country Home there was so much excitement that Elvis Presley who was shooting on another set came rushing over to have his picture taken and there was tremendous publicity. We really had a great time with all those old timers. Most of them, like Tim McCoy, for them it was actually their last movie.

So it was a fun film to do?

Yes, they had so much fun. Johnny Mack Brown and Raymond Hatton and Fuzzy Knight hadn't seen each other in ages – they had made so many picture at Universal and Monogram together – others hadn't seen each other in years and they really had a wonderful time. That was really a great experience.

It's a shame that so many television stations don't show as many black-and-white films as they once did.

The young audiences today seem so imbued with the idea of color that very often if a picture is in black-and-white they will refuse to see it. One of the questions asked is if the picture is in color, which is a pity because that way they miss an awful lot of good pictures. You see before the days of television all the major companies thought they would have no further use for their pictures so they neglected them and allowed them to completely lie away and lapse without proper care without proper ventilation and humidified atmosphere and so on. With the rare exception of a few they thought would make reissues, like a James Cagney picture or a W.C. Fields or Humphrey Bogart or Marx Brothers they really let these pictures rot.

In 1968 I suggested to [20th Century] Fox that I should come in there and try to find their lost films. Some 750 films they couldn't account for going back to 1914 and I became a one-man operation trying to locate these films in archives all over the world and try to get some kind of preservation job done.

There was complete enmity at the studio. They just didn't want anyone to interfere and they were self-conscious that these things had rotted all these years and exploded with the nitrate flammable film that was used before 1952.

However out of 750 lost films I did manage to find 350 including rare works, well 14 films directed by John Ford. John Ford's career always had these gaps in them by people studying it or writing books about him. For the first time these great films by Ford like *Three Bad Man, The World Moves One, Judge Priest* and other things became available for study. Howard Hawks films, F. W. Murnau who made *Sunrise,* I found his film *City Girl* jammed behind a radiator in some basement at Fox and this was nitrate. Films of Janet Gaynor and Charles Farrell, like *Seventh Heaven,* the films of Will Rogers and one of the greatest treasures, the films of Tom Mix. Since the silent days, no Fox Tom Mix pictures have been found. They all thought the Tom Mix pictures were lost but out of 86 films Tom Mix made at Fox, I found 14 in the Czechoslovakian film archives. We worked out an exchange and when we got the films they had Czechoslovakian titles so those had to be removed and the English language titles had to be put back in again.

For the first time the Mix films became available to new generations and this was a tremendous discovery. Unfortunately, of the Buck Jones films only two of the, one directed by John Ford in 1920 and one directed by Frank Borgaze in 1926 called *Lazy Bones,* which is a great picture were found. The others were lost.

When I got through with Fox a new regime had come in 1978 and the preservation program had to stop. Gene Autry offered me a job to work for him full-time in charge of his movies, television shows and music publishing companies. So I came back in again and have come full circle. That's what I'm doing now. We are preparing the 88 Gene Autry films for television release for the first time in their full-length version because 32 of them had never played television at all and the others only in cut 53 and half-minute versions when MCA released them. For the first time then we will be releasing all 88 Gene Autry pictures in their full length versions and some of them are available on Republic Pictures home video including a color film, *The Big Sombrero.*

TED BONNITT

2002

David F. Friedman and Dan Sonney, the renegade filmmakers profiled in Bonnitt's film, passed away in 2011 and 2002, respectively. Bonnitt's film is available through Amazon.

***

Here's a challenge: produce and package a feature-length film for about $150,000 and get rave reviews from the *New York Times, Variety,* and *TV Guide.* Ted Bonnitt took that challenge, although he had no idea when he started his production that he would be a trailblazer.

Bonnitt is in the vanguard of a film making revolution. The fledging director and producer's new documentary on two retired exploitation moviemakers has received great reception from critics and audiences and yet Bonnitt didn't expose a foot of film stock.

His documentary – with the intriguing title of *Mau Mau Sex Sex* – was shot 100 percent digitally. Although no film print exists of the production, Bonnitt has used ingenuity similar to the roadshow pioneers he profiled to get his film to an audience.

Bonnitt is following in the footsteps of filmmakers Stefan Avalos and Lance Weiler who made the first all-digital movie, *The Last Broadcast.* The low-budget horror film was the first digital film to be presented in theaters through satellite transmission.

His friend Eddie Muller, who wrote a definitive book on the subject, *Grindhouse,* introduced Bonnitt, a veteran radio commercial producer and performer with a background in journalism, to the exploitation film scene.

Muller's book examined the Adults-only films made in the 1920s through the 1970s. Following a rigid formula, these films routinely promised to educate its audiences about a social ill by presenting a sordid story. Billed as precautionary tales, films such as *Mom & Dad* and *Reefer Madness,* titillated their audiences more than taught them of the dangers of premarital sex or the use of marijuana.

Produced by a group of renegade filmmakers who operated far out of the reach and censorship of Hollywood's Production Code, these films played burlesque theaters, independent theaters and drive-ins. More important than the actual film was how it was sold to the public and the producers – who called themselves *The Forty Thieves* – showed mainstream Hollywood how to sell the sizzle and skimp on the steak. They were shameless in how they hyped their often laughable productions.

Bonnitt was introduced to one of the key figures in the exploitation scene, David F. Friedman, and took a liking to him. Bonnitt immediately realized that Friedman closely resembled a character of an unscrupulous talent agent he had played for laughs on radio.

"My jaw dropped," he recalled with a laugh.

Friedman had started in "legitimate" show business doing publicity work for Paramount, but was attracted to the carny atmosphere of The 40 Thieves and worked for the biggest "thief" of them all, Kroger Babb. Eventually Friedman began producing films on his own.

On a business trip to Alabama, Bonnitt visited Friedman, who agreed to participate in a documentary. The budget stood in the way, though. Bonnitt took a year to research his budget and discovered that shooting 35mm – the industry standard – would cost him about $500,000.

"I stumbled across a digital movie camera in 1997-98 and people told me it was a toy and it would work," said Bonnitt.

His budget problems were solved by the new digital technology.

His next problem was convincing his other subject, the late Dan Sonney, to be in the film. Sonney's father, a former police officer, had made a film about a wanted criminal he had apprehended and toured vaudeville houses with it. He soon discovered that crime might not pay for the criminals, but he could make some money from it. Louis Sonney spent the rest of his life making road show films.

Dan entered into the family business and worked with Friedman on a number of. productions. Sonney, an accomplished businessman, was skeptical of Bonnitt's project, but the two became close friends and he assisted Bonnitt.

"Dan questioned my sanity in my making this film," Bonnitt said.

Bonnitt shot interview footage with the two men in just five days when Friedman made his annual trip to California to visit Sonney. Another two days were spent following Friedman around his Alabama hometown, and Bonnitt shot an additional interview with film historian and director Frank Hennelotter.

"I thought the film was an ultimate character study. These guys were cunning, and smart and they laughed all the way to the bank," said Bonnitt.

Bonnitt didn't whitewash his two subjects, though, and the film does present the clash between two family men and the often-sordid films they produced.

After shooting, Bonnitt then bought digital editing programs and equipment and set out to edit the film and hire a composer for the score.

"I was never set for a theatrical release; maybe a video. But every theater [owner] who saw the film wanted to book it," he said.

"I was working with a totally unproven technology. It was like a genie in a lantern, I didn't know where it was taking me, but we were going somewhere," he added.

Bonnitt struck a deal with Sharp Electronics, which supplied him with two state-of-the-art video projectors for promotional purposes. When a theater booked the film, Bonnitt simply shipped them the 15-pound projector and a DVD of the film. Theaters in New York, Los Angeles, Chicago and Philadelphia, among others, presented the film. Bonnitt now sees that, like Sonney and Friedman, he was road showing his film.

"Those old guys taught me a lot of tricks," he said affectionately.

Now Bonnitt's film is playing around the world and he has made a number of international television sales. It's now available on DVD through Amazon.com.

Dan Sonney recently passed away, but not before he saw the film become a success.

The film's title refers to one of Dan Sonney's few box office flops, a pseudo-documentary on the bloody Mau Mau uprising in Africa during the mid-1950s.

Sonney mused on camera that the film, titled *Mau, Mau,* would have done better if it had been called *Mau Mau Sex Sex.*

Both men thought Bonnitt's use of phrase was crazy, until they saw the film's reception.

And, like the showmen they were, they declared they loved it.

LLOYD KAUFMAN

2003

Is Lloyd Kaufman feeding me a line? He tells me that if I hold the DVD of *The Toxic Avenger IV: Citizen Toxie* up to a light, I can see the image of Jesus on one disc of the two disc set and Satan on the other.

He must be smiling on the other end of this telephone interview.

The patter is typical Kaufman, a movie director who has taken lessons on promoting himself from masters such as William Castle and Alfred Hitchcock and ratcheted up the hype to meet these jaded times.

You haven't heard of Kaufman and his company Troma Entertainment? Well, the studio's flagship franchise, The Toxic Avenger, just made the top 50 cult films of all times list published recently by *Entertainment Weekly*. In fact, Toxic Avenger – or "Toxie" as he is affectionately known – has not only appeared in four films, but has been the star of an animated television show and several comic book series as well.

Besides heading the independent company with his partner Michael Herz, Kaufman has directed a number of the key Troma releases, and has written two books about the tribulations of independent filmmaking. In the grand tradition of the classic Hollywood studios, Kaufman and Herz have established a highly recognizable style. Warner Brothers was known for its films "torn from the headlines," while Paramount's films boasted a European elegance and MGM had "more stars than there are in heaven."

Troma has brought gratuitous violence, gore and sex to levels that are almost surreal. In fact, Troma's films have captured the attention of mainstream critics because of their no-survivors satire that is in the tradition of Jonathan Swift's *A Modest Proposal*. In fact, some film writers have stated that without Troma paving the way, bad taste and mainstream comedies such as *There's Something About Mary* may never have existed.

Troma titles include films such as *Class of Nuke 'Em High, Fat Guy Goes Nutzoid, Sgt. Kabukiman NYPD* and "*Terror Firmer*. Its latest film, which is now being produced, is *Tales From The Crapper*.

There's no doubt about it that Troma is not for everyone, but Troma fans are highly dedicated to the company. The studio's web site (www.troma.com) features a gallery of photos from fans who have pledged their loyalty with a tattoo of the Toxic Avenger. When were the last time you heard of someone putting Julia Roberts or Harrison Ford on their forearm?

The company's most recent film, *Citizen Toxie* – now out in a double disc DVD edition crammed with extras – boasts of scenes with such over-the-top material this writer barely can start describing them in a family publication. The plot revolves around our hero The Toxic Avenger, the hero of Tromaville, who finds himself transported into an evil dimension. The hero of that dimension, the Noxious Offender, is now in Tromaville killing at will and turning the town into his own criminal municipality.

Where else than in a Troma film could the hero be a former health club janitor who thanks to being dropped into a vat of toxic waste has been transformed into a superhero? In what other movie could porn star Ron Jeremy be cast as the mayor of a town or the late Hank the Angry Drunken Dwarf play God?

And this DVD version is unrated. You've been warned.

If nothing else, the film takes the "what if" story formula so popular in many of today's mainstream films and shows it for the lazy storytelling device that it is.

Troma is celebrating its 30th year in business, something of which Kaufman is proud, especially considering that there are few other independent companies around with that kind of staying power.

It has been an interesting journey for the Yale student majoring in Chinese Studies, who decided after graduation to pursue a career in film. Kaufman told The Journal/Bravo that rather than going to film school, he decided to "attach" himself to a director and learn by doing.

As an aside, Kaufman said that the pleasure and pain of film making fit right into the Taoist philosophy he had studied.

In his case, Kaufman's instructor was John G. Avildsen, the director of such films as *Rocky, Joe,* and *Slow Dancing in the Big City.* Kaufman began work with Avildsen on *Joe,* a low budget politically charged film produced in 1970 that starred Peter Boyle. Boyle played a working class conservative who reacted violently to the social changes of the Vietnam War era.

Kaufman said that on his first day as a production assistant, he realized that "this guy [Avildsen] is talented. I worked for free on that movie in order to learn." The film was a surprise hit and Kaufman continued his association with Avildsen with his next film, *Cry Uncle,* a detective comedy, which earned an X rating for its sexual content. Kaufman said, on that film, he "jumped a few rungs" up the career ladder from production assistant because he helped raised money for the production.

Kaufman and his Yale friend Michael Herz had formed a partnership that slowly but surely began producing their own films while working on other productions. For instance, the Troma Team - as Kaufman calls his crew - shot the exteriors in Philadelphia for *Rocky* and he recalled zipping around the city in eight days making sure his non-union crew wasn't spotted by union representatives. At a Los Angeles screening of *Rocky*, Kaufman said, "Union guys were trying to remember when they shot that footage."

Another acclaimed director used Kaufman's services, on the art house classic *My Dinner With André*. Actor André Gregory was so impressed with the economical shooting of a comedy titled *Waitress!* Kaufman and Herz made that the late Louis Malle hired Kaufman as his production manager for that shoot.

Although Kaufman worked on a mainstream film such as *Saturday Night Fever* – he scouted the New York locations for the film – he is not a Hollywood type of guy, and has a lot to say about establishment filmmaking. Guerrilla movie making seems to be the basis for the Troma style. Kaufman said that Troma tries "to have total freedom" and that the company is "anti-elite." Kaufman believes in the idea that "the purpose of art is to reflect the spirit of the artist."

"Troma has a loyal fan base. Some people may hate or love our films, but they never forget them," he added. Kaufman dismisses many mainstream Hollywood films as "baby food," and said that Troma's success shows that people want "half pepperoni on their cultural pizza."

The indifference expressed by corporate media conglomerates over Troma products hasn't helped the company. Kaufman explained that Blockbuster Video would not stock Troma movies, even in R-rated cuts. He charged that attitudes such as this one have "totally marginalized independents."

Kaufman believes there has been "a conscious effort to economically blacklist" the studio. He said that The New York Times refused to run a review of one of his books despite the advocacy of the Times' own film critic, Janet Maslin.

Kaufman's style is blatantly New York, and his promotion of Troma is definitely of the "in your face" variety.

Warner Brothers may have its signature water tower on its Hollywood lot, but Troma's 9th Avenue building in Manhattan has the Toxic Avenger painted on its exterior.

Kaufman's two books detail his adventures in filmmaking, and have encouraged people to become filmmakers themselves. In fact, the most recent book, *Make Your Own Damn Movie,* takes people step by step through the process from financing to distribution.

In the book's press release, Kaufman said, "I want to give young filmmakers a step-by-step guide to making low-budget independent movies so that they can use what works for us and learn from our mistakes... although in Tromaville, we don't call them mistakes. They're impromptu script deviations." Troma films have relied on free labor provided by people who are seeking an education or simply a break into the industry. On the Troma website right now are notices calling for interns and volunteers to help further the Troma cause.

That's right, you may only be a mouse click away from schlepping coffee or holding a light for a Troma film crew or appearing at a comic book store as Toxie.

Although he is definitely a showman, Kaufman doesn't take himself very seriously. The second disc of the *Citizen Toxie* DVD has a feature-length making of documentary which I found just as – if not more amusing – than the film itself. The documentary shows Kaufman directing the film and many of the cast and crew complaining about him.

Kaufman doesn't mind though. He said nice things about his crew on the movie's audio commentary and explains their criticism as "the truth as they see it."

For him the documentary is "a window into what it's really like to make an independent movie."

Like his movies or not, one has to give the devil his due. In this era of media giants, Kaufman and Troma Entertainment keep getting away with thumbing their nose at the big boys.

And, by the way, you can't see Jesus or Satan on the *Citizen Toxie* discs. Kaufman made me look.

***

A few months after I did this telephone interview, I found myself at the Sundance Film festival in the spring of 2004. An experience that I wouldn't want to repeat, none the less, I did enjoy stumbling across *Troma Dance,* Kaufman's combination of a publicity stunt and alternative film festival.

I was the only member of the press when I was at the festival, which was conducted in the basement of a bar on the main drag of tiny Park City, Utah, and the various filmmakers dying to get some attention greeted me warmly.

Kaufman was speaking with the late actress Karen Black, who had directed a film and was going around to the various filmmakers and audience members with a video camera shooting footage for a *Troma Dance* DVD compilation.

It was an appropriately Troma experience – equal parts ballyhoo, balls and cheese.

MARTY LANGFORD & WARREN AMERMAN

MAGDELENA'S BRAIN

2004

I've never had the opportunity of covering the creation of a feature length movie from start to finish, but when my friend Marty Langford began shooting a science fiction film locally, I had the chance of seeing first hand the triumphs and the lessons learned by independent filmmakers.

***

It's in the mid-afternoon of the fourth day of shooting, and the director of photography is carefully lining up and rehearsing what appears to be a simple shot. The camera is to glide through a set of computer equipment with the lead character walking in the background. One person carefully guided the dolly on which the camera is mounted while two others keep the wires attached to the camera out of the path of the dolly's track.

After trying several variations of the camera movement, the director positions the actress, gives her instructions and quietly said, "Action!" Peering into a video monitor enclosed in black shroud, the director said that the movement is too fast, while another take it is too slow. After a few more moments, though, the desired shot – lasting only a few seconds – is achieved.

Marty Langford, producer and co-writer of *Magdalena's Brain*, whispers to me, "Look at the light pouring through the window. This is going to look great."

The crew quickly breaks down the camera and goes to an adjacent part of the set for the next shot. The continuity person makes notes to be used to match this shot with others, and the make-up artist is finishing shaving the side of actor Sanjiban Sellew's head.

This isn't Hollywood, but if Langford gets his wish, Western Massachusetts will become a center for independent film production.

The set is on the third floor of Mill #2 of the Open Square complex in Holyoke, Mass., and will be the hub of activity for Glowing Screen Inc. for most of the month. The fledging production company is shooting a script written by

Langford and Warren Amerman. Amerman is directing and Langford is producing.

And while this is the company's first feature film, the crew is all film production veterans. Langford, an Agawam resident, is a hardcore movie fan who went into the business. He is a producer at Veritech in East Longmeadow, Mass., working on commercial and business films and he also teaches a screenwriting course at Westfield State College.

Amerman, a musician who runs the Rotary Records recording studio in East Longmeadow, has directed short films in the past. The rest of the crew has professional experience behind the camera and hails from Western Massachusetts communities such as Chicopee, Springfield, Monson and Tolland.

Langford said that he and Amerman wanted to write a script that was feasible to shoot on a low budget, so they devised this dramatic story with science fiction undertones about a once promising brain surgeon who has retreated from society after an accident that nearly killed her husband.

The husband had been working on a device that transfers memories from one person to another, but something has horribly gone wrong and he is now bound to a wheelchair unable to communicate, except for an electronic device that he wears around his throat. She is continuing his work, though, in an abandoned factory building.

"This is a real moody piece, a dark moody piece," said Langford.

Langford and his crew have set up shop on the un-restored third floor of the mill building. Along one wall is a make-up area and the sets are built on the opposite end. There is a lounge for the cast and crew on the next floor.

Langford said that about half of the $25,000 budget goes to rent the camera and to pay for the lead of the film, Los Angeles-based actress Amy Shelton-White. The rest of the cast and crew are donating their services or deferring their payments because they want to work on the feature. Open Square owner John Aubin has donated the use of the space.

If he had to pay for everything, Langford estimated the budget would be between $125,000 to $150,000.

"Everyone has been so cool and helpful," said Langford.

Shelton-White came to Langford and Amerman's attention thanks to Springfield native Mark Sikes, who has been a casting director in Los Angeles for a number of years. Langford and Amerman went through many audition tapes of actresses on both coasts before settling on Shelton-White. The actress has had numerous roles in independent films and on television productions and said that she is attracted to productions where there are "people of quality."

Later in the week, there will be location shooting at a robotics lab at UMass, a local hospital and outdoor locations. Too much traveling can tax the resources of a low budget production, Langford noted.

Langford said the shooting schedule allows the crew to be flexible and to take their time, unlike many independent productions, which by financial necessity must rush from one camera set-up to another. Technical quality is very important to the company and the rented camera is the same model used by George Lucas to film the last two *Stars Wars* films.

Langford and Amerman's immediate goal is to have the film ready in September to enter it in festivals such as Sundance. They want to get the film in a number of festivals later this year and next year in order to increase its exposure and to find a suitable distributor.

"I'm confident we can get this film on the shelves," he said as two different camera operators buzzed around the set with their own cameras shooting footage that undoubtedly could become a "making-of" feature for a DVD release.

The long-term goal, though, is to make one or two features a year and build a film making community in Western Massachusetts, explained Langford. Although mainstream films ranging from *Cider House Rules* to *Malice* to *Stanley and Iris* have been shot in the Valley, Langford envisions a group of local filmmakers who could provide a talent pool for each other and utilize the area's scenic resources.

Looking at the crew work, Langford, beamed, "This is what I've wanted to do my entire life."

***

Local filmmakers Marty Langford and Warren Amerman are now hard to work putting the finishing touches on their first feature-length film *Magdelena's Brain*.

As previously reported, principal photography took place this summer in locations in Holyoke and Chicopee. Langford, the producer, and Amerman, the director, are now working on the final version of the film, including the musical score and final sound effects. The two men co-wrote the screenplay.

They are preparing a final version for an invitation-only premiere at the Basketball Hall of Fame theater later this month. They are also submitting their film to several film festivals, including Sundance and Slamdance, which is their first step in marketing their production.

The team invited this reporter for an advance look at the film and for a discussion on how their first feature turned out.

The film is an under-stated but involving character study of a young woman whose husband has suffered a debilitating accident, during a medical experiment. With several significant twists and turns, this film bridges the gap between a drama and a thriller and has a science fiction undertone that plays very realistically.

Amerman's style as a director is to eschew the kind of camera tricks and editing stunts that characterize many films today. The stylishly composed photography and the crisp editing keep the emphasis on the film's story and performances.

Shot with the same kind of high definition digital camera used by director George Lucas for his last two *Star Wars* films, *Magdelena's Brain* has a sharper image than many low-budget films are able to achieve.

The photography and production design doesn't betray the tight budget – under $30,000 – and the 14-day shooting schedule. The biggest expense, Langford said with a smile was feeding the cast and crew.

"The shoot went well," said Amerman. "Many disasters could have happened, but there were no knock-out blows."

"We all had to wear many other hats," said Langford. He added that his biggest job on the film was making sure that Amerman could focus on the actual shoot. In turn, Amerman said his biggest challenge was to know when to "move on" from one scene to the next.

Both men heaped praise on the film's lead Amy Shelton-White whom they hired from Los Angeles, CA. While they said the supporting cast of local actors were fine, that Shelton-White "brought everyone else up," said Langford.

Amerman said that she would stay in character "until she heard the word 'cut'" even if the action in the scene was over. "She was wonderful," he added.

In order to build a reputation for the film, Langford and Amerman are researching film festivals in order to decide which would help advance their marketing campaign. They said there are literally hundreds of festivals and the issue is to find out what significant movies have appeared in the past at which festivals.

"We both like the idea of a successful festival run," said Langford.

2006

In a digital-editing suite at Veritech Corporation, Marty Langford is editing footage from his science fiction thriller *Magdalena's Brain*. Langford isn't working on the feature itself; he's preparing deleted footage for the extras section of the film's national DVD release.

Langford and his partner, Warren Amerman, recently signed an agreement with Heretic Films, a San Francisco-based distributor. Their locally produced feature should be at retail outlets such as Best Buy, Amazon.com,

Sun Coast and Virgin for sale and for rent at Hollywood Video in July.

With a North American distribution deal set, the team has set their sights at exploring foreign distribution deals and domestic and foreign television sales.

Magdelena's Brain was shot in the summer of 2004 in several locations in Hampden County, but primarily at Open Square in Holyoke. Langford produced the film and Amerman directed it. They collaborated on the script.

Starring Amy Shelton-White, the film is a story about an experiment in artificial intelligence gone terribly wrong and the toil that it takes on one woman.

Prior to the interview, Langford was working on amending the credits of the film and preparing a group of deleted scenes. The distributor had requested that Langford and Amerman produce a group of extras and Langford noted that there weren't many scenes not used in the low-budget film.

He showed one scene in which Amerman shot two different versions with different actors. At first, the team thought the first actor was the problem in the scene; however, with the second version, they realized that the scene as written was the problem, not the performers. Langford noted that deleted scenes were not included in the final cut of a movie for a reason.

Langford and Amerman recently recorded a commentary for the film and he said it was a fast-moving experience. Neither man had seen the movie for several months and they sat in Amerman's recording studio with a bottle of wine.

Langford said, "No one cares about me or Warren on a personal level," so they didn't focus their commentary on stories that would come across as self-indulgent. Instead they used the commentary track as an opportunity to share some of the lessons they learned during the shoot.

"We talked about how to work around restrictions," Langford said. He added that the recording period sped by and they were tempted to do another track to include more information for fledgling filmmakers.

The two men found their distributor by soliciting companies that had a catalog that included films similar to theirs. They sent out a number of copies of the film and two companies expressed interest. Eventually, they signed on with Heretic.

Langford and Amerman are now considering their second feature. Langford noted that many directors break into the business with a horror film because horror fans are the "least discriminating." As long as a director includes the story elements that please the fans, its audience can deem his or her film a success. Langford said this with a smile, as he is a fan of horror films, himself.

Their next feature will be a heist movie, a genre both men enjoy. Langford described it as "a group of everymen with no specialties who must work together."

LANCE WEILER

2006

Head Trauma, the new film from producer, director, and writer Lance Weiler, will be released on DVD on Sept. 26, and Weiler has avoided the sophomore curse.

Weiler and Stefan Avalos made history in 1998, when the pair produced *The Last Broadcast,* the first motion picture that was shot digitally and then transmitted by satellite to theaters, which used a digital projector to present the film.

What made the pair's accomplishment so impressive is that they did it as independents working far outside of the studio system.

While other filmmakers have tried to obscure this milestone, Weiler and Avalos made movie history. They also made a good movie, the premise of which was stolen by the producers of *The Blair Witch Project.*

The Last Broadcast is being re-released on DVD in a new edition packed with extras on Sept. 26 as well.

Weiler is now back with his second film, which is a taut psychological thriller. Undoubtedly one of the savviest independents making films today, Weiler has been touring the nation with a theatrical release of *Head Trauma* prior to the home video release to build up a buzz among critics and fans.

Head Trauma tells the story of George Walker, a homeless man who returns to his late grandmother's house after a lengthy absence. Walker hopes to fix up the now condemned house and turn his life around.

It's not easy as there is a neighbor who wants the house demolished and Walker has no real resources to do the work that needs to be done.

What's worse though are the dreams he is having about a figure in a parka who clearly wants him out of the house. Walker increasingly is having problems distinguishing whether or not the hooded figure is actually real.

Anyone who has waken from a sound sleep wondering if what they experienced was just a dream will identify with Walker's situation.

The film is well directed and keeps viewers off-balance, as any good thriller should. Josh Cramer's editing and Sam Levy's photography matches the tone of the story perfectly.

Shot in an actual condemned house in Scranton, Penn., the film transcends many other current horror and thriller films by actually being about a man's redemption. Vince Mola as Walker is quite good in conveying the desperation of a man who yearns to be "normal" but has problems that prevent him from doing so.

Although Weiler could have added the elements that have become standard in the horror and thriller genres – sex and explicit violence – he avoids them. He opts for a clever story and a solid lead performance instead to carry the film.

Head Trauma shows what the potential is for independent films. In an era when bloated Hollywood films can fail to deliver the story-telling goods, Weiler proves again you don't need $50 million to make an enjoyable film.

Weiler shot *Head Trauma* on a 90-day schedule that was stretched over much of 2004. The complete production budget for the film was $126,000 peanuts by Hollywood standards.

The film's story was inspired by a very bad car accident that Weiler had 12 years ago. His car was struck head-on by a garbage truck and Weiler spent five days in intensive care. He had very lucid dreams that he couldn't tell if they were real or not.

After spending two and half years and $1 million developing a television show for FOX only to have a new executive regime kill it, Weiler said he wanted to work on something over which he had complete control.

Based in Pennsylvania, Weiler asked city officials in Scranton if they could help him find an abandoned house that would be the centerpiece of the film. Since the city has lost 75,000 people with the closing of nearby coalmines, Weiler had many houses from which to choose.

"They were incredibly disturbing and disgusting," he said. He noted that the house he chose made the crew uncomfortable and few wanted to work in the house by themselves.

Weiler joked that working on the film "felt like head trauma."

True independent filmmakers, unlike those whose projects are backed by major studio boutique labels, have to "wear 15 hats," he said.

"Film making is problem solving. You're always trying to find creative ways to solve problems," he said.

JOHN KRICFALUSI

2006

John Kricfalusi is considered one of the "bad boys" of contemporary animation and is the creator of *Ren & Stimpy*. He was also very frank and open about his adventure with corporate politics.

Talk to people in the animation industry today and ask them about their influences. You'll hear names such as Max and Dave Fleischer, Chuck Jones, Bob Clampett, Tex Avery, and among the younger generation, John Kricfalusi.

Kricfalusi is the creator of *Ren & Stimpy,* a cartoon that was a phenomenon in the early 1990s. An outspoken advocate of creativity, Kricfalusi rejected the state of animation in the 1980s television programs produced by committees that recycled tired gags and premises and revived the concept of a strong director who worked with a team of artists and writers.

For the first time in many years, Kricfalusi established a style and look that was singular. Like them or not, there was no mistaking a Kricfalusi cartoon.

Conflicts with *Ren & Stimpy's* cable home, Nickelodeon, led to his being removed from his own series. His team of Ren, the psychotic Chihuahua, and his soul mate Stimpy, the affable but idiotic cat, maintained a loyal fan base and influenced a new generation of animation fans and professionals.

In 2003, Kricfalusi was asked by Spike, the cable channel devoted to programming for men, to bring the series back, only this time there would be no restrictions on content. The show would be part of an "adult" animation block that included *Stripperella* and *Gary the Rat.*

The network only aired a handful of the new *Ren & Stimpy,* shows before cancellation and there were completed shows that never saw broadcast.

Now, however, *Ren & Stimpy* fans will get a chance to see what Spike didn't want them to see. The new two-disc *Ren & Stimpy: The Lost Episodes* has just been released by Paramount Home Video. The collection contains three episodes seen on Spike and three that were not aired. Kricfalusi, as well as some of his animators, introduce each cartoon.

The introductions are funny and pull no punches. Kricfalusi speaks his mind about the shows and about the status of animation today.

There are also some great extras that show Kricfalusi's animation process such as storyboards and pencil animation tests.

The cartoons themselves are a mixed bag. The strengths of the original *Ren & Stimpy* shorts rested in their outrageousness and liberal use of non-sequitur humor. Anything could happen in a *Ren & Stimpy* short.

Kricfalusi loves the Three Stooges and explained in one of the introductions he always liked how the lives and professions of the Stooges could change from short to short something he adopted for his characters.

Kricfalusi didn't shy away from gross-out humor in his original shorts – remember the Magic Nose Goblins? – and with the network's initial encouragement he pulled out the throttle on these type of gags in the new cartoons. From nudity to body functions, the new shorts have it all.

These *Ren & Stimpy* shorts were not designed for children, make no mistake.

If that kind of humor puts you off, then this collection is not your cup of tea. There are some great *Ren & Stimpy,* moments in the collection, though, and *Firedogs 2* has the distinction of featuring another bad boy of animation, Kricfalusi's mentor Ralph Bakshi, as an animated character.

Kricfalusi said that the very thing Spike executives wanted him to do caused the series to be cancelled.

"The executives told me to make them as outrageous as possible," he said.

He said that, unlike other networks with in-house censorship offices, Spike didn't offer him any parameters for content.

Their method of censorship, he added, was to pull the show off the air. That move surprised him as he pitched all of the story ideas to the network execs and "they laughed all through it."

Kricfalusi took many of the new cartoons from story ideas that had been rejected by Nickelodeon and produced them with no-holds-barred.

He's proud of the quality of animation in the series, some of which was done by Carbunkle Productions in Canada. A studio in Korea completed other animation. Kricfalusi said he had to have re-takes done, as the Korean studio animators didn't understand his method of animation.

Kricfalusi based his animation on "poses" key drawings that begin and end an action that carry a lot of dramatic or comic impact. This technique mirrors how animators made cartoons in the 1930s and '40s, the height of theatrical animation.

The popularity of *Ren & Stimpy* cartoons in the 1990s spurred a revival in creator-driven animation but Kricfalusi sees a big change in the animation scene today.

"It's a lot worse the way I see it," he said.

He noted that "stars," the creative people, used to have the power in the entertainment industry. Today, though, "the executives are in control."

"I see a lot of sad faces in animation today," he said.

Today he thinks that animated shows are "bland." He added that today the characters can swear, though.

"Bland characters telling immoral stories" is his conclusion.

He admitted with a laugh that probably this is "partly my fault."

While many people working in animation today have embraced trying to be outrageous, they've "left out characterization, good drawing and pleasant music," he said.

Will there be more *Ren & Stimpy?* Kricfalusi said he has at least 100 more story outlines and has done considerable work on a half-hour *Ren & Stimpy* special titled "Life Sucks." He said that his production staff has told him the new special is the "best *Ren & Stimpy* ever."

Kricfalusi sees the future of the characters on direct-to-DVD productions. He noted that the previous collections have been "selling lots of DVDs."

"Yes, I'd like to make lots more," he said.

BRANDON DAVID

2006

After this interview was initially published, Brandon Paul changed his name to "Brandon David."

***

The Mardi Gras gentlemen's club seemed at first glance like an unusual location for a first-look at a new independent movie, but it made sense once it was known that the bar's owner, James Santaniello, is one of the executive producers of the film and that the Springfield, Massachusetts bar, is one of the local businesses featured in *Bristol Boys.*

The gritty urban morality tale about a young man trying to escape his dreary working class life by selling marijuana was based on a true story set in Bristol CT., but was shot largely in the Springfield area last summer.

This was the second time that writer, director and editor Brandon Paul had come to Springfield to shoot a feature film. His previous film, *Six Figures,* was also co-produced by Santaniello.

Paul explained that the version of the film presented on Wednesday night to members of the cast and crew was "close to being the final version." He intends to complete the editing and then start submitting the production to film festivals. Eventually, Paul would like to sell the film to a cable television network and then strike a deal for a release on DVD.

Paul said that his contract with the Screen Actors Guild also requires him to have a theatrical release of the film in New York and Los Angeles.

When the film is released, local audiences will recognize Springfield businesses such as Balise Auto Sales on Columbus Avenue, as well as People's Pawn on Worthington Street, and Agawam Tire and Auto. Footage was also shot at the former York Street jail.

Well-edited and fast paced, *Bristol Boys* has a topical story that, if produced 70 years ago, would have starred the likes of James Cagney.

The story is based on that of Kevin Toolen, another executive producer, on whom Michael "Little Man" McCarthy, played by Tom Guiry, was based.

McCarthy, the working class guy stuck in a series of dead-end jobs. His drug-addicted mom contributes to his woes and he sees selling marijuana on the side as a way to get out of Bristol.

Guiry has appeared in a number of feature films, from big budget films such as *Tigerland* and *Blackhawk Down* to independent movies such as *Scotland, PA*. Guiry has also made guest appearances in television shows, such as *Law & Order S.V.U.*

He is supported by a cast of newcomers, with the exception of Max Cassela, who has been acting since his teens and was first noticed as a co-star on the sit-com *Doogie Howser, MD*. Casella has been playing Benny Fazio on the hit program *The Sopranos*.

The film is dedicated to the late Harold Murphy, a Springfield resident who played a major role in Paul's *Six Figures*.

Paul is now researching another crime drama and has been riding along with a detective unit of the Hartford (CT) Police Department.

While he is moving back to Los Angeles after a year on the East Coast, Paul said he wouldn't rule out Springfield for another film shoot.

STANLEY NELSON

2007

When doing research prior to the interview I found a site that bitterly criticized the film and the director's approach. The author of the blog believed

Nelson was trying to whitewash Jim Jones and not portray him as the deeply disturbed man he obviously was.

This film tries to strike a balance between the natural freak show aspects of the story and trying to humanize the Jonestown experience. I think he did a fairly good job, although I do have certain criticisms.

People remember that the 1978 deaths at Jonestown in Guyana in South America as the largest mass suicide in recorded history. Filmmaker Stanley Nelson wanted audiences to remember more than just the hideous end for over 900 people, he wanted to explore what brought them to an isolated section of the South American jungle.

Nelson's new documentary, *Jonestown, the Life and Death of Peoples Temple,* will make its television and DVD debut on April 9. It will be seen on PBS stations as an episode of *American Experience.*

Charismatic preacher Jim Jones and his social experiment have been the subjects of films before. A wildly exploitive drive-in movie *Guyana: Crime of the Century* was released in 1979, while a more sober television production, *Guyana Tragedy: The Story of Jim Jones,* won an Emmy in 1980 when it was broadcast.

Nelson spent almost three years working on the film that weaves interviews with 25 people, two of which actually escaped from Jonestown, with archival footage and sound.

Nelson said he remembered hearing about Jones and the Peoples Temple on the radio in the 1970s. He said that members of the San Francisco-based church were living out socially progressive ideals.

"It sounded so sane," Nelson recalled in a telephone interview.

That perception changed when the 1978 mass suicide and the murder of Congressman Leo Ryan was reported. Nelson said the story of "the crazy man" stopped with his death and the deaths of many of his followers.

In his research Nelson found that Jones was "a very complicated man. It was hard to make it simple."

Nelson went back to Jones's Indiana hometown and said that Jones "was never normal. He was a strange guy who hid [his true feelings]."

As an adult Jones became a controversial preacher who broke down racial barriers and fought for social change. He and his wife adopted African-American and Asian children, making them one of the first multi-racial families in his home state.

He formed a successful commune in California and then decided to bring his ministry to a large city, San Francisco, where he became a political force.

Although Nelson said that "on the surface, [the church] was very, very attractive" to many people, there were problems revolving around Jones's sexual practices and faked healings, among other issues.

With his church under greater scrutiny, eventually Jones decided that he and his congregation could only practice their brand of religion and socialism outside of the United States. Jones acquired property in Guyana and built a small town there.

Nelson believes there was no one trigger to Jones's deteriorating mental state that led to the move to Guyana and the abuses that culminated in the suicide. He thinks Jones's problems started with childhood and grew more severe.

"With more and more power, things got worse," Nelson said. "In Guyana, he was totally isolated. He built a little kingdom."

Nelson said that people who have seen the film have been affected by it.

"It's such a dark story. People joined [the Peoples Temple] with all of the best intentions and were led astray."

"There's no happy ending to it," he said. "It's a cautionary tale."

***

There's an old saying in show business that a performer should always leave an audience wanting more. I'm not sure if that's the best approach in documentary filmmaking, but at the end of *Jonestown: The Life and Death of Peoples Temple* I did want more.

Nelson's film goes a very long way in humanizing the people who joined Peoples Temple. Through numerous interviews, it becomes clear the congregation was not made up of people who could be simply be written off as mindless members of a cult. Instead these were people who were swept up in the idealism of the 1960s and early '70s and saw this church as a true vehicle of change.

The film is also effective in showing how Jim Jones, undoubtedly plagued with mental health issues for most of his life, slowly went from being a preacher with ideas to a paranoid who said he was the reincarnation of Jesus and Buddha.

The filmmakers interviewed Jim Jones, Jr., who was away from Jonestown the day of the suicide, and I wanted them to ask him what kind of man his father was, how did his mother figure into the Peoples Temple and how his life has been for him in the years since the suicide.

They didn't broach those subjects and the film is weaker because of it.

The film doesn't try to whitewash Jones nor does it vilify him. It is a very sad, melancholic production because we know the ending of it. And Nelson is right in saying it is a cautionary tale. In turbulent times, another Jones might be around the corner.

KEN BURNS

For such an acclaimed filmmaker, Burns is pretty easy-going. I told him I had seen him once in a Chinese restaurant in Brattleboro, Vermont, and had wanted to come over and say hello. That, however, would have meant breaking one of my cardinal rules concerning celebrities. Burns quickly said that I should have and told me if I saw him again to do so.

I've interviewed him three times to date.

2007

For Ken Burns, the award-winning documentary filmmaker, his approach to the story of America's involvement in the Second World War wasn't to focus on the presidents, prime ministers or generals, but instead to report it through the lives of ordinary people.

Burns is quick to add the men and women who experienced the war were not "ordinary."

Burns said that in producing the film, the first thing one had to do was shed any idea of a standard documentary format for the production. The goal was to make "an authentic film."

That task was daunting because Burns added World War II was "the biggest event in human history."

Burns wanted to approach the subject through four communities – Luverne, Minnesota; Sacramento, California; Mobile, Alabama.; and Waterbury, Connecticut. – and their citizens. Once the communities were selected Burns and his colleagues spoke to over 600 people – individuals who saw combat and those waiting for their loved ones to return from combat.

From that group, about 40 on-camera interview subjects were selected. They ranged from people who fought in the Pacific and European theaters to Americans who were imprisoned behind enemy lines to young women who found themselves working in jobs that supported the war effort.

Burns said it was a privilege to speak with these people as it allowed him to see what it was like to experience the war.

Many other documentaries have discussed the leaders and the events of the war and Burns thought this approach "keeps you away from what really happens in war."

The production took seven years to make and involved going through thousands of hours of archival movie footage – some of it was truly horrific – thousands of photographs and hundreds of hours of interviews Burns said.

Burns wanted to put viewers into the shoes of Americans living during the war by cutting from scenes about the clash in Europe to the home front to the war in the Pacific rather than covering those events in separate parts of the film.

"Americans were overwhelmed by news," he said.

With uncensored war footage and frank interviews with veterans and others, Burns hoped to strip away the romance that has surrounded "the good war."

"The good war was the worst war ever," he added.

Burns noted, though, one can draw some of the most positive examples of human behavior from the war.

"The good stuff is only made better when you lift up the carpet and sweep out some of the dirt," he said.

The ultimate result is a film that has made a deep impression on its viewers. Burns said he has received thousands of calls and letters from veterans who have told him that finally someone has portrayed what being in the war was like. Burns has received gifts such as dirt from Omaha beach and sand from Iwo Jima from viewers.

"It's been an amazing, amazing outpouring," he said.

With America currently involved in a war started with an event that has parallels with the attack on Pearl Harbor, Burns noted Americans today haven't been asked to make any sacrifices unlike their countrymen of 60 years ago.

He said that at signings he always asks how many people know someone who is serving in Iraq or Afghanistan and he said only about two percent raise their hands.

He said the lack of involvement of most Americans in today's conflict has resulted in a separate military class.

During World War II, Americans were in the fight together, he said.

"Today we're all individual free agents," he added.

He said we might be today "a richer nation, but we feel a poverty of spirit."

2010

Behind Ken Burns's new documentary *The National Parks: America's Best Idea* is a message.

Burns said in a press conference before his speech at the Springfield Public Forums on Dec. 1 that he wants families "to understand this valuable sense of ownership of the parks and that they would act with their feet and take their families there and do what so many of us who have visited the parks have, [gathered] not just memories of spectacular places, but memories of spectacular places experienced with the people closest to us."

Burns is perhaps the most honored documentary filmmaker in cinema history. His famed production of *The Civil War* was honored with more than 40 major film and television awards, including two Emmy Awards, two Grammy Awards, a Producer of the Year Award from the Producer's Guild, a People's Choice Award, a Peabody Award, a DuPont-Columbia Award, a D.W. Griffith Award and the $50,000 Lincoln Prize, among dozens of others.

Burns, a 1975 graduate of Hampshire College in Amherst, received an Academy Award nomination for his 1981 film *The Brooklyn Bridge*.

The new documentary series aired on PBS explores the history of how the parks came to be and is more than just a travelogue or tips on how to visit the parks, Burns later said.

He admitted that picking a favorite park is difficult as they are "so beautiful, they're like your children – you can't choose one."

He told the near capacity audience at Symphony Hall that filming the sequence on Yosemite Park awakened a long-forgotten memory of his father taking him, at age six, to visit Shenandoah National Park in Virginia.

Burns stressed the unique place in history the American system of national parks have. "For the first time in human history large tracts of land were set aside not for kings or noblemen or the very rich but for everyone," he said.

"It's an utterly democratic idea," he added.

The parks are facing many threats, Burns said, from budgetary problems, including an estimated $8 billion in deferred maintenance. Climate change is also a real concern, especially at Glacier National Park in Montana where the glaciers are disappearing "at a terrifying rate."

Apathy is the biggest threat to the park system according to Burns, who while he was in production on the series, met many people who assumed the parks had always been part of the country and would always be part of the country. The parks system was formalized in 1916 by legislation signed by President Woodrow Wilson that created the National Parks Service with the charge to maintain and protect the then 40 national parks and monuments.

Burns said that in all of his films he addresses the division between Americans but seeks to "figure out a way to speak to all sides."

Burns has not been tempted to follow in fellow documentary filmmaker Michael Moore's footsteps by producing a movie with a readily apparent point of view.

"I wish to engage everybody," he said.

While he readily admitted to having points of view that are easy to see in his own films, he said of Moore's documentaries, "I don't believe his films make any converts."

While he said that Moore was talented and funny, he couldn't share Moore's approach.

"I just think it's important to me to speak to as many people as possible," he explained.

There has been a proliferation of documentary filmmakers, and Burns did acknowledge the success of his production of *The Civil War* "had a kind of dramatic sea change coming as it did at the real explosion of cable [television]."

"All of a sudden there were all of these channels and what you needed to fill them with wasn't expensive drama but so-called reality," he continued.

Burns was quick to add with a laugh that shows featuring people choosing their mate or eating bugs wasn't "reality" to him.

The digital revolution in film making technology has also contributed to the increase in documentaries, but Burns noted, "you can put a camera in everyone's hands, but that doesn't make them a filmmaker."

"You have to figure out how to tell a story," he added.

Burns is currently working on six projects all in various stages of production. His new films will include a sequel to his popular *Baseball* series, *The 10th Inning;* a production covering the 1989 Central Park jogger rape and attempted murder case; a biography on Theodore Roosevelt and his cousin Franklin Roosevelt; and a history of the Vietnam War.

2013

Many people might not have heard of the late photographer Jerome Liebling, but they have heard of one of his students, Academy Award and Emmy winning documentarian Ken Burns.

Burns was the name that drew people to the opening of *A Walk Through Holyoke [Massachusetts]* an exhibit of photographs taken in the city in 1982 by Liebling that made its debut on April 4 at Open Square, a benefit for the construction fund of the Holyoke Public Library. The collection will be split between the library and Wistariahurst Museum and will be on exhibit through April 28.

The photos had not been exhibited before and Burns carefully walked around the gallery space looking at each print before his address. The photos depict portraits and cityscapes, ranging from the industrial buildings of the city to the Whiting Reservoir.

Burns called the photos a "revelation." Describing Liebling's skill, Burns said the ratio between what a photographer takes and what he or she shows is always high. "With Jerry it was far less," he added.

Liebling, who was a faculty member at Hampshire College in Amherst at that time, was an internationally acclaimed photographer who had received two Guggenheim Fellows and a National Endowment for the Arts Photography Survey Grant. His works are in the permanent collections of the Museum of Modern Art, the Whitney Museum of American Art, and the Metropolitan Museum of Art, all in New York City, N.Y., as well as the Boston Museum of Fine Art, the Museum of Modern Art in San Francisco, Calif., and the Fogg Museum of Harvard University in Cambridge. He died in 2011.

Speaking to the press, Burns said, "It's hard to put into words what he meant [to me.]"

He added that there was "no greater influence" on his career than his former professor.

"He brought respect for the single image asking us to look into this photograph and see," Burns explained.

Liebling "was seminal in re-arranging my direction," Burns said. He noted that from the age of 12, he had wanted to "go to Hollywood" and be a director such as Alfred Hitchcock and John Ford.

Burns said that Liebling was "very, very tough as a teacher," but was kind and supportive as a friend.

The man who produced and directed films such as *The Civil War, Baseball, The War* and *National Parks: America's Best Idea,* among many others, Burns believes his mentor was "secretly pleased" with his success.

Although Burns said, "you never say never" to working on a fictional film, his schedule for up-coming documentaries is full for years. *Central Park Five* will be broadcast soon on PBS, he said and his production of *The Roosevelts,* which examines the life of Theodore, Franklin and Eleanor Roosevelt, will be completed by 2014.

He is also working on a seven-part film on the life and career of Jackie Robinson, a film on the Vietnam War and another on country music with the title of *I Can't Stop Loving You.*

Ask him which one of his films is his favorite, and he is quick with an answer: it's the one on which he is currently working.

Burns shed light on how Apple Computers received permission to name an effect in its video editing program "the Ken Burns effect," after the trademark manner in which Burns photographs still images. Burns said the late Steve Jobs asked for his permission to use his name, but Burns refused, as he doesn't do commercial endorsements. They subsequently struck a deal, though, in which Apple donated "tens of thousands of dollars" of computers to Burns who then distributed them to schools.

When asked if he was concerned whether or not people confuse documentaries with reality television, he said yes and added, "What we call 'reality television' is not. No one proposes [marriage] before 50 million people."

He described them as "bread and circuses" and added that [documentary filmmakers] spend up to 10 years to try to get it right."

CHICAGO 10

BOBBY SEALE & PAUL KRASSNER

2008

With the national political conventions looming, the DVD release of director Brett Morgen's documentary on the trial of the Chicago Eight, titled *Chicago 10,* seems appropriate – once again the country finds itself involved in an unpopular war and the sitting president is not seeking re-election.

In 1968, a protest aimed at the Democratic Convention in Chicago arranged by members of the Yippies and other groups opposing the war in Vietnam went from a media circus to bloody confrontations with police.

Following the protest, much of which was seen live on television, some of the organizers were charged with crossing a state line to incite a riot: Jerry Rubin, David Dellinger, Tom Hayden, Rennie Davis, John Froines, Lee Weiner and Bobby Seale. These men became known as the "Chicago Eight." Later, Seale's trail was separated from the rest and the group was redubbed "the Chicago Seven."

The film's title refers to the original eight defendants and their two lawyers. Although the group was not convicted on the charges, all were sentenced for contempt by Judge Julius Hoffman. These contempt sentences were later overturned.

Morgen's film seeks to recreate the events leading up to the protest through archival footage and reconstructed scenes. The bulk of the film, though, centers on the trial of the eight people who were accused of planning the civil disturbance.

What makes the film unique is Morgen's use of animation for the re-enactments. Normally, documentaries either use contemporary interviews with participants or observers to fill in the gaps or stage re-enactments with actors.

While the animation itself could have been more polished there was more traditional cel animation used as well as computer generated imagery

(CGI). It is significant that animation was chosen for this purpose. From an animation point of view, I was disappointed in the crudeness of the CGI footage. With CGI as the new favored medium of the art form, audiences demand much more "realism" that what this film's CGI offered. It was service-able, though, and was used to depict the courtroom scenes.

What struck me about the event was how Abbie Hoffman and Jerry Rubin, two of the key Yippie organizers, saw how comedy and satire was part of their strategy in planning the protest and then their reactions in the court-room. In hindsight, their almost absurdist approach seems at odds with the seriousness of what the anti-war movement was all about.

I would have loved to see archival follow-up interviews with either of them, but both died well before the film's production. I did not see a finished version of the DVD release, so perhaps material of this nature will be included in the extras.

The documentary's focus is defined to the protest in the street and its evolution. There are very few references to the Democratic race culminating at the convention a race that was marked by the murder of Robert Kennedy, nor is there any mention of how journalists were treated while covering the convention. I think for many people seeing the film today who did not live through that time, a wider context would have better served the material.

These criticisms aside, the film provides some interesting links to our nation today, as noted by one of the defendants in the case, Bobby Seale, and as well as Paul Krassner, an acclaimed writer who was part of the planning of the protest, but who was not charged with any crime.

Both men spoke with me about the film and the protest.

Seale, the co-founder of the Black Panther Party, said the film's history of the protest was quite accurate, but the movie didn't show that Judge Hoffman had him manacled and gagged for as many days as he actually was. Seale wanted to represent himself and Judge Hoffman refused the request. Ultimately, Judge Hoffman had Seale chained to a chair in the courtroom and silenced with a gag.

Seale recounted that the Sixth Amendment of the Constitution gave him the right to represent himself.

"I had that right," he said. "For seven weeks the judge and I went round and round."

Seale, who is now a lecturer, author and barbecue expert, believes American society has changed since 1968. He's reminded that people were murdered during the civil rights movement in the 1960s. He noted the number of African-Americans elected to public office has increased, but believes there is much progress to be made.

One of his concerns is the erosion of free speech in the last 10 years with the advent of "free speech zones," fenced off areas at public events where protesters are allowed to gather.

When Seale lectures at colleges today, he knows that the young audiences don't know about the Black Panthers and what the group was attempting to do. He said he gives an hour-long speech followed by an hour of questions and answers.

"When I'm introduced there is polite applause," he said. At the end of his speech, though, he receives a standing ovation.

Seale is currently working on another book, one that describes his time in jail.

Krassner is also seen in the film and said he liked the film.

"It captured the flavor and the emotions we felt," he said.

Krassner has been known as one of this country's premiere satirists and commentators. The founder and editor of *The Realist,* a political and social commentary publication that figured prominently during the counter culture movement. Krassner, like Jonathan Swift before him, used savage cutting-edge satire to make political observations.

He writes today for publications such as *The Onion* in its A.V. Club section, *The Nation* and *High Times.*

In 1966, he also became well known for publishing after the death of Walt Disney a poster titled "The Disneyland Memorial Orgy," in which the pantheon of Disney characters are seen in various illegal, unethical and inappropriate behaviors. Amazingly, Krassner was not sued then, a fact he attributed to a report he heard that lawyers for Disney thought a suit would only give the artwork more public attention.

He now has a colorized version of the poster on sale on his Web site and still is awaiting legal action.

He wrote several of the scenes in the film and did use some creative license. He explained that in one scene he substituted a joint for a cigarette because he "wouldn't want to send that message [that tobacco is OK.]"

He said that 1,200 people a week die from complications due to smoking tobacco while the worst byproduct from smoking marijuana is people "raiding the neighbor's refrigerator."

He also noted that in one scene poet and political activist Allen Ginsberg is seen levitating while meditating also an example of the freedom of animation.

The use of animation also allowed the filmmakers to use audio of Abbie Hoffman's telephone calls to a radio host in New York City and provide a split screen image between Hoffman speaking at a phone booth and the host in his studio.

Krassner had hoped to supply his own voice in the animated sequences, but was unable to do it because of scheduling conflicts.

Comparing America in 1968 to today, Krassner said, "In my lifetime this is the worst I've seen."

"It's a challenge to be happy in these times," he added.

When asked who was the worst president Lyndon Johnson, who escalated the war in Vietnam; Richard Nixon, who trampled on the Constitution; or George W. Bush Krassner replied, "That's the easiest question I've been asked my whole life, including my pre-natal period: George Bush!"

MICHAEL SPORN

2008

Michael Sporn was an animator's animator. Based in New York City, Sporn was an independent who was not just an artist, but also a historian of his medium. He died in 2014.

***

For many people, animation is broken into nice little categories. There are the big feature films that are much heralded from Disney or Dreamworks. There's the stuff for kids and television that always seems to be searching for something innovative to copy. There are the anime productions from Japan and those non-Japanese productions that clearly try to imitate them.

And then there are animators like Michael Sporn. Sporn is one of a relatively small group of independent American animation producers whose subject matter and techniques put this productions in a far different category: art.

Now, by saying, that I don't want to scare anyone off. Two new DVDs released by First Run Features have two half-hour productions each that are truly memorable and accessible to nearly all members of the family. *The Marzipan Pig* is coupled with *Jazztime Tale*, while *Abel's Island* is double-billed with *The Story of the Dancing Frog*.

For anyone who enjoys animation, these two DVDs are a must for one's collection. Of the four films, the one that challenges you the most and has the lushest look is *The Marzipan Pig*. With its oddly linear story, and its introduction from a candy pig that has fallen behind a sofa, the film has a dreamy, hypnotic quality. I was really intrigued with what was going to happen next.

Abel's Island, adapted from the book by acclaimed illustrator William Steig, was a treat. A Robinson Crusoe-style tale of an urbane mouse on a desert island, it was the kind of story that, in other hands, would surely have been turned into a bloated musical of some sort. Sporn preserved the story's purity and the film is better for it.

Within animation circles, Sporn is well known. He is a two-time Emmy winner, a two-time Cable Ace winner and has been nominated for an Academy Award. Carefully adapting children's books to animation as well as presenting stories of social relevance in animation has distinguished his work. He was honored with a retrospective program last year at the Museum of Modern Art in New York.

Sporn also has one of the best blogs on animation on the Internet today. It can be read at www.michaelspornanimation.com/bios.html.

I visited Sporn in his Greenwich Village studio earlier this summer where, among other things, he discussed his first feature film, an animated biography of Edgar Allan Poe.

Originally, Sporn thought he would do six half-hour productions for HBO, but that concept didn't pan out. Instead, he is planning a theatrically released feature.

Sporn is using four of Poe's celebrated short stories to illustrate parts of his life. He said that *The Black Cat,* in which a murderer is revealed by his own guilty feelings, is being used to show how Poe became guilty that he couldn't prevent the death his young wife from tuberculosis.

Poe's life and reputation has been hurt for years with false impressions and assumptions, much of which came from a biography written by a man who swore to get revenge on Poe, Sporn noted.

As is the case with any independent film, the production's pace has been dictated by the availability of funding. One of Sporn's animation mentors, Tissa David, has worked on the film and there is a ten to fifteen minute demo reel.

Sporn cast up and coming British actor Hugh Dancy as the voice of Poe and said the actor did a "brilliant turn."

Sporn admitted he was concerned about the end of the film, which uses one of Poe's lesser-known books that critics have dubbed as one of the first science fiction novels. The book addresses what Poe thinks God is and Sporn described it as "almost an epic poem." He said it is very positive and uplifting.

"I wasn't sure it was going to work," he said. With Dancy's reading of the piece, though, Sporn added, "I knew I had a perfect ending."

Other cast members include Alfred Molina and Dianne Weist, both of whom perform multiple roles.

One point of interest in Poe's life that fascinates Sporn is how the author died. Poe had gone to the train station to travel from Baltimore to Philadelphia, but never made it to his destination. Instead he was found in a coma in Baltimore in clothes that didn't belong to him. Sporn said there is one theory that Poe had been involved in a common voter fraud scam at the time of voting multiple times in different polling places. This part of Poe's life might make it into the finished film, he said, with Weist as Poe's mother-in-law telling the story.

With financing in hand, Sporn said the film should take a team of three animators about 14 months to complete.

While computer technology will play a hand in the production, Sporn is not rushing to embrace the latest trend in animation: computer generated images (CGI).

He cited *Kung Fu Panda* as a CGI film that could have been "graphically more interesting" than what it was if it had been done with traditional animation forms.

Of the legion of CGI animated features, he said, "Everything looks like a Viewmaster."

He admitted he is rarely impressed by animation today and said that CGI is great for special effects animation such as fields of grass waving in the wind.

While he said the career he has chosen "is really hard at times," he noted that both PBS and HBO have been great supporters of his work.

He added with a laugh, "I've nothing to complain about."

JOHN LANDIS

2009

I was shocked to see one of the most commercially successful directors in American film signing autographs for $20 a pop at a horror film show, but I took the opportunity to interview him. Landis graciously gave me some time and at the end I bought an autograph.

He is one of my favorite filmmakers and I asked if he would mind if I emailed him the article. He told me that he had long given up seeing any reporter write an accurate piece, but gave me his email.

I sent him the link to the story on line and he sent a nice reply.

***

In the celebrity autograph area of the annual Rock and Shock horror film convention in Worcester, Massachusetts, there is a collection of the usual suspects – actors who have made their mark in horror, science fiction and fantasy films.

Sid Haig, the character actor who has a new career thanks to *House of 1,000 Corpses* and *The Devil's Rejects* was in one corner and Malcolm McDowell, the star of many films including *A Clockwork Orange,* was busy greeting fans as well.

There is one person who seemed out of place in this group – John Landis, a director whose films have earned hundreds of millions of dollars. The man who brought *Animal House, The Blues Brothers, Trading Places, An American Werewolf in London* and *Coming to America,* among many other films, to the screen just didn't seem to be in the same league with the guy who portrayed Jason in the last remake of *Friday the 13th.*

But Landis seemed to enjoy the interaction with fans and with his neighbor at the next table, Jason Mewes, best known for his appearances in Kevin Smith movies as "Jay." Mewes had covered the paper blanketing the top of his table with graffiti and has left a message for Landis at his table that reminded the director he should cast Mewes in all of his movies.

Before anyone thinks that Landis, whose last theatrical releases were *Susan's Plan* and *Blues Brothers 2000* in 1998 is some sort of has-been, it should be noted the director has been busy in the last several years with television work as well as making two acclaimed feature-length documentaries: *Slasher,* about a salesman who specializes in liquidating car inventories, and Mr. *Warmth: The Don Rickles Project.*

He also directed two installments in the popular *Masters of Horror* series on Showtime, experiences he said he enjoyed.

He is also going to begin shooting a new feature film based on the notorious grave robbers Burke and Hare. When one fan asked him about the project, he replied in a loud, but friendly, voice, "It's *Burke and Hare.* Look it up! Google it."

For the uninformed, Burke and Hare supplied medical students in Edinburgh, Scotland, in the 19th century with corpses. When there weren't fresh dead bodies available, they made their own.

After consenting to an interview between signings for fans, Landis said the film is being produced at the venerable Ealing Studios in Great Britain and will star Simon Pegg and David Tennant. He said the film would be "a romantic comedy with all 16 murders intact."

Speaking with Landis is like getting a crash course in the realities of the film industry. When I ask about his ability to move a project forward because of his track record, he interrupted with "A track record means nothing."

"But your films have made millions of dollars," I said.

"It doesn't mean anything. You're being rational," Landis said with a smile.

"So Hollywood isn't rational," I said.

"It never was," Landis replied. "The movie business has changed like newspapers and television because everything is now corporate. It's corporate in a way that's truly bizarre. If you look at the product coming out of Hollywood in the last two years you'll see it's made for the lowest common denominator. It's depressing."

Landis began his directing career in 1973 with *Schlock,* a low budget horror comedy. With the advent of digital technology, Landis believes the production of films is easier today, but the distribution side of the business is in "chaos."

"The platforms are changing, but it will all settle down," he said.

With changes in corporate ownership in Hollywood, how difficult is it for established directors to receive a deal?

"It's very difficult for everybody, for everybody," he said. "Stephen Spielberg, Tony Scott, Michael Mann, Robert Zemeckis [can get deals]. There are very few people the studios will hire. They'd much rather hire hacks. They'd much rather hire people with no opinions."

Landis disputed the importance of having a good script as the basis for a good movie.

"Here's what I tell people. It gets me in trouble. It's not the story. People misunderstand that. A good story is a good story. It's like jokes – it's not the joke, it's how the joke is told. The best example I can think of are westerns or samurai movies where there'll be 25 movies with the exact same story, but in the hands of John Ford or Kurosawa or Preston Sturgis or Robert Aldrich – so many directors do it differently. It's a fascinating thing. It's something the studios, the conventional management, doesn't understand. It's not about high concept. It's only about execution."

And the budget of a film plays less of a role than most people think.

"The idea that budget affects the filmmaking process comes out of ignorance. You often hear critics say they spent too much, they spent too little. They don't know what it cost. The truth is the cost of a film has nothing to do with the quality of the film," Landis asserted.

"The cost of a film has nothing to do with the quality of a film just like genre has nothing to do with the quality of a film. I've made huge moves and

I've made little moves. I've made big budget movies and low budget movies and the director's job is exactly the same: put the camera there and you guys do this," he added.

Just like actors, Landis has been typecast as a director of comedies.

"Producers are much more comfortable offering me comedies because I've made a lot of money with comedies than with other genres. I mean I love westerns, musicals. I love everything. It's easier for me to get the money for a comedy than it would be for a serious drama," he said.

Landis added that there are "many" projects he has in the back of his mind.

One of those he is currently trying to launch is a movie on the life of publisher William M. Gaines, the man who is best known for bringing *MAD Magazine* into the world.

Since he has worked with both fiction and documentary films, does Landis have a preference?

"I'm a filmmaker. I like making movies. I don't care what they are," he said.

He learned from *Slasher* that pre-conceived ideas about a documentary subject could be easily changed due to the reality a director is shooting.

"In some ways the documentary is more experimental," he said.

He said he enjoys appearing at horror film conventions such as this one, although this is only his fourth or fifth time. He believes it's a way for performers to make some additional money from their work, since studios make so much, and he enjoys meeting the fans.

***

Landis directed *Burke and Hare* but Andy Serkis replaced David Tennant. It received scant theatrical release in this country and is available on DVD. I recommend it.

NINA PALEY

2010

Sita Sings the Blues is a highly improbable film. It is an animated adaptation of a revered story from the Hindu tradition told from the perspective of its non-Indian creator. Unlike big studio animated features, the film has four different art styles and much of the action is accompanied by vintage jazz songs performed by the late Annette Hanshaw.

By commercial standards, this low budget animated movie has no business being successful and yet it has garnered enthusiastic reactions from reviewers and audiences alike and its manner of release may revolutionize the independent film industry. Now that it is on pre-recorded DVD anyone interested in independent film or animation should check out this remarkable film.

Cartoonist and animator Nina Paley chose to put a version of the Indian epic *The Ramayana* on film – a story she described as "the greatest break-up story ever told" – after her own marital split. *The Ramayana* is about Sita, a goddess separated from her beloved lord and husband Rama. Rama questions Sita's purity after a rival king abducts her and although Sita ultimately proves she has remained true, she is banished to live in the forest.

Paley tells this story on four artistic levels. There is a rough "cartoony" narrative relating her own story, another looking like ancient paintings, one more that uses a more contemporary depiction of Hindu deities and a final one that is used for the musical numbers.

In many ways, the musical numbers resemble the classic Fleischer Brothers *Betty Boop* cartoons with the construction of Sita with a Boop-like series of circles and the evocative recordings by Hanshaw.

This shifting of styles might be a bit jarring at first for some audiences, but I found it very playful. I love it when animators take chances with their story material and audiences and Paley does that in spades.

The result is a must-see animated film for adults. Paley has tested the boundaries of animated stories farther than any of the commercial studios.

Speaking by phone from her home in New York City, Paley said the origin of the film was a series of random events. She was married to a man whose work brought him to India, where she was first introduced to *The Ramayana*. During a business trip she made to New York City, her husband broke up with her through e-mail.

Stranded in New York, she recounted she was reading *The Ramayana*. She recalled, "I was obsessed with the story" – and found comfort in it at the same time she was "sofa surfing" – staying at the homes of friends while looking for a place to live in New York. One of those friends was a record collector who introduced her to the recordings of Hanshaw.

"All these happened at the same time," she said.

Paley said that, like Sita, "If there had been a funeral pyre I would have thrown myself on it."

Her emotions, though, became channeled into the creation of her film.

A veteran cartoonist but a novice animator, she began work on the film and "did three years of work over five years of time." Animating the film on her home computer she was essentially a one-woman studio. She supported herself as a freelance artist and her project was awarded a Guggenheim Fellowship.

She also asked for donations from friends and the general public through her Web site. She said that including her living expenses for the time period, "Sita" cost about $270,000. In comparison the Pixar hit *Monsters, Inc.* reportedly cost $115 million.

A considerable amount of the budget went to licensing the music about $70,000 and the manufacture of a 35mm print for theatrical showings. The print cost Paley $30,000.

She said the use of different artistic styles was due to several factors, the first being "to keep myself from getting bored."

"There is a huge breath of 'The Ramayana' art in the world and I wanted to give a little taste [of it]," she added.

Although this writer saw a strong influence from the classic Fleischer Brothers *Betty Boop* cartoons – from its flying monsters to characters gently bouncing to the beat of the music to the anthropomorphized moon Paley said, "Everything I've seen is an influence. I wasn't thinking of *Betty Boop* when designing those segments."

An integral part of the film is commentary on *The Ramayana* from three animated Asian shadow puppets that provide commentary and analysis of the story. Interestingly enough, they sometimes bicker a bit and disagree about the details of the story and its implications.

The dialogue for the three characters is bright and spontaneous and Paley said it was a conversation about *The Ramayana* from three Indians living in the United States recorded for the film. Paley called the non-scripted dialogue "an experiment."

"Obviously, it was perfect," she said with a laugh.

She said the three people all grew up with the story and were from different parts of India and had their own views on it.

There has been criticism of the film's depiction of the story from Hindu fundamentalists and Paley said that many of the negative reviews have come from people who haven't seen the movie. She doubted the film would ever be released in India because of state censorship issues as well her refusal to sell exclusive rights to a distributor.

The film is being seen in India, however, thanks to the way Paley has released the film, a method that has attracted more mainstream attention than the film itself from such media outlets as *Time* and *The Wall Street Journal*.

Typically, a distributor would buy exclusive rights to getting a movie into theaters, while separate deals would be made for DVDs and television screenings. These distribution deals also are usually for one country, so a filmmaker must make multiple efforts to have his or her film seen worldwide.

Paley has said that one distributor of independent films offered $20,000 upfront, hardly enough to cover her costs. She added she has learned that a distributor "can keep a smaller film down."

With a standard distribution contract, "no one can compete with them [distributors] to make [a film] available."

"This was highly influential in my decision to free the film," she added.

So "freeing" the film meant she did not copyright it. She allowed WNET in New York City to stream it on its Web site. She encouraged people to download the film and make copies.

She has made "endorsement deals" with several DVD companies, which have released the film to the home video market. These arrangements are not exclusive and Paley gets a significant percentage of each DVD sale.

She explained she is not signing over her rights to the film but signing over endorsements. The downloading and sharing of the film has resulted in an underground marketing effort. Generally, she said, about half of a movie's cost goes to marketing. By taking her approach, she said she "is getting tons of free advertising when people see it."

"If it hadn't been free, the film would have been at the mercy of a marketing director," she said.

People who have seen it on-line have sought out ways to buy the film on DVD and other "Sita" merchandise.

By last October she had earned $65,000 through this arrangement.

Reaction from the animation community was at first hostile. She was called a "freak" and a "traitor."

Her success, though, has changed some minds.

"With success more and more people have been writing 'She may have something,'" she said.

Paley also went through a copyright dispute over the use of the

Hanshaw music and through her struggles with the songs and with her decision to "free" the film, she has become a leader in the "Free Culture" movement. She has joined others in questioning if art and culture should be controlled by monopolies.

"The whole struggle with our broken copyright system turned me into a Free Culture activist. I'm actually going to release all my old *Nina's Adventures* and *Fluff* comics under a Share Alike (copyleft) license too. I saw what happened to Annette Hanshaw's beautiful recordings: they got locked up so no one could hear them. I didn't want that to happen to my film. My first concern is art, and art has no life if people can't share it," she said.

For more information on the film and on the Free Culture concept, log onto www.sitasingstheblues.com.

R.O. BLECHMAN

2013

You may not know his name, but if you've watched television or read *The New Yorker,* the *New York Times* or the *Huffington Post,* you've seen – and will recognize – his work.

R.O. Blechman's distinctive squiggly line is featured in a new exhibit at the Norman Rockwell Museum called "R.O. Blechman: The Inquiring Line" through June 30.

Blechman has received a Lifetime Achievement Award from the National Cartoonist Society, won an Emmy in 1984 as the director of the PBS animated special *The Soldier's Tale* and has been featured in an exhibit at the Museum of Modern Art, among other honors.

Blechman has also done a series of children's books, and has collected many of his cartoons in the book *Talking Lines.*

In his statements made at the opening of the exhibit, Blechman marveled the exhibition even existed.

"A museum for a *Saturday Evening Post* illustrator? That's important. Me in that museum? That's fantastic," he said.

The exhibit features a wide selection of original examples of Blechman's work from New Yorker covers to advertising work. Some of his animated productions play on a monitor.

Perhaps no two artists could have such different style as Blechman and Rockwell. Blechman said growing up in New York City in the 1930s and '40s, his world didn't resemble the warm images of small town America that were the herald of Rockwell's most famous work.

He came to appreciate Rockwell more, he added, when the painter's liberal politics came through in later paintings in the 1960s. Blechman also said that he really rediscovered Rockwell when his mother and father-in-law moved to Stockbridge and he visited the predecessor to the current museum.

"It was a revelation ... that guy could really paint, really paint and he could design," Blechman said.

Blechman described himself as a self-taught artist who did some cartooning for his college newspaper. After graduating from college and serving in the military, he drew what would now be called a "graphic novel," *The Juggler of Our Lady* in 1953. Published by Henry Holt, the book was a huge success, which Blechman said actually negatively affected his growth as an artist.

Ask him what his favorite medium has been and he answers it before this writer could finish the question.

"Animation," he said snapping his finger for emphasis.

The medium combines his interests of telling stories and illustration, he explained.

He has an idea for an animated feature that he would love to produce.

Animation was the first step in his career as a professional artist. He began as a storyboard artist for acclaimed animator John Hubley who was impressed with *The Juggler of Our Lady*. Blechman wanted to animate, but he said, "I could not draw in those days."

The Juggler of Our Lady was later made into a cartoon as a collaboration between Blechman and directors Gene Deitch and Al Kouzel. The British Academy of Film and Television Arts nominated the production as best animated film.

He was pleased with the results and later turned down an opportunity to remake the story in color with animation director Chuck Jones. Today, he expressed his regret not to have worked with Jones, but said with a laugh he wouldn't rate his mistakes.

Blechman is still busy working, but he admitted, "I've lost projects because I'm told [my style] is old fashioned."

He added that while more realistic illustration may be in favor now, he believes the pendulum will swing back to more idiosyncratic styles.

"[Johann Sebastian] Bach was lost for 150 years," he noted. "Illustration will come back."

Although he expressed concern for the future of two-dimensional animation, he is no Luddite. Of digital techniques he said, "I love the stuff. It can be well used if you have eye [for design]."

Digital techniques can enhance hand-painted art, Blechman said. For him an understanding of design is essential no matter what medium is used.

"If you have an eye, the hand will follow," he said.

His own squiggly line is part of his design, which he admits was sometimes a challenge for his animation staff when he operated an animation studio. The Ink Tank produced numerous television commercials including a memorable one for Alka Seltzer in which a man and his stomach argue about his love of spicy foods.

"[My drawing style] was very difficult to animate, but I was fortunate enough to deal with two animators who took to it as if it was their own," Blechman said.

On his Emmy Award-winning production *The Soldier's Tale,* Blechman recalled the best animators "supplemented, not just complemented" his designs.

Blechman was effusive in his praise for the late animator Tissa David who worked at his studio starting in the 1970s, calling her a "great animator, an animated filmmaker." He said she could look at a scene in real life and "animate in her mind."

The most obvious question this writer reserved for the end of the interview: how he did develop his own distinctive drawing style?

He admitted that it is both natural and designed.

"My stuff was so stiff and dead," he said. The non-straight line work "loosens" his compositions.

After decades of drawing in this style, Blechman said, "Now it's natural. I don't even think twice," he said.

MIXED BAG

WILLIAM M. GAINES

1975

I wish I could remember how I decided to interview the publisher of the legendary line of *EC Comics* and *MAD* magazine, but as a student at the University of Massachusetts I sent him a letter to ask for an audience and he responded favorably.

This is an example of the first rule of interviewing: it doesn't hurt to ask.

I came to reading *MAD* late in the day. My mother believed that most comic books – she made an exception for Disney titles – and *MAD* were somehow bad for kids. I'm sure that her attitude was fallout from the comic book scare of the 1950s created by the infamous book *Seduction of the Innocent*.

By junior high school, though, I was a complete comic book fan and started reading *MAD* in high school. In my mind, *MAD* was essential reading and was far more counter culture than anything the dreaded hippie movement created.

MAD taught me and several generations of young people to question what we saw and read. It stands as a body of work with the best of American popular humor and satire and is in the tradition of Mark Twain, Sinclair Lewis, and Ambrose Bierce, in my humble opinion.

I had no idea what to expect when I went to the *MAD* office and was certainly a bit nervous. I felt some relief when I noticed the door to the office had a small sign under the slot for letters that read "Plastic Man's entrance."

After the following piece ran first in my fanzine Inertron, with an edited version being one of my first professional sales, I visited Gaines once more in New York. I came with a manuscript in hand for a *MAD* piece and Gaines introduced me to one of the editors.

He sat me down and read the script on the spot. It was the longest five minutes of my life. He didn't crack a smile. At the end of it, he told me what I had written was very funny, but I had written in the style of a regular *MAD* contributor and that I needed to develop my own voice – good advice.

Gaines was noted for his avuncular manner and he showed that to me when I asked him what he thought of the magazines that imitated *MAD*, such as *Cracked*. Look for his answer here.

I did another short piece on Gaines in 1980 by phone and he was gracious as usual. He sent me a note with an advance look at a two-page apology to the *MAD* readers for the magazine putting its name on the comedy *Up the Academy*.

Gaines died in 1992. *MAD* goes on in a form that he probably wouldn't have liked much as the magazine now accepts advertising, something Gaines had forbidden so that *MAD* could make fun of anyone and anything.

***

Looks can be deceptive. The building at 485 Madison Ave. in New York City look like a typical complex: a lobby with marble walls and a jovial uniformed elevator attendant. Only by consulting the registry could one discover that this building houses *MAD* magazine.

Well, you think if the building is conventional, then the *MAD*-men must be cut from the same executive cloth.

This assumption is definitely refuted when you meet the publisher of *MAD*, William M. Gaines. If seen on the street, Gaines might inspire words such as "bum" or "Hippie freak." A man in his fifties, Gaines is dressed in a simple combination of baggy grey pants and a solid blue shirt. A chubby man bordering on fat, Gaines wears his grey hair shoulder-length and has a full beard. Horned-rimmed glasses complete the picture.

I started my talk with him on the subject of his first success in publishing, the Entertaining Comics line of horror comics in the late 1940s.

How did you come up with the idea of the horror comics?

Well, my editor at the time was Al Feldstein and we were working on a line of rather bad books and Al was taken with some of the stuff that was on television at the time, such as *Lights Out* and *Suspense* and he proposed putting something like that in the crime books. This jogged my memory and I remembered the radio programs I listened to when I was a kid, notably things like *The Witch's Tale*. Al liked the kind of story that had a logical ending and I rapidly pushed him into doing stuff, which did not necessarily have a logical ending, something of the supernatural. Although as the years went by, to get ahead of the story, we developed our own kind of rules for the stuff we wanted to run.

We felt that vampires, werewolves and walking corpses were logical but ghosts weren't. We found stories that fit our fantasy belief rather than those that other people would have done. That's how they got started. After running one such story in each of the four crime books, we decided to throw out the crime books and put out complete horror books.

This illustration by Michael Moyle graced my fanzine when I published the interview in 1976.

And they sold very well?

Actually when we did this, we didn't know how well they sold because you don't known that quickly in comics. We just got enthusiastic about what we were doing on the basis of four little stories and we decided that everybody has crime books, but no one has these – so that started something new.

By 1954 Gaines's line of horror comics (along with his science fiction, suspense, humor and war titles) were extremely popular with fans, but extremely unpopular with parents who started well organized protests against Gaines and his publications.

Did the charges that your books were smut bother you?

Oh, it bothered us, but I can't honestly say I was surprised. In those days, a lot of people objected to a lot of things in the way of literature, television and movies, which today are taken pretty much for granted. I didn't think you can really comprehend the differences in the attitudes toward sex in any of the media and even towards horror stuff. Sex was just out and out so immoral and so bad that people would get into a frenzy just thinking about it and it's understandable because for most of the history of man, sex has been a taboo subject that seems to generate differences. But all the fuss about horror stories was a shocking thing; as I say, I wasn't surprised, people are that way, but ah [pauses] it was disheartening."

Gaines was forced to give up his tales of revenge and the supernatural. Was he strapped for new ideas when the horror comics ceased?

Oh now, we had lots of ideas, but [pauses] let's say the stuff we published between 1950 and 1954 came from the heart. We were publishing things we loved. I loved the horror books. I loved the science fiction we published. I loved the suspense stories and Harvey Kurtzman came along and he loved the war books. I never loved the war books, but that was all Harvey's and he did them by himself.

The other books Al and I collaborated on and we both have the feeling or it. We plotted the stories together. We wrote them and edited them together.

Did you have the same affection for "MAD" when it first came out?

Not when it first started out. Again this was something that Harvey handled pretty much by himself when he was editor. I got an affection for it later on. Actually I think that the first issue of *MAD* was rather bad. If you read it and occasionally I go back and read it, I don't even chuckle. The later issues of *MAD* get me hysterical even at this late date. But it was the beginning of something new and different and it developed into a very good magazine and I got very fond of it later.

But to answer your question, we had lots of ideas, but they were forced ideas. Now we had to drop the stuff we loved – ah, we came up with a tremendously craftsman-like line of comics. They were extremely unsuccessful, but not because they weren't good comics. They were unsuccessful due to the various pressures. The wholesalers were attempting to put me out of business by not distributing my magazines. These magazines sold 20 percent, which was catastrophic and almost unheard of even in an industry that has had some catastrophes. I didn't think anything ever sold as bad as my "New Direction" comics because they just were returned unopened. This bankrupted me about 1956.

Then MAD pulled you out?

MAD pulled me out.

Although "MAD" is the best known and most widely read humor and satire magazine *in the country, does "National Lampoon" cut into "MAD's" audience?*

I'm sure it's cutting into our market. What seems to have happened is that *Lampoon* has taken a lot of the college age readers that *MAD* used to have. I still think that *MAD* still has a lot of the college age readers and I'm sure that there are a lot of readers who read both. But I'm sure that some readers read only Lampoon that otherwise would still be reading *MAD*. *MAD*'s sales have continued to go up and this past year hit new highs so that Lampoon hasn't hurt us. It's just that we might have gone higher if *Lampoon* didn't exist.

On the other hand, nipping at our other end is *Cracked* and possibly *Sick* and maybe *Crazy*, which are fringe books that appeal to very young kids and perhaps they have taken some sales away in the same way. There are ten-year-old kids who might have bought *MAD* except that *Cracked* is around. I'm sure that a lot of them are buying both. So we have the very elementary kind of [pause] – I'm groping for a proper adjective to describe *Cracked* and I can't come up with a nice one – but we have that at one end and Lampoon at the other with the ultra-sophisticated sex and sick humor that they specialize in. It hasn't hurt us, but we might have a higher circulation if it weren't for both of them.

Do you read Lampoon to see what they are doing?

Frankly, no; some of the staff does, but I don't.

What do you think of the "MAD" parody they did?

Some of it was pretty funny, and some of it was in very bad taste, and well, that's the story of the *Lampoon*. Sometimes the *Lampoon* is very funny and sometimes the *Lampoon* is in dreadfully bad taste. So they are really putting out what some people think they want. As a matter of fact I stumbled on that article in advance and here's a funny story, which most people don't know. In a way that I'm not ready to reveal, I found out the story was in preparation. It was purely by accident. So I sat down and I wrote them a letter and I said something to the effect of I'm looking forward to seeing this wonderful thing and I signed it – ah what do they call me, I forget?

"Citizen Gaines"

Citizen Gaines, right and then I said, "P.S. My spies are everywhere."

Well I understand there were giving, practically giving, lie detector tests to people trying to find out who had blown this thing and nobody blew it.

Is there an animosity toward competitors such as "Lampoon?"

Oh sure. Listen when you get into business and this may be something that simply hasn't occurred to you, but it will when you get out of school and start competing. When you get out in what I'll call "the real world," for lack of a better term, you're in competition with everyone around you. Your bread and butter, and your family's bread and butter depend on what you're doing and [that] what you're doing survives and prospers. Of course, there's a feeling of competitiveness and at times animosity against any imitation of what we're doing. We feel that *MAD* is ours. We started it and our company owns it and we live off of it. Of course, if someone comes along and rips you off you're not going to be happy about it. I feel that both *Cracked* and the *Lampoon* on many occasions have lifted ideas from old issues and used them. Jerry DeFuccio can give you examples of this. I don't keep track of them.

What do you think of the renewed interest in the old EC comic books?

It's tremendously flattering to us. We love it. Actually my happiest days were back in the old EC magazine days because I was creative then, I was doing something creative then. With *MAD* I've been nothing more than a business-man and while that's fun too, it's different.

Would you rather be at the creative end of "MAD" now?

I can't be because I'm not creative in a *MAD* way. I was creative for the kind of books we were putting out. I'm not creative for *MAD*. I couldn't possibly write or edit *MAD*.

"MAD" has increased its price recently. Did it bother you to do that?

It kills me. I hate to raise prices and I always do it with great reluctance. The only thing I can do is to give you some comparison, which I always give myself to make myself feel better. When *MAD* was a quarter, hot dogs were 15 cents. I always measure everything in terms of hot dogs, so this is perfectly valid. *MAD* has now doubled its price, but the old nickel frankfurter, which was 15 cents at Nathan's when *MAD* was a quarter, is now 50 cents. The Nathan's frankfurter has tripled its price whereas *MAD* has only doubled its price. So I think we're not doing too badly.

Recently one of DC Comics' titles, "Weird Worlds", stopped production because of a paper shortage. Has a paper shortage affected "MAD" as yet?

No, because we don't use Canadian newsprint. We use a special paper made for *MAD* magazine called "Great Northern *MAD* Jet." You say *Weird Worlds* has been dropped?

The phone rings. Gaines answered it and asked that I turn off my recorder. While he is talking I marvel at his office. Impeccably neat, it reflects Gaines' interest and personality. Suspended from the ceiling are about 11 different models of zeppelins. Hung in the window is a tremendous sculpted face of King Kong, which Gaines later tells me was made by "MAD" artist Sergio Aragones. Original oil paintings of EC horror comics characters are hung on the wall, along with numerous caricatures of Gaines. On a cabinet behind me is a hinges frame with photos of silent comedian Fatty Arbuckle and Virginia Rappe, the starlet he was wrongly accused of murdering.

Gaines finished his call and makes another to Carmine Infantino, the publisher of DC Comics, best known for characters such as Superman and Batman, and the late "Weird Worlds".

Hello, Carmine, what's this about *Weird Worlds* being cancelled because of a paper shortage? Oh, oh, okay. What? Oh, a fan wanted to know [to me]. It wasn't selling and they just didn't want to do it. It wasn't making money and they had to kill it and that's something every publisher hates to do.

"Lampoon" has a radio show and an off-Broadway show (something "MAD" also had several years ago). Have you considered doing more "MAD" things in different mediums?

Yes as a matter of fact, ABC has produced a *MAD* television special. It cost them a reputed $300,000 to produce it and it's sitting in the can because they've decided not to run it.

Do you know why?

Well, no, they won't tell me. I suspect one of the reasons they won't run it is because one of the features is the "Automobile Manufacturer of the Year." [laughs] *MAD* accepts no advertising and we have no censorship problems from anyone. We do anything we want and the only thing that we are bound to is the law of the United States. When you go into the area of radio or television you have to have sponsors and accept advertising, and you have to please advertisers, which is one reason I never wanted to go that route. I wasn't particularly anxious to make a television special, but these people offered me an awful lot of money and so I said I'd try it and we tried it. I got paid and they got paid and the only people who didn't get paid was ABC, who lost. They paid and they have the option of killing it, if that's what they want.

Is it done with live actors?

No, it's all animated; a half-hour animated show. At the moment we're examining the possibilities of an off-Broadway show. By and large I always felt that *MAD* would translate brilliantly into something else. A perfect example of that is Laugh-In, which was tremendously successful. They tried to put out magazines and paperbacks, but were complete flops. It is not impossible that *MAD*, which is tremendously successful in the print field, would be a flop in those fields.

MAD is now owned by a large corporation. I've always had a negative image of corporations.

I don't blame you. We do too and thus far *MAD* has maintained complete autonomy. We run ourselves the same way we always have.

Do you have to fight for it?

You bet we do! [laughs] All the time! No, it [corporation interference] has never really been a problem and the day it does become a problem I'll probably walk out. But it does take a little cursing and screaming now and then [laughs].

***

William M. Gaines
485 Madison Avenue
New York, N. Y. 10022

NOV 7 1975

Gaines sent me this note of appreciation after my first interview.

The *MAD* television special has never been released, however it is available to see on YouTube. To this date it has never been officially available to *MAD* fans, although the magazine has inspired two successful television series, the late night comedy *MADtv* and an animated show on Cartoon Network.

DON McLEAN

1982

Singer and songwriter Don McLean came to my hometown several years ago to play with the Springfield Symphony in a pops concert. I was given a pair of comp tickets since my paper had published an advance piece on the show that included an interview with McLean.

I didn't conduct the interview as I had spoken to him many years ago and found it to be such an unsatisfying experience that I swore off listening to his music for many years.

I had been a huge fan of his and when *American Pie* was released I thought in my dopey junior year of high school kind of way that he was speaking to me. I loved his stuff.

I saw him perform at Springfield College in the 1970s at a concert marred by some heckling. He was good, though.

I had an idea in 1982 to start up an alternative weekly newspaper for Springfield and decided to do up a dummy issue. When I heard McLean was going to be performing at Riverside Amusement Park (now Six Flags New England) I thought an interview would make a good story to add to the prototype issue.

I made the arrangements and was joined by several other writers at the park. We all watched him perform and then approached him for the interview time.

He said he and his band wanted to ride some rides before they had to do the next show and so we all waited 45 minutes.

When he returned, he ignored us and started jamming with his group. Finally, I walked up to the stage and told him that if he didn't want to talk with us then he should have the decency to tell us so we could go home.

He stopped playing to say that he really didn't like to do interviews, but he knew he had to do them. He then spoke with us.

The alternative newspaper went nowhere. The story and photo were never published until now.

Eventually I started listening to his music again, breaking one of my cardinal rules about pop culture: I loathe supporting jerks.

How was his recent show? Well, he has maintained much of his outstanding vocal quality and actually spoke to the audience a little with some humor and charm. The hall was almost sold out and there were a lot of hard-core fans there. Overall, it was a treat.

But I didn't stand in line to buy a book or CD.

***

Singer-composer Don McLean was riding high in 1971 when his monster hit *American Pie* was released. Although McLean has said he could have had a very profitable career if he played the recording industry's game, he

Don McLean between sets at the former Riverside Park in Agawam, Massachusetts in 1982. Photo by G. Michael Dobbs

chose to do it his way. Even though he released five albums since *American Pie*, he has not appeared in the musical forefront until last year with his remake of Roy Orbison's *Crying*.

Now, McLean's career appears to be gaining momentum with his new album, *Believer*.

How does it feel to be in the spotlight again?

Well, I supposed I never worried about it, you know. I figured it would happen eventually. I have a lot of faith in myself where that's concerned. To be here a while and to be gone a while; I kind of like that actually. I don't think I'd like to be in the middle of everything all the time. I'm happy I've got the chance to sing for a lot of people now. If it changes back to the way it was, that's okay, too.

I've made some wonderful world tours; been all around the world many times and have made a large following in a lot of countries in those years.

Now, my country is coming around to my music.

Have you learned to cope with the popularity of "American Pie?" Have you had audiences unwilling to give other songs a chance?

No. Did you see the show today? Certainly they liked a lot of the material today, and a lot of the people there weren't fans, but were just people here at the park. So, I feel that's a pretty good acid test.

I'm used to playing for the public, and there's lots of songs I've written they think highly of, such as *Vincent* and *And I Love You So*. So, when I start singing them, I think a lot of people don't realize I'm responsible for them. They just know *American Pie* and now *Crying*. That's the purpose of a concert anyway, to get more specific about your music.

Why haven't you had a hit record since "Vincent?"

There are several factors involved when you have a record company promoting you, determined to break you, so to say, break your career – make it happen. There's a lot of artists in the past 10 years, I think, who can say this. They were on big record labels in the early '70s, and now are gone. They're still out there. I was lucky I had record companies still interested in me after all these years.

I wasn't on that many labels. I was on United Artists for six years, and I made six albums for them. Then, I was on Arista for one album, and that was supposed to be a three-album deal, but Clive [Davis, president of Arista] didn't like the work I did in Nashville [on the "Chained Lightening" album] so I decided to look elsewhere and that took a year and a half. There had been a real change in the taste of the record people, and singer-songwriters were a thing of the past.

Do you think your career would have been much different if you had been given more help from your record companies?

I think, probably, if the record companies had worked with me during those years, that all the things that are happening now would have happened then because people have known me for many years. It's that if you can't get those people who bank on you to work with you, and then you're out in the cold until you break in again, and that's what I did.

I felt inside that this was the right time for me, and for a song like *Crying* because it shows people what I can do musically from a whole other perspective.

You once termed disco as "musical masturbation." What trends do you see in music now and what do you think of them?

Well, they're still masturbating. It's just that they've found different ways of doing it, I guess. I don't hear much in the way of freshness out there. A lot of people imitating Bob Dylan, that's what I hear everywhere.

I never asked their [the music industry's] permission. I just sort of did it [his career]. I don't give a damn if I fight with a record company or if they get behind me. If I have to wait five years to do what I have to do, I will. It doesn't matter to me because I have a lot of faith in my abilities to communicate with music.

BOB BACKLUND

1984

Perhaps this is the interview with the oddest context that I've conducted so far, as I mentioned in the introduction to this book.

I had been a professional wrestling fan since childhood and even though as I grew older I was more and more aware of the show business aspects of what I was watching, I had great admiration for what these men and women did in the name of entertainment.

My first chance to speak with a wrestler was when I brought my tape recorder to Mountain Park, a long since closed but beloved amusement park in Holyoke, Mass. Walter "Killer" Kowalski would perform there along with students from his wrestling school.

Kowalski was an intelligent articulate man who willingly posed for a photo with me taken by my father-in-law. As soon as the camera was ready, he assumed his wrestling persona and lifted me by throat onto my toes. I smiled but I secretly feared for my life!

I was able to initially interview Backlund when he and a group of wrestlers were in a small town high school nearby. Before the advent of nation-wide broadcasts, wrestling was a regional enterprise. The World Wrestling Federation actually only operated on the East Coast from New England and New York state south to Pennsylvania or so. Backlund was the world heavy-weight champion of this group – there were many other heavyweight champs in other promotions.

Even then, wrestlers of Backlund's stature would appear in smaller venues and I spoke with him for a few minutes at the match. He seemed to be an even-tempered person until I brought up the subject of whether or not professional wrestling is faked. I asked him how he reacts to critics who allege this.

His response was to take his index finger and strike my recorder with it for emphasis while saying something along the line of "How do you react when someone says the contests at your radio station are faked?"

And that was pretty much the end of the interview.

I did a freelance story on wrestling for a local arts weekly in the early 1980s and got some quick quotes from several wrestlers back stage at the Springfield Civic Center. Wrestling veteran Pat Patterson candidly told me, "If the money wasn't that good, I wouldn't take all the punishment and all of the traveling."

I chatted with Pedro Morales, Angelo "King Kong" Mosca and with the one and only Captain Lou Albano. Backlund was there, as well, but while the other wrestlers were socializing or having a smoke, Backlund stayed to himself. He actually did stretching exercises with a broomstick.

So, why Backlund chose me out of the blue to speak with me months after he had lost his heavyweight title to the Iron Sheik on Dec. 26, 1983 is still beyond me. I never asked him why he called and queried if he could come on my show. Why look a gift horse in the mouth? After an initial interview, I opened up the phones for calls from my listenership. It was almost two hours of effortless radio with fans even coming to the station to see him.

***

How did you make the transition from collegiate wrestling? [*Backlund had wrestled for North Dakota State University and had won the Division II NCAA Championship at 190 pounds in 1971*]

I trained in Minneapolis for about a year with a professional wrestler. He showed me the different submission holds. You have to learn to land as flat as you can when somebody body slams you or suplexes you, so the weight is displaced over a large area rather than landing on your shoulder or hip or your feet so you won't hurt that one body part.

You have to learn how to perform in the ring instead of a mat. You don't have to think about losing any points because in amateur wrestling you're always thinking, "Geez, the guy can't take me down because he's going to get points." In professional wrestling there's no points.

You have to learn how to deal with people who are in it for just one thing and that's the money.

I know that you maintain a busy schedule with the WWF, but did you catch any of the Olympic wrestling?

I just got back from the Olympics three weeks ago. I spent a week with the Greco-Roman wrestlers. They asked me to come out and help train them. My training program is very, very tough and I didn't find anybody who can go through it all.

I went out and helped train them and wrestled with their heavyweight Jeff Blatnick while he wrestled at Springfield College. Two years ago, he had Hodgkin's Disease and he recovered from that and won the gold. To me, that is one of the best things that could have ever happened to an athlete.

You perform what is known in the business as "scientific wrestling" with holds and counter-holds. Would you like to see professional wrestling go in this direction?

Well, I think people like George Steele and different people in professional wrestling are a disgrace and you can't be proud of man like that. I can't go home and say to my family, "Geez I had a heck of match with George the Animal Steele." I'm not going to be able to do that.

I can respect a match with somebody like, he's not well known up here, Jack Brisco, a two-time national champion, a great wrestler in professional wrestling. [Also,] B. Bland Bear, I wrestled him in Hartford and it was a heck of a match, a match I could be proud of.

Yeah, I would like to see it go in that direction a little more, but it's not going to. Right now I'm not in professional wrestling anymore. A few weeks ago Vince McMahon told me my morals are too high and after he told me that, I told him, "I don't belong in your profession."

And we're no longer together. The WWF and I are separated.

Would you consider wrestling in another league or promotion?

You see they wanted me to change. They wanted me to yell and scream more. Maybe they wanted me to have green hair. And I'm not going to do that. I try to help a lot of kids get into amateur wrestling. I tell them to be champions within themselves, which is my motto.

I'm not going to change no matter what anybody says. No matter what it costs me. Because I feel I'm going to let myself down, I'm going to let your kids down and I'm going to let my kids down. And, by golly, I'm not going to do that. I'm not going to conform.

Right now, I'm fighting the system. I'm not conforming. There's a possibility I would go to another organization but they would have to understand that Bob Backlund is nobody else than Bob Backlund. I don't have a fictitious name. I don't have a fictitious weight. My hair is red and it's going to stay red.

I recently spoke to Walter "Killer" Kowalski and asked him what he thought of today's wrestling. He said he doesn't watch very much because it's too violent. It was violence for violence's sake. It wasn't holds and counter-holds, it was really brawling. So the WWF wanted you to change your scientific style?

I feel I'm still a champion. I resented your introduction of me. And you didn't know it but the only two ways you can lose a championship is by a pin or by a submission and that didn't happen the night I wrestled the Iron Sheik in Madison Square Garden. I wasn't pinned and I didn't say, "I give up." And I still lost the championship. I feel I still have the title. They took the belt away from me.

You felt you were cheated out of the title according to the rules?

Well, if I was pinned, I would have gave up and then I would say no, I wouldn't been [the champion]. For as long as I've been in professional wrestling and I've talked to a lot of old timers it's always been that way. You can only lose it of you get pinned – one, two three. Or you submit. That did not happen to me.

But that's not the reason I'm not involved with the WWF. When a man tries to change what I believe in, it's time for us to separate.

What are you doing now? Introducing more kids to Greco-Roman wrestling?

Well I have a league that's named after me, The Bob Backlund League. I'm going to do a lot more work in that. I'm going around doing speeches to different organizations. I'm going to New York City next week and work out with the New York Athletic Club wrestling team. Talk to them a little bit about training and diet, staying away from drugs.

I've been very interested in having a program sort of like Jack LaLanne has. I've been speaking to some people about that.

Would you consider doing a workout tape?

I'm speaking to a few different television stations and seeing if they would be interested in airing a program I would be on. I would do exercises on the program and talk a little bit about the importance of an education for the kids and the importance of diet for the adults. It would be geared toward people in general, but especially the youth. I really enjoy being with kids and helping children – seeing them mature and try to help them in the right direction.

Do you think, considering how the WWF is now buying time on WTBS in Atlanta and displacing the wrestling program that originated there, there will eventually be just one national wrestling organization?

I don't think so. You follow wrestling closely so you may know that Vince McMahon Sr. died this summer – as a matter of fact I was the only wrestler at the funeral. He was a great man and perhaps the greatest promoter in professional wrestling. And nobody will ever replace him. Nobody will ever be bigger than he is. Nobody will ever be able to fill his shoes.

If he thought there ever could be one organization in professional wrestling, he would have done it.

I talked to him quite frequently and he was disappointed in what was happening in professional wrestling in his last few days.

ANTONIO FARGAS & MARK METCALF

In 1984, I was able to speak with two visiting artists to a theater company in Springfield, Massachusetts called Stage West. The director for the company at the time was Timothy Near, the sister of the singer and activist Holly Near.

She brought a new energy to the company and took some risks. Antonio Fargas, the African American character actor perhaps best known for playing *Huggy Bear* in *Starsky and Hutch* was cast by Near as "Starbuck" in a production of "The Rainmaker."

Not only was an African-American performing a role that was traditionally played by a white actor, Fargas's versatility proven from his career on the stage was not known locally. Most people had either seen him on the television show or in black action movies.

His kissing of the heroine of the story on opening night actually brought gasps from some of the blue-haired older women from suburban communities.

Near cast Mark Metcalf in the central role of the Arthur Miller play "All My Sons." Again she brought a talented actor to a role that was outside of his public perception. Metcalf was best known at that point for his role as the villainous "Neidermeyer" in "Animal House."

Both men turned in compelling performances.

ANTONIO FARGAS

How did you get started in acting?
Oh boy, well, I have to start by stating my mother said that as an infant when I cried it sounded like I was singing so she thought I always should be in show business.

I'm one of 11 children and was considered from a young age to be the lawyer in the family, the sensitive one who could bring people together. So I put all of this together [and] when I was 13 and a half they were casting a film about gangs in New York called *The Cool World* directed by Shirley Clark, They were going around to different neighborhoods, settlement houses, interviewing people because they wanted a real documentary look and they didn't want people who had acting training, but could adapt.

So at my mother's urging I went down and tried out for one of the roles. I always tell young people one of the reasons I think I got one of the roles is because I could read well. I had one of those fundamentals down and I was able to interpret the script and show my natural abilities for the craft.

After that I started studying in New York and here I am 25 years later.
Most people identify you with the role of Huggy Bear. One local station is running "Starsky and Hutch" five days a week.
It never dies.
Has that hurt your career or helped it?
There are negatives and positives to it. The most negative part is not the public per se but the people in my business who I think should know better. They are just as brainwashed by a character you showed them for many

years on a TV series. They sort of pigeonhole you more than even the public. The public will accept whatever areas you go in.

I've been doing a soap opera recently and the public says, "Oh, Huggy Bear is doing a soap." I think the business is more guilty of pigeonholing an actor after he's done a role like Huggy Bear for a while.

I've been very fortunate in that, one being a black character actor, I've been able to do a variety of different types of things, all in the character vein but very different. I've also been able to segue between film, television and the stage, which has helped my versatility and helped people think I can do different things.

Did you pattern your role of the piano player in the film "Pretty Baby" on legendary jazz performer Jelly Roll Morton?

I listened to some of the tapes from the Library of Congress on Jelly Roll Morton but I think it was locked in by the screenwriters and I just tried to fulfill what they had put down on the page. It was patterned after Jelly as well as Tony Jackson who wrote the song "Pretty Baby." He was a flamboyant character, homosexual, but a very great "professor" in the district in New Orleans as well as Jelly.

[It was a] combination of the two, but primarily Jelly since his music was predominant in the film.

Many of your roles have been interesting and thoughtful in films that could spark controversy. Has that been deliberate or has it just worked out that way?

It just has worked out that way. I think a lot of my peers wouldn't have touched some of the work I've done because they have problems about what their image is and what direction their careers are in. I feel I'm in a special situation because I'm a black character actor and there aren't that many as far as I know.

So, I think it's luck as well as the fact I really like working at my craft, creating roles and I will take a chance. I'm the sort of actor who gets hired because the director knows I can handle the material. I don't get directed too much because I bring what they want. That's a nice feeling to know that people trust your work and they'll hire you because they know you'll go for that character. You're not going to let inhibitions and all kinds of other things stop you from achieving a mirror image of something in life that people can recognize. That's my forté I guess.

Many people in show business have observed that race is still a consideration for many roles in films and television and there are not enough good, solid roles for those performers.

I think not only do the producers think of it that way but a lot of my peers. I've probably been guilty myself, of also thinking that way. Both sides [must] start thinking an actor for a role and not thinking about [an] ethnic background. A lot of times they have to deal with pressure groups and balancing of characters and they really haven't taken that in consideration that there are ethnic groups all through our society who are doctors, lawyers, who own things who are very rich who could probably be on *Dynasty,* or even on *Dallas.* I think the public is ready for it. We're so hung up; the industry is so hung up.

I also think there is some unwritten conspiracy to a certain degree. We all know during the period of black exploitation films that blacks flocked to the theaters. Blacks support the soap operas. I sort of feel the industry turns its back on the money that would be generated by giving blacks and other ethnic groups a chance of showing what they can do. It would turn a profit. They say, "Nobody would watch it." They sort of feel blacks are going to watch the soaps anyway and blacks are going to watch *Dynasty* whether they are represented on it or not.

I tell people if they want something on television or film they should write because the networks and the producers count a letter as 1,000 people...if you want to change something, pick up your pen. If you write in, they take that as big step toward what the public really wants.

Your role in "The Rainmaker" here is an example of an actor and a role without consideration of ethnic background.

I take my hat off to Timothy Near for that. Most of the time that kind of situation takes place in regional theater. It doesn't happen in New York or Los Angeles, I wouldn't probably be cast in the role in New York even today, unfortunate to say that but it's true.

I think it's a special place for an actor. There are so many people who want to see live theater and to get a chance to do *Hamlet* in Springfield or where else is special to me ... I'm not one who has be starring in plays or whatever, I just like working at my craft and I'll go anywhere to do it.

I had to audition for Timothy and I found it a good challenge to come to Springfield to do this role and I'm really enjoying myself.

Which is your favorite medium?

I think it's very romantic to say, which is true for me, that stage is my first love. It's the kind of work I would do even if I wasn't paid because of the instant rewards you get, the rewards you get every night and the danger of doing something live in front of an audience every night and there's no take two and no cut.

Theater is my special love and I think film would be next and television if I would line them up. What's best for an actor, to be well rounded in this business is to work on all those fields. I've been fortunate so far to be able to do that and keep my muscles sharp.

Another thing about working in Springfield or different places, for me coming from California having been there nine years and not doing so much stage work, that my muscles had sort of gotten atrophied for stage. It's a frightening thing to walk out on a stage when you're not prepared. So I was able to do a play at the Hartford Stage and a couple of theaters in New Jersey. Now I feel I'm getting in shape again because it takes time to really build yourself up – your confidence as well as picking up the little things you need to be effective on stage.

What are the disciplines that different types of acting require of an actor? In films, an actor has to wait between scenes or takes. Is it difficult to maintain your edge?

Consistency and keeping that edge and knowing where you are mentally – that's the hardest part of [being] an actor.

Actors have to be, number one, in shape. Anyone who says that partying and having a good time is the only thing an actor does, [well] I go to the gym and try to work out. These are new disciplines for me, as I get older, also ... I work best in the morning, sometimes a shot takes all day. For me sometimes I have to take off my make-up and wash my face, take a shower and try to get that crisp bright-eyed look again.

And it's tough. Sometimes you have to retake scenes because sometimes some actors also work better in the morning ... Doing *Starsky and Hutch* I saved them a lot of money because I was good at being very quick with my work. They could be all day with those other guys and when they get to my shot at the end of the day it would be boom, boom, boom, and we're finished.

To be able to be on your job and be ready and it takes only one or two takes to get a scene down makes them very happy because time is money in this business.

MARK METCALF

I began speaking with Metcalf about his preparation for the lead in *All My Sons* and made the embarrassing admission that on opening night I didn't recognize his name or photo in the program. I was impressed by the fact I watching a well-crafted and moving dramatic performance from "Doug Neidermeyer," one of the "Hitler Youth" from *Animal House* (1978). He took my confession with a laugh.

He did reveal he gained 20 pounds for that role by eating pancakes and drinking beer.

***

What was it like to work on that film? Universal had no expectations for that movie, did they?

Almost everyone in the film was not a known quantity or a regularly working quality in the business before it, except for John [Belushi] and Tim [Matheson] who had done a lot of TV series before that and John had done *Saturday Night Live.*

Almost everyone from that cast has gone on to work most all the time in theater or television and back and forth – it was great to work on it because of that, because we were unknown quantities. There were no stars among us. Everyone was working pretty much for scale and nobody knew what it was going to be.

We were out there in Eugene, Ore. and when you do a film on location, especially a film like that, you're sort of like an outlaw: you've got no past, you have no future. People seem to like the movie business and you get a lot of attention. We had a great time. We didn't tear the town apart or anything like that, but we gave it a good go.

Was any of the film improvised?

No, it was very heavily scripted, specifically scripted by Doug Kenny who is dead now, and Chris Miller and Harold Ramis had come in and sort of cleaned it up. When we all got there we had about a week of rehearsal and every day we'd rehearse scenes and do a certain amount of improvisation. Basically the scenes all remained exactly the same. Some lines would change and by the nature of some of the kinds of performers, people would sort of throw a line in. Once cameras were rolling, everything was set.

It was a good meld and Doug Kenny and Chris Miller were there all the time. When we were rehearsing we would throw a few more things in and Doug would say, "I like that, but could not you say it this way, say it this way." [He would] change it and reshape it – accommodated to our personalities and our performing styles.

Were you typecast in Neidermeyer-type roles after the success of "Animal House?"

Yes, they asked me to do the TV series [the short-lived *Delta House*] and I didn't want to do that because I didn't want to land too much in that. To a certain extent, as soon as I was finished with the film I stopped acting for two and half years. I did a little. I did a movie called *Where the Buffalo Roam,* for the same people basically, for Universal. They wanted me to play a Neidermeyer kind of character named Dooley, press secretary to Richard Nixon. Anyway I did that.

Because I quit acting for two and half years to produce a film I didn't really ever get the sense I was being typecast, but when I went back to acting to a certain extent it exists, but not really. It had been long enough. They forgot about it.

I had done a lot of different kinds of things on stage. In *Chilly Scenes of Winter,* the film I produced, I did a pretty different kind of character; still one of the guys stuck on the outside because he's a little too straight like Neidermeyer is, but he's certainly the kind of bully or fascist Neidermeyer was. He's just a big dumb jock kind of guy.

Yeah it happens, but because I took myself out I never really had to bear the burden of being typecast.

Tell me about your film. I admit I haven't heard of it. Was it released widely?
"Chilly Scenes of Winter" was released in 1979. The film was directed by Joan Micklin Silver and starred John Heard, Mary Beth Hurt, Gloria Grahame and Peter Riegert. Metcalf's co-producers were Griffin Dunne and Amy Robinson.

It was released by United Artists but not in a real wide release. I don't know if it ever played Springfield. It played in Boston and was a real big hit.

It was released originally as *Head over Heels,* and United Artists changed the title on us at the last minute. It was always called *Chilly Scenes of Winter* from a book by Anne Beattie. They changed the title at the last minute and advertised really poorly and it really sunk pretty quickly. It played a month in New York, a month and half in L.A. and various other cities. It played cable. It had a cable showing. And then we got it just a year ago last August we got it re-released as *Chilly Scenes of Winter,* the real name, the name it was supposed to be. It had a really nice art house run.

It's kind of European movie, European in style. We wanted to make that European realistic, naturalistic, low key, no car chases, no sex scenes, no guns, no knives no violence. It is a movie about people having a relationship, not pushing the comedy, not pushing anything – a piece about people.

So it ended up in the art house and got a good critical response. I didn't get rich off of it. It seems to be becoming a cult films in certain areas. In Seattle, they love it, Boston, New York, they like it in certain theaters, play it again and again. It's doing all right.

I will do it again. I'm involved with the people who produced it. There were three of us. They went on and I helped them at the beginning stages of producing John Sayles's last film *Baby, It's You.* I didn't line produce it. I helped develop the script and set up the deal and then pulled out because I wanted to act. They are now this summer shooting a film tentatively called

Lies, which they are making in New York. I will probably be acting in it and maybe doing a little background producing on it.

I'm trying to get more and more back into acting because it gives more immediate satisfaction and more long-range satisfaction. I'm not quite built for being a salesman and that's what you are when you're a producer.

How frustrating is it when you've worked a project two and half years and then the distributor changes the name of the film and botches the advertising?

It's a killer. I think it's probably one of the main reasons I wanted to get out of it and go back because it was so debilitating. It was so insulting. There seemed to be no way to get through to these people, to make them understand. It's like taking your child to somebody, turning your child over to somebody and they say, "this isn't a boy. It's a girl" or saying, "God you have an ugly kid." That's basically what they said. They said, "I don't know what this movie is. How do we do it?'

They're used to handling *Moonraker,* James Bond pictures or *Rocky.* They don't know how to handle a little picture that has the same kind of qualities as *King of Hearts.*

Short of hanging them out of their eighth floor offices by their heels, there's no way to get through to them and we weren't about to do that. It's really a killer. It's embarrassing. You feel a great deal of shame that you weren't really able to bring this thing through all the way to completion. You completed making the movie, but advertising, the salesmanship part of that game is not something I'm attuned to. It's not something I want to be involved in but you have to be if you're going to produce a film because you have to get it into the theaters in the right way. You want the right people to go to see it, to appreciate it.

Do you think cable television will open up new vistas for people with small films who want to reach a particular audience?

It should and eventually will. It seems to me that what's happening with cable is what has happened to TV and films in that they are interested in money. It's a business for them. They want to get their investment back. It costs a lot of money to make a movie, even a low-budget film and they want to get that money back.

So, they are going with what are considered reputable box office stars, not necessarily the right actors or directors or cinematographers for the right project. So there is a lot of heavy compromise going on up front dealing with cable people. They have a lot of hours to fill and they're going to have to let people – and some of them are [doing this] – encourage people who are not known.

We had no business producing. It's amazing we got a chance to produce. We were three actors no one had ever heard of and we did it but not taking "no" for an answer.

It takes that type of determination from the creative people. I think cable will break open a little bit more because there are so many hours to fill with creative work. What I see happening right now because they're trying to get more and more stuff done with a limited number of people. They're still ignoring different kind of creativity. They still want the *Three's Company, The Hart to Hart* [kind of shows]. They're looking for that to put on cable. They get the same writers, the same kind of product and they're doing it just as fast as they do it for prime time TV. You're leaving out some of the good stuff.

HAROLD RUSSELL

1984

If you've seen the 1946 film, "The Best Years of Our Lives" then you've seen the remarkable performance of Harold Russell, the WWII vet who lost both of his arms in a training accident. Director William Wyler chose Russell after he saw him in a documentary short subject and cast him in the film that told the story of returning service men and their effort to re-adjust to civilian life.

In light of our growing number of veterans today and the problems they face, this film is still relevant and packs a real emotional punch.

Russell won an honorary Oscar for his performance in 1947 and then, in an upset, was chosen as Best Supporting Actor. He did not pursue a show business career and only returned to acting in the movies, *Inside Moves* (1980) and *Dog Town* (1997). He also appeared on the television shows *Trapper John M.D.* in 1981 and on *China Beach* in 1989.

For about 20 years, Russell served in the voluntary position of chair of the President's Commission on Employment of the Handicapped and was a nationally known advocate for the rights of the disabled.

When I asked him about the status of the disabled in the workplace, he said the nation had made "tremendous progress," although the number of Vietnam vets who had come home suffering from injuries was the highest in the nation's history – twice as many amputees from Vietnam than WWII and the Korean War combined.

***

I've got to ask you about your unusual acting career. How did you happen to be selected for the role in "The Best Years of our Lives?"

I was in Walter Reed Hospital in the later part of 1944 and the surgeon general at that time wanted to do a documentary, which would address itself to the problem of rehabilitating amputees. I luckily happened to be the only bilateral amputee in the hospital and they wanted to concentrate on that. They asked if I would stay in the service for six months to make this film and work for the people who were making it and I did.

The war ended and the film was later used for a theme for War Bonds sales after World War II and they were casting for *The Best Years of our Lives* at that time.

[Director William] Wyler had come back from World War II as a pilot and [Sam] Goldwyn had seen it and they decided maybe I should have a chance to work in it. I came out to Hollywood and I read for the part and I was photographed. It turned out pretty good and I got the role. It's an unusual way to get into the film business but it worked in my case [chuckles].

Were you nervous to work with people like Fredric March and Dana Andrews?

[Laughs] I was scared to death. I really was. When I got out there I was frightened to death. Of course I had seen these people, Dana and Freddy, in all these wonderful films. I just couldn't conceive a little guy coming out of World War II working with these people. I soon found out they were very kind and generous and very supportive. One of the great things about *The Best Years of our Lives* is that we had a wonderful team of people, both in front of the camera and in back of the camera. Everybody was working to make a good picture, including the director William Wyler, who himself was disabled. He suffered from deafness from World War II.

They were out to tell a story and I think one of the reasons the picture was so successful was in a sense everybody who came back from WWII one way or another could relate to one part of the film – either to the army sergeant played by Fredric March or the Air Force Captain Dana Andrews or to myself who was disabled. There was a kind of relationship, kind of spirit who everyone could say, "Hey, I remember this or I remember that because it happened to me or it happened one way or another."

There were no heroes in that picture. It was a team effort with Wyler leading the team. It was great. I don't think I had seen anything like that before. It was wonderful.

I saw you in "Inside Moves" and I thought it was a very good picture about people who were overcoming their disabilities.

I did too and I felt that John Savage did an unbelievable job as the young disabled person. I thought he was fantastic. I was very disappointed when he wasn't up for an Academy [award]. I thought he deserved it.

Dick Donner was a very low-key director, wonderful guy to work with. For the most part we had a script to work with and everyone knew the script, but he let us go ahead and improvise and let us work as we felt. Obviously a lot of stuff was not used, but enough was used to make at least what reviewers felt was a good picture, maybe better than good.

I was very interested in it. I was especially interested in the reaction of young people. I spent a lot of time on the campuses of universities around the country and it was funny how many young people related to those four guys in the film ... most of all to the reaction to disability. It was very funny, Mike, there was only one reviewer in this country, I shall not name, who said it [*Inside Moves*] had a wonderful narrative, but it was not realistic because handicapped people didn't make jokes upon themselves [laughs].

That was another effort where everyone enjoyed coming to work. It wasn't work to make a film; it was kind of a fun thing.

FIRESIGN THEATER

1985

The Firesign Theater may be the most influential comedy group in American popular culture and yet there is also a good chance you may never have heard of it. David Ossman, the late Peter Bergman, Philip Proctor and Philip Austin have created a huge body of work that has included dozens of recordings, stage appearances and a few films and television appearances.

The group's initial comedy albums such as *Waiting for the Electrician or Someone Like Him* (1968) and *How Can you be in Two Places at Once When You're not Anywhere at All?* (1969) placed them square in the center of the counter culture movement at that time. Their stream of consciousness style was married to both sharp political commentary and to affectionate references to popular culture.

Unlike other acts that became identified with the late 1960s, the Firesign Theater survived being a topical act and continued to record and perform up until 2011. They all had their own careers and there were members who departed from the group for a short time. The group changed permanently when Bergman died in 2012.

I had been a fan for many years and had the opportunity of speaking with members of the group three times. The first time was in 1985 with Proctor and Bergman about a revolutionary technological development: the compact disc.

The Firesign Theater as they appeared on their PBS special "Weirdly Cool" in 2002.

***

Since the late Sixties, the Firesign Theater has been on the cutting edge of comedy and satire in the United States and now they are turning their efforts not only to new audio productions, but video as well.

Famed for albums such as *Don't Crush that Dwarf, Hand me the Pliers* and *How Can You be in Two Places at Once When You're not Anywhere at All?* the group's new projects include an interactive game recorded on compact disc, a comedy special for Cinemax, and the first comedy album recorded digitally for compact disc.

"The history of the Firesign Theater," said group member Philip Proctor, "is that we have been afforded the opportunity, because of the kind of forward thinking aspects of our own comedy viewpoint, to work in the state of the art technology. And this is the first time that we have actually been in involved in the state of the art before it was stated it was art."

Proctor and his fellow Firesigners, Philip Austin and Peter Bergman, started work two years ago on an interactive game for the compact disc player.

"Now this is going to be complicated so I hope everyone tells jokes to one another while I'm doing this," Proctor explained." But basically, the compact disc has the capacity to contain pictures – not moving pictures, but kind of like an illustrated book. We were hired to develop some of the prototypes for this new system, which at this point, two years ago, hadn't been even developed yet."

The game is called *Eat or be Eaten,* which served as inspiration for their Cinemax Comedy Experiment show and also their comedy compact disc.

Their Cinemax show, which will be released by RCA to their home video market next year, concerns the strange rural town of Labyrinth, where an innocent television talk show host finds herself in the middle of a yearly virgin sacrifice to the kudzu vine. Proctor has the lead male role, with Bergman and Austin not only acting but also serving as executive producer and director respectively. It was the first video project that the group produced completely on its own.

Although many pop culture historians have credited the group with pioneering the type of complex humor which some now call "conceptual," the Firesigners really don't know what they are.

"Do we consider ourselves conceptual humorists?" Proctor asked Bergman, who is in the office with him. "The concept confuses me," is his reply.

"The Firesign Theater has always done what amuses it," Proctor explained. "The group, when it was a four man group and now that is a three man group, still garners most of its inspiration out of our partners' responses to the ideas we come up with. And we find that all of us as a unit – or as a eunuch, because sometimes we feel emasculated trying to work out ideas – anyway, of the ideas we are dealing with amuse us all and the comedy flows and we're having a good time, generally speaking, that is the thing we'll develop."

Proctor believes their brand of humor has lasted now nearly 20 years because of the varied interests of the group and because "all of us were inspired by the madness of American society and the vernaculars it was creating."

America is still mad enough to inspire the group, as are the demands of recording on digital compact discs. There is no way to "fake" on a digital compact disc, according to Proctor. Sound effects must be actual and not pre-recorded. Proctor recounted the group driving around Los Angeles recording a scene in a car in order to get the sound of driving.

Their new comedy album, to be released by Mercury in November, will be available in both compact disc and regular record formats and Proctor assured Firesign fans that they will be able to hear "every thing." The group is legendary for laying one track of sound onto another for startling comic effect and the new recording technology has allowed them to do this with even greater clarity.

Although they may not be the most famous of the comedians spawned by the 1960s, they are probably the most contented.

Bergman said, "I think the most satisfying thing I've done with the Firesign Theater is just the 20 years of being with the Firesign Theater. I can't pick out one particular project – it's a body of work and that's what I've been most happy about. Just to work with these fellows, to work under conditions they make possible. It's friendly. It's fun. It's an artist's dream. I can remain a child and still get some serious work done in the world."

***

In December of 2002, I had another opportunity to speak with members of the Firesign Theater. That year marked the broadcast of their television special *Weirdly Cool* on PBS stations as well as the release on DVD of that special and the long-awaited DVD release of *J Men Forever,* (1975) a unique film project from Proctor and Bergman.

Weirdly Cool was quite mainstream for the Firesign Theater and segments of the program were introduced by people such as Robin Williams and John Goodman. It underscored the considerable effect the group had on American comedy even if they were not household names.

J-Men Forever is a particular favorite of mine. I saw the film two or three times during its brief theatrical release in 1974. Thanks to its broadcast on *Night Flight,* the film became a cult classic.

I first spoke to Ossman about *Weirdly Cool* and then talked to Proctor about *J-Men.*

Regrettably, I'm missing the first section of the interview with Ossman.

***

Abbreviated versions of the first Nick Danger episode as well as *High School Madness,* and *How Can You Be in Two Places at Once* are among the features of the program. While each segment is true to the original material, the authors included up-to-date jokes swell.

Ossman said that the group writes for the audience; and they enjoy the fact that in a live show people will say the lines along with them.

"It's far from disconcerting," he said with a laugh.

He added that he also likes playing with the audience's expectations by changing the reading of a line, fooling the chorus in the audience.

Ossman said there was a sense of history in the production of the show as it was taped at CBS's Television City complex in Los Angeles where the classic Jack Benny and Carol Burnett shows were taped.

"The vibes [in the studio] were great," Proctor said.

The *Weirdly Cool* DVD not only features the television special, but also has a clip from the group's video production of *Every Thing You Know is Wrong,* a set of wonderful non-sequitur commercials from the late 1960s for a Volkswagen dealership, a short documentary on the group made at the time of their 15th reunion, and an audio recording of a writing session from *Give Me Immortality or Give Me Death.*

The last extra, the audio recording, gives an insight into the group's writing process.

"It [writing] is very tough, but because we've done it so long, certain aspects come easier," explained Ossman. "It's like writing a novel with four hands," he added.

The group has had its ups and downs, with members periodically breaking up and re-grouping and all having careers on their own.

"It has been hard and contentious [at times]," admitted Ossman. "If the four of us are clicking there was nothing like it. It is magical."

***

Two of the Firesigners have regularly teamed up for a variety of projects on their own. One of the collaborations between Phil Proctor and Peter Bergman is a film that has reached true cult status.

J-Men Forever is a hilarious re-editing and re-dubbing of Republic Studios movie serials from the 1930s and '40s into a new film detailing a secret war against the world from the leader of the Moon, the enigmatic Lightning Bug. The Bug was using rock and roll and drugs to corrupt wholesome middle class America.

Receiving limited theatrical release in 1975, *J-Men* didn't attract its audience until several years later when television producer Stuart Shapiro brought the film to his *Night Flight* program on the USA cable network. There it played many times, with fans making sure they set their VCRs to tape the film.

It was only released once legally on home video and has been a favorite of bootleggers.

Proctor recounted that producer Patrick Curtis had established a relationship with Republic Studios when he had produced an homage film to B westerns, another film genre that Republic produced.

"We thought it would be fun to do the serials," Proctor said.

He and Bergman watched the serials and then wrote the new screenplay. They also supervised the new soundtracks, performing some of the voices themselves and casting other performers such as deejay Machine Gun Kelly.

An influx of funding allowed the pair to shoot new wrap-around footage featuring them as the federal agents coordinating the fight against the Lightning Bug.

The reception the film received was so impressive that it inspired two spin-offs, a Cinemax special *The Mad House of Dr. Fear,* and *Hot Shorts* for RCA Home Video, which used the other members of the Firesign Theater.

After *Night Flight* ended its run, the film was relegated to cinematic limbo.

"For years I tried to get it out," said Proctor, "but we couldn't find a good print. It was more important to have it look right. Then Stuart Shapiro came up with a print."

The DVD features a rambling and affectionate interview between Proctor and George Wallace, the actor who played Commando Cody in several Republic serials, and a dialogue between Proctor and Bergman on the making of the film.

***

Like all of the members of the group, Proctor has developed a solo career and is kept very busy as a voice actor for animated productions, including *Rugrats* and several of the Pixar animated features. Despite his schedule, he still tries to "make time for Firesign."

Although another tour, like their one in 1993, may be out of the question, because of the money it takes to underwrite such a venture, the group doesn't wish *Weirdly Cool* to be their swan song.

Ossman hopes to see the 22 hours of XM programs they produced released on CD.

"Phil Austin said there will always be a Firesign Theatre. Since it will always be there we might as well work with it," Ossman said.

MELANIE KINNAMAN

1985

When you are writing for a local or regional publication one type of standard interview story that is among the most intriguing to readers is the hometown kid made good. Here is one from 1985 and another from 2013.

***

Some of the Valley residents who saw *Friday the 13th Part Five* earlier this year went to the film not so much to gawk at the splatter as to check up on one of their own: a Valley native who has taken the chance on becoming a successful actress in films and television and who is making it the hard way.

Holyoke native Melanie Kinnaman was the star of the film taking the role even though she never liked that kind of film. It was a realistic career compromise for a 28 year-old actress who started her career straight from high school by moving to New York and competing for stage and soap opera roles.

If you harbor favorable ideas on the glamour and romance of show business, talking to a person like Kinnaman is revealing. She is a working actress, not star, and her job is not so different than anybody else's.

"I learned that every new place you go to, no matter what city it is, it's like starting all over again, no matter what credits you have," Kinnaman said.

"Getting that one job, the first job, was difficult and a struggle, in each different medium, it was the same thing as film, getting that first thing. Once you get the first, it snowballs for you. Getting the momentum going is very difficult. It's like getting into the inner circle. It's not just show business, it's in every business. I meet different people in different businesses and they tell me it's the same."

Kinnaman has wanted to be an entertainer most of her life and transferred from Holyoke [Massachusetts] High School to the Williston-Northampton School in Easthampton, Ma. partly because of its theater activities. After graduating, she made the decision to pursue an acting career by moving to New York City to find work and to study.

Although her mother was very worried, "like all mothers worry," Kinnaman said, she was supportive of the move and Kinnaman spent seven years in New York learning her craft.

She did soap opera, off-Broadway, and off-off Broadway, but she eventually decided that to break in films and television, she would have to move to Los Angeles.

"I felt that I had done everything I could possibly do in New York, other than Broadway, which is very difficult to get into. And I knew at that point I didn't want to do one soap opera and go on to the next one and then do an off-Broadway play."

Her credits did not impress Los Angeles casting directors and Kinnaman had to start her career all over, She lived in Los Angeles for eight months before her first TV job, a 13-week stint on, ironically, another soap opera, *General Hospital.*

After her West Coast soap debut, her career picked up its much-needed momentum. Other small TV roles followed, and then Kinnaman was offered her first movie role.

In Cannon Films' *Thunder Alley,* Kinnaman has a major role as a model with a drug problem. A rock and roll musical that was shot a year ago this past March, Kinnaman noted with some regret in her voice, the film has yet to be released.

"It's a rock-and-roll story, and they use a lot of music in the movie. They had a few legal battles [over performing rights]," she said.

Cannon Films is Hollywood's top independent studio, making hugely profitable exploitation films such as the recent Chuck Norris epics and the *Break In'* musicals.

"They're not nice people," Kinnaman said discreetly. She hopes *Thunder Alley* will be released in September.

Kinnaman is currently under contract to Paramount Pictures for another movie, part of her agreement when she signed for the *Friday the 13th* film, So far, no script has been picked. Kinnaman is staying busy, though, with a role in the play *Diamond,* now in rehearsal and opening in August.

"Ed Ames is playing the lead, my love interest. I enjoy doing theater again. I did so much in New York and there's so little of it in L.A. I jump at the chance to do it," she said.

Her next big movie break came in chapter five of the *Friday the 13th* saga. Kinnaman was offered the role of the therapist who tries to help a youngster who is imitating the grisly behavior of the supernatural killer Jason, and although she was no horror film fan, she took the job.

She said, "I went in knowing what those kind of pictures are like. I had never seen any of them, but I knew. After I got the role, I did see one of them. I guess it was 'Part Four.'

"What made me happy about the picture was that a lot of people liked it. I went to see it at its major opening in L.A., and the audience just went crazy, and that is when I felt good about it. I suppose if I sat in a screening room by myself and watched the picture. I would have said, 'What is this?'"

"But I sat there in a full house and these kids were on their feet. They enjoyed it from beginning to end. When they came out of the theater, they were all excited. They had gone through some experience like a roller coaster. I hate roller coasters. A lot of people hate them. A lot of people love them. That's the same way I feel about that movie. It's not for everybody."

Although *Part Five* was no critical favorite, like the first four films in the series, it was a financial success. Kinnaman believes that no one takes these kinds of films seriously, although she noted that her fan mail from the film was "just amazing."

"I was shocked at some of the imaginations out there," she said with a laugh.

To make it in the film industry, Kinnaman firmly believes in having a strong sense of self.

She said, "If you don't have that, you can be eaten alive. I had to learn about that. I don't know if people naturally have it. I know I didn't naturally have it. That came through a series of shocks; trial and error.

"You have a lot have a lot of confidence in yourself in what you can do, maybe not in everything that you do, but in that basic talent you know you have. The rejection every single day is unbelievable. I have people who started with me who are no longer in the business. Perseverance is the key here. Very talented friends of mine have dropped out and will not work in the business now.

"The difference is I persevered and I had that basic feeling I had something to offer.

"I think you need to be very intelligent in what you do. In show business you can't make a lot of mistakes, because they follow you. People don't forget them. People in the business will not allow you to forget them," she concluded.

SABINA GADECKI

2013

Think a life in show business is easy? Just ask Chicopee native Sabina Gadecki.

Gadecki is co-starring as the female lead in the new film *Freaky Deaky,* an adaptation of the Elmore Leonard novel of the same name. Although she has had success modeling, as a commercial actress and has landed guest shots on television series, being selected for her first prominent role in a motion picture is something for which she has worked a long time.

Gadecki explained how her involvement in the film, which co-stars Billy Burke, Christian Slater, Michael Jai White and Crispin Glover, came about.

Gadecki recently made the move to Los Angeles, California, for both professional and personal reasons and when she went to the audition for the film she was impressed by the sheer number of actresses in the room.

"I looked at every other girl and I wondered how the heck I'm going to stand out from everyone else," she said.

Her answer was to be prepared for the audition as best she could.

Sabina Gadecki

Gadecki was trying out for the role of *Robin Abbot*, the ex-con and political radical who is looking for revenge. She read for the part and then took a flight to Brazil to attend a family wedding.

What she heard next from her agent was both the best and worst news she could receive: the filmmakers wanted her to come back in for an additional audition.

She had just arrived at her hotel when her agent contacted her and flying back to Los Angeles wasn't an option. Gadecki explained that she always carries a small video camera and tripod. She asked her agent to email her the pages of the script she needed and had them printed out. She then took a look around the hotel room for a blank wall with a neutral color. The only one she could find was in the bathroom.

She set up her laptop, contacted her acting coach through Skype who read the lines for the other characters. Five hours later, she had a videotape of her performing the character that she sent to the producers.

She didn't find out until weeks later that she had been selected for a role, but not for the one she thought. Instead of the bad girl, she received the female lead part of *Greta*, the woman whose plight drives the plot of the film.

She said that originally Brendan Fraser and Matt Dillon were cast as the male leads. Eventually, Burke, one of the stars of the NBC series *Revolution*, was cast in the role of the police officer who befriends Greta instead of Fraser and Slater as the pyrotechnics expert that Dillon was going to play.

She didn't learn of the changes until she flew to Detroit, Mich., where the film was going to be shot. For the first four days, she was the only cast member there.

"[On a film] you don't know how many changes are made at the last minute," she said.

The shoot took two and a half months and at first the cast, although cordial to one another, would retreat to their trailers between takes. Gadecki said the cast started to warm up to one another and as a group did everything in their time-off from going to art galleries and museums to the local casino.

"It organically happened," she said, adding that she really appreciated both Burke and Slater for "looking out for me."

"I was very, very nervous," Gadecki said. "They couldn't have been more professional."

Glover, who has been known for eccentric roles on camera, was the actor that Gadecki knew the least at the start of the shoot. She said he was very kind to people, but very professional about the role and the work.

"He took the process so seriously," Gadecki recalled. She added that Glover frequently suggested bits of business to director Charles Matthau, whom she also praised.

The old line in the film business is that "you're only as good as your last picture," and Gadecki has been hard at work finding roles during "pilot season," the time during which television networks produce pilots for potential series.

Although she would prefer working in movies, Gadecki has been busy auditioning for television series. She said getting a comedy series would send her "through the roof," as she loves comedy.

Gadecki came very close to landing a role in a comedy pilot for ABC. She said that 40,000 actresses submitted their resumes to the show's casting directors. Out of that pool, four actresses were selected to make a screen test and Gadecki was one of them. Out of that four the decision came down between her and another actress and they chose the other performer.

"I didn't get it. I was so upset," she said.

Her agent pointed out to her that she had accomplished a lot by coming so close.

Despite the disappointment, Gadecki is undaunted. She said all of her professional experiences have led her to her current status in show business.

In 2007, she was the host for the *World Poker Tour* series and while she said she was grateful for the opportunity to be a television host, it "was just not for me." She noted the difficulty she had when interviewing poker players who had just lost millions of dollars.

"No one wanted to talk to me," she recalled.

As a model she is represented by Ford Models, but she said at age 30 she is "getting older."

"I've worked really, really hard to be a trained actress," she said. "Modeling and hosting has helped me a lot but acting has always been number one."

ANNE RICE

1986

The current boom in vampire fiction, movies and television series can be traced back to one writer: Anne Rice. I doubt that all of the current incarnations and versions of vampires would ever have happened if Rice hadn't decided to write vampire novels from the perspective of the vampire, rather than any humans in the story.

I introduced the best-selling author as a writer with a sensual and "languid" style that resulted in a very different kind of vampire story. At the time of this interview, her book *The Vampire Lestat* had just been released to paperback.

***

Thank you, I like that word "languid." What has always appealed to me about vampires is that they were seductive and sensuous and really the charmers of the supernatural world. In writing about them I try to convey some of the spell they exerted over me to the reader.

Lestat was first introduced in "Interview with a Vampire."

He is the villain in *Interview with a Vampire.* He's the aggressive, supposedly evil vampire who makes the hero Louis into a vampire. He gets sort of a bad rap in *Interview with a Vampire.* Then in *The Vampire Lestat,* he tells his own story and, of course, he goes back way back into the history of the vampires and gives the answers that weren't available to the characters in *Interview with a Vampire.*

They were interested in finding out where they come from and why they are here and whether they were meant to be evil in some grand design. They never found those answers and Lestat really didn't find them either; he did find out a great deal more about where the vampires came from.

Of course this is my own fictional mythology.

How much research did you do for your books? Do they reflect the mythology of vampires that first started in the Middle Ages?

I started with the popular concept, the image right out of the movies. You know I wanted to bring alive that image: the cape-wearing gentleman. I wanted to know what went on in his mind. We had so many movies and stories that focused on the victim. I wanted the vampire to talk and tell us what it was like to be a member of the living dead, what it was like to be important, what it was like to have to take life in order to live.

I really didn't do much research at the outset because I was working with that concept, working with that cliché. I was determined to bring it to life. A lot of things I used in the novel came right out of the movies. The idea, for example, that the sun can destroy my vampires is really a Hollywood idea. It's not part of the legend from Eastern Europe about real vampires.

I didn't know that, but I love the idea and I'm very glad I adopted the idea. These creatures can live forever but they can never again see the blue sky and the sun. I think it's a beautiful idea. It's the price they pay for immortality.

I later went and did some research and I found out, of course, there are vampire legends from all over the world, but most of them come from Eastern Europe. That's where people actively believe in vampires even now. There are peasant superstitions alive in Eastern Europe. I really didn't do too much with that material.

Another form of research was to go and look at all the films and short stories, all the novels that had ever been done, and there I found the vampires I had responded to. My vampire is really a literary creation.

Did you watch the films of Bela Lugosi, then?

The one I saw as a child was a sequel called *Dracula's Daughter.* I loved that film. I saw that film as a little girl at a neighborhood show in the years right before television.

I just adored it. I loved the foggy atmosphere of nighttime London in that film. Dracula's daughter was, of course, conscience-stricken and in agony of what she was. She wanted to get rid of the curse, but she couldn't. She was hundreds of years old. In the end when she's destroyed she turns to ashes. I just loved it.

That really was one of the strongest influences on me. It was that whole milieu I was responding to. Later when I wrote my book and I wrote in a very spontaneous and unconscious way – I didn't think too much about what I was doing.

So movie vampires like Christopher Lee didn't have much influence on your work?

I was just working with this vague concept and my characters began to develop and they developed their own personalities. Lestat was the impulsive action-prone one who leapt in where angels fear to tread. Louis is the passive more Hamlet-like character who asks "What is this nightmare we're in?"

The female vampires Claudia in *Interview with a Vampire,* and Gabriella in *Lestat* turn out to be very ruthless and pragmatic creatures. They had been so disillusioned with mortal life; they were really just thoughtless killers when they became vampires.

All of this was kind of happening. If anything I was trying to create the vampire novel I had never been able to find in the library. I was making the movie for myself that I had never seen, if you know what I mean. I had never been satisfied with what had been done with these characters so I was trying to do what I wanted to have done.

You don't seem to like to use scenes of explicit violence in your books, is that intentional?

Yes, the thing that has always delighted me about vampire fiction and films is that they happen in a very unreal atmosphere. You can slip away from literal violence and the headlines that upset us every morning over the breakfast table. You can slip away from all of that into an imaginary world where there is good and evil. You remain comfortable just as the audiences of Elizabethan times could do when they went into the Globe Theater and watched *Hamlet* on the stage. It didn't have anything to do with the pressures of their everyday life in the streets of London. They could get away for a while and enjoy this great drama about good and evil and then go back to their daily lives somewhat enhanced by what they saw.

That's what good fiction always does, as far as I'm concerned. Even if it's low level entertainment fiction, even if it's very high literary books that are more up front about their philosophical content; it takes you away and lets you come back. You haven't really been hurt, but you've worked with all these things that trouble you mentally.

If you put a lot of literal violence in there, you ruin that basically. If you bring it close to the raw reality of life, you disrupt somewhat. So, I've never really liked to do that. I've always despised these slasher pictures and so called horror movies where people are killed one after another in gory ways. The whole thing seems to want to stun you and shock you. That to me is not an escape. It's too real.

Do you consider yourself to be a horror writer or are you just a writer who happens to be involved with characters such as vampires?

I think both. Ten years ago when I first wrote *Interview With a Vampire* I didn't want to be called a horror writer. I was afraid people would dismiss the book if they called it horror fiction. I kept saying to people, "But listen this is really serious. This is as serious as any contemporary novel that I could have written. Please pay attention."

But now, after ten years, I don't worry about that any more, because one of the things I found out is the horror fans out there, the readers of Stephen King and Peter Straub and many others, are very literate, very intelligent people. If anything they read their books more carefully then mainstream readers who read literary books.

They are in many ways very appreciative of all the little poetic things that happen in a book of psychology, of the twists and turns. So I'm proud at this point to be called a horror writer. I've found the horror readers and science fiction readers are just a wonderful group of people.

So, I see the book, I hope, fulfilling all the requirements of that genre of being a good horror book and also transcending it appealing to readers who aren't particularly interested in that genre.

Both "Interview with a Vampire" and "The Vampire Lestat" has been very successful. Have you been approached about turning either into a movie?

As a matter of fact, *The Vampire Lestat* is in development right now. I was just speaking to the screenwriter in Hollywood. Unfortunately, I can't release any names about this; only the studio and the producers can do that. It's very exciting what's going on. We're talking about a big movie; a big wonderful full-bodied film and I couldn't be more thrilled. They haven't hired anybody yet – big stars or unknowns – but so far everyone looks wonderful to me. I'm completely excited.

Interview with a Vampire we're talking about doing it on the Broadway stage.

It's a very ambitious vision and it's all up in the air and I hope it all works out.

Do you think you'll have any control over the film?

I don't think I have any control. What I do have is a very good relationship with the people involved and a lot of opportunity for a lot of informal input. Really I don't want any more than that. I found from experience the best thing I can do is stay home and write the third book. I really don't want to be a scriptwriter. I've had a couple of cracks at that. And I don't like writing blueprints for other people to build. I like doing the whole thing at the typewriter.

I'm just going to stay here and concentrate on writing the third book, which will be entitled *The Queen of the Damned* and just sit back and enjoy what happened in Hollywood. I know inevitably there will be some painful moments, no matter how good the film might be I'll see things I don't like or hurt or so forth. But that's inevitable. Again I have great confidence in these people. I think they're going to do something wonderful.

***

The film project based on *The Vampire Lestat* never happened as Rice described it and it wasn't until 1994 when director Neil Jordan's version with Tom Cruise and Brad Pitt was made. Rice wrote the screenplay. The stage version of *The Vampire Lestat* wasn't produced until 2006 as a musical with music by Elton John and lyrics by Bernie Taupin. It closed after 39 performances.

JUNE FORAY

1998

June Foray is a legendary voice actress in the animation business and who is still active in her nineties. I conducted the following two interviews two years apart from each other and for two different publications. She is a wonderful person and a very comfortable conversationalist.

***

Few people know that Rocky the Flying Squirrel is a native of Springfield, Massachusetts.

For that matter, most people are unaware that Tweety's protector," Granny, also hails from the City of Homes.

In fact, Natasha Fatale, Witch Hazel, Jokey Smurf, and Nell Fenwick also have ties to the city.

That's because all of these cartoon characters have been given their voices by June Foray, long considered one of the premiere voice actors in the animation industry. Now, Foray has another role that of "Grandmother Fa," in the new Walt Disney Pictures animated feature *Mulan*, which opens today in theaters.

"My agent called and said they wanted me," Foray said in an interview from her home in California. "They liked the texture of my voice and they needed a particular voice, one that could be strident and yet soft and gentle."

Mulan re-tells an ancient Chinese myth concerning a young woman who saves her father's life and her family's honor by disguising herself as a man and serving in the emperor's army.

Foray plays the title character's grandmother, who is viewed as outspoken and unconventional and serves as the young woman's role model.

While some actors couldn't imagine spending their careers in relative anonymity, Foray said that acting with just one's voice is a high form of the art.

"The voice actor is the nexus between the animator and the audience," she said. "It's extra important to create an emotional connection."

Foray recorded the role of Grandmother Fa in six recording sessions over a three-month period. While the casts of most animated television shows record their dialogue as an ensemble, Foray noted, "in a feature you don't work with anyone else. You always work alone. It's more difficult in a way, unless you're an experienced actor, because people like the give and take of an ensemble,"

Unlike her colleagues who act before a camera, Foray must rely solely on her voice to create the character designed by an artist.

"You don't have the benefit of using your eyes and body motion," she said.

Foray was born in Springfield and lived at 75 Orange St. She said she has fond memories of the city and recalls walking to Forest Park and ice-skating on Porter Lake.

She said she knew she wanted to be an actress since she was 6-years-old and her parents helped her by sending her to acting lessons.

By the age of 12, she had made her professional debut acting on the former WBZA radio station and was asked to join the station's acting company at 15.

Her family moved to the Los Angeles area in the late 1940s when she was 17, and Foray had her own show, *Lady Make-Believe,* two years later. She also worked on a number of network radio shows originating from Los Angeles such as *Lux Theatre, The Danny Thomas Show,* and *The Jimmy Durante Show.*

In 1950, she received the role that changed her life. She was chosen to make the feline noises for Lucifer the cat in Walt Disney's animated feature *Cinderella.*

Cinderella and her work on children's records with the late Mel Blanc, the man who created the voice of Bugs Bunny, Daffy Duck, and almost all the rest of the Warner Brothers cartoon stars, led to work at Warner Brothers on Tweety and Bugs Bunny shorts.

Foray really hit her stride when she was cast in a number of roles in the *Rocky and Bullwinkle Show* in 1958. The long-running animated television series was a hit in its original run and is currently seen on The Cartoon Network.

She not only played Rocky, but also one of Rocky's nemeses, the evil spy Natasha Fatale, Nell Fenwick in the *Dudley Do-Right* shorts, and assorted heroines, children, and fairy godmothers were also among her roles on the show.

Foray has become a well-known advocate of animation and has appeared at festivals promoting the medium throughout the world. She is now serving her sixth term on the board of Governors of the Academy of Motion Pictures Arts and Sciences and continues in her role as chairman of the Short Films branch.

Despite her position in the industry, and her credits, which include hundreds of appearances in animated cartoons, radio programs, and recordings, Foray isn't about to rest on her laurels.

She maintains a busy schedule with voice work for television shows, and recording audiotapes for children. She just completed narrating several *Mulan* read and sing-along tapes, and has a deal with Turner Publishing to record her Lady Make-Believe stories.

Foray continues to take great joy in her art and said, "There's a little bit of me in all the characters that I've done."

2000

A prominent role in a major film and a star on the Hollywood Walk of Fame are the latest accomplishments of Springfield native June Foray. The voice actress is reprising her role as Rocky the Flying Squirrel in the new movie *The Adventures of Rocky and Bullwinkle* and will be honored July 7 with her own star on the Walk of Fame.

Foray said she would be only the second voice actor honored by a star from the Hollywood Chamber of Commerce. The late Mel Blanc – the voice of Bugs Bunny, Daffy Duck and other Warner Brothers cartoon characters – is the only other voice actor with such an honor.

Foray has been called the "female Mel Blanc" by acclaimed animation director Chuck Jones. Her name may not be familiar, but if you've watched cartoons in the last 45 years you've heard her work.

Besides Rocky, Foray has been the voice for Granny, Tweety's protector; Witch Hazel in a number of Bugs Bunny cartoons; Natasha Fatale, the spy in Rocky and Bullwinkle; Nell Fenwick in Dudley Do-right; Ursala in *George of the Jungle*; Grandmother Fa in *Mulan*; two roles in *Who Framed Roger Rabbit*; and numerous roles in animated television series.

The new *Adventures of Rocky and Bullwinkle*, which opened last week, is described by Foray as "very funny, very fast; it has the essence of 'Rocky and Bullwinkle.'"

The film also has received the approval of the family of the late Jay Ward, the show's original producer.

The film combines the live action performances of Robert DeNiro, Jason Alexander, and Renee Russo with the animated moose and squirrel.

The animated cartoon show is considered a classic and made its debut in 1959. It ran until 1964 when it entered re-runs which lasted until 1973.

Re-discovered on video, the show has a new generation of fans thanks to its current broadcast schedule on The Cartoon Network.

Foray recorded her lines as Rocky over a period of a year, often with fellow voice actor Keith Scott who provided Bullwinkle's voice and the voice of the narrator. The late Bill Scott was Bullwinkle's original voice and the late William Conrad – better known for his television series, *Cannon* – was the show's announcer.

Foray explained that the voices are always recorded prior to the animation work, so the artist can accurately match the lip movements to the voices. Although she and Scott did ad lib a bit, she said that they "basically followed the script."

After the animation was finished Foray and Scott were called back to add additional exclamations such as Rocky's famous line of "Hokey Smokes!"

In the new movie, Rocky's archenemies, Boris, Natasha, and Fearless Leader, manage to escape the world of cartoons and attempt to take over the "real" world. The plot gave Foray the chance to see one of her cartoon roles played by another actor. Renee Russo is the sexy Eastern European spy Natasha Fatale.

Russo was a little intimidated by Foray's presence, but Foray readily gives Russo her stamp of approval.

"She sounds like me and looks like Natasha," Foray said with a laugh.

Russo is quoted in publicity materials as saying "At the table reading, I was so nervous. I walked in the door and there was June Foray. She did the original voice of Natasha and I thought, 'Oh good, they have June here to make me look like an idiot.' I asked June if she could read a couple of lines for me, and she did, she was so gracious. So I got the accent down, the Russian accent, for which I lowered my voice."

Foray has become a well-known advocate of animation and has appeared at festivals promoting the medium throughout the world. She has served six terms on the Board of Governors of the Academy of Motion Pictures Arts and Sciences.

Foray recently recorded her character of Granny for several Rhino Records projects featuring the Warner Brothers characters, and appeared on a CD-Rom featuring characters from the *Ducktales* television series.

She is currently working on an Internet-based cartoon series titled *Elmo Aardvark, Outer Space Detective.*

"I seem to be working all the time," she said.

***

At the time of this writing, at age 96, June is still working.

LESLIE GLASS

1995

One day, I was going through some files and happened upon a piece I wrote (and never got paid for) for a magazine distributed to strip clubs. It's much more about low-budget filmmaking than anything else, certainly than the T & A biz.

I love interviewing people about filmmaking and Glass was happy to speak with me in between her sets as a featured dancer at a local club.

She died a very untimely death of cancer in 2000 at the age of 36. She was fun to talk with and had much more going on in her life than just being in the fringes of show business.

***

The long dark hair. The finely shaped features. The creamy complexion. Acclaimed Penthouse model Leslie Glass has got what she describes as "the Anne Rice look."

"Don't you think I'd make a good vampire?" she asked with a laugh.

Well, at least Leslie makes a fine vampire vixen from Venus. Leslie stars with Michelle Bauer, Theresa Lynn, and J.J. North in the Ted Bohus horror spoof *Vampire Vixens from Venus,* which is now available on home video.

"I really wanted to get into acting," explained Glass on why she made her acting debut in the low-budget romp.

The tall brunette model who has graced the cover and interior pages of the acclaimed men's magazine many times, and has been in several of the Penthouse videos, has long harbored an interest in acting. She hadn't acted on her ambitions until Bohus's production company contacted Penthouse looking for talent.

"They called Penthouse, and told them they needed some models with good bodies," recalled Leslie, who fits that casting call, as any reader of the magazine certainly would agree.

Don't ever make the mistake of thinking that Glass is just another centerfold star and would-be "scream queen." She is bright, articulate, and uses much of her earnings for the passion of her life, helping animals.

Glass has founded a non-profit center in her native Baltimore, MD, to care and treat stray and abused dogs and cats. This center is the dream of her lifetime, as over the years she had helped 600 animals get the medical treatment and the homes they need. Still under construction, the center will open this year, and will feature the world's second cancer treatment center for dogs and cats. Penthouse publisher Bob Guccione has helped by allowing her to use the trademarked "Penthouse Pets" name in her fundraising "Pets for Pets" campaign.

Get into a conversation with Glass, and it's easy to understand why Penthouse has often asked her to represent the magazine in various public appearances around the world. Besides being a knockout, she's a smart and savvy spokesperson. Her recent promotional trips have included Russia and Hong Kong. So popular is Glass that she holds the title 1994 International Pet of the Year. But, does she ever have problems with people who think of a centerfold model as a "bimbo?"

"Sure, but if you talk with me for any more than a minute, you'd know I'm not a bimbo," she said emphatically.

Describing her as "goal-oriented" is something of an understatement. She has worked hard to achieve her fame at Penthouse, and to reach her personal goal of building her animal shelter and clinic. There is a new world for her to conquer, though, and that is acting.

Although she's had plenty of experience in front of a camera with her appearances in Penthouse videos, she realized she needed more experience, and gladly accepted the role in "Vampire Vixens from Venus."

The film was shot in two weeks in July 1994, and features Glass as one of the three title characters. She admitted she had some doubts about the movie during production.

"I thought it was cheesy," she said candidly. "But when I saw the film I was pretty impressed. The special effects were great and it was really comical."

The film does feature several topless scenes, and although she has appeared nude in print and on video before, she'd rather do roles in which nudity is not included.

Glass, Theresa Lynn, and J.J. North star as the titular vampire vixens. Their mission on Earth is to extract the liquid part of human bodies, and to do that they transform themselves from their hideous natural state to forms more pleasing to horny men. Once a guy is interested, they waste little time strapping a helmet to his head extracting his precious body fluids and leaving him resembling a pitted prune.

As they leave a trail of dried remains around New Jersey, the police begin to investigate under the barely competent leadership of one Detective Lieutenant Oakenshield, played by Peter Grimes. His efforts to get to the bottom of the mysterious deaths is sidetracked by a not-so-chance meeting with a lovely woman played by scream queen favorite Michelle Bauer, who just happens to be the ugliest Venusian of them all.

The emphasis on comedy rather than t-and-a or gore is refreshing to see in a low-budget genre film, and that's what director, writer and special effects artist Ted Bohus had in mind. Bohus, who has made a name for himself with films such as *The Regenerated Man* and *The Deadly Spawn,* wanted to do something "light" instead of horrific, and wrote the script for the science fiction comedy.

Bohus is a big fan of Michelle Bauer and he was impressed with Theresa Lynn, and J.J. North. For the last alien, Bohus had decided on actress Stacey Warfel, but she had an untimely motorcycle accident, which sent him looking for a replacement.

After sending out casting notices, Leslie auditioned for the part, and Bohus knew he had his fourth alien. "She was very enthusiastic, looked great, and carried some weight with her title of 1994 International Pet of the Year," he recalled.

Although she lacked acting experience, she did impress Bohus in front of the camera. "She came prepared," Bohus said. "With a low budget film, actors have to come prepared and know their lines."

The production of the film went smoothly, according to Bohus, except for a scheduling mix-up, which prevented Glass from being on the set the night the opening scene was shot. This scene introduces the three aliens who transform themselves into beautiful women. Without Glass there, the scene couldn't work, and on a low-budget film, time is most definitely money.

"I went through the roof," Bohus admitted. " I told everyone to leave me alone for a while and I thought of a way to work this out." Bohus's solution? The transformation device for the third alien isn't working correctly. When Glass was able to join the production, Bohus shot a scene in which the vixens manage to get the device to transform one ugly Venusian into the beautiful Glass.

Bohus was impressed enough with the newcomer that he would certainly consider her for another role.

For the time being, Glass is taking her new acting career one day at a time, and is very grounded about her future.

"I've got to start at the bottom, and work my way to where I want to go," she states. Yet she is going to tackle acting the same way she has worked in modeling: on her own terms.

By living in Baltimore, she believed she "misses a lot of roles," but yet she doesn't want to live in Los Angeles.

"I don't want to get caught up in the politics of it all," she explained, alluding to the competitive pressures of getting a role. "I know a lot of the women out there are clawing each other on the way to the top."

How does she evaluate herself in her first acting job? "I was impressed with myself," she said with a laugh. "I memorized everything in the script."

Hard work doesn't bother her nor does paying her dues, and this writer is willing to bet "Vampire Vixens from Venus" is the start of her new career.

"WEIRD" AL YANKOVIC

1999

If your image of recording star "Weird" Al Yankovic is that of an accordion-toting wild man willing to poke fun at some of the most popular songs and biggest acts in music, you'd be right.

But speaking on the telephone Yankovic seems scarcely weird at all. In fact, the interview with the Grammy-winning humorist is a low-key affair with Yankovic giving thoughtful, and occasionally funny, answers.

Yankovic took time out from his lengthy tour supporting his tenth studio album, *Running With Scissors*, to talk with me.

Yankovic has carried on a tradition in American music led in the past by Spike Jones, Stan Freberg, and Allan Sherman. His new album not only has hilarious send-ups of songs such as *Zoot Suit Riot* and *Pretty Fly for a White Guy*, but also very funny original compositions.

A native of southern California, Yankovic began sending homemade recordings of parody songs to the nationally syndicated Dr. Demento radio show in 1979 while he was a college student.

One early effort, *My Bologna,* parodied The Knack's hit *My Sharona.* It received a lot of attention from the show's listeners and the popularity of several other submissions to Dr. Demento helped land him a recording contract several years later.

Yankovic maintained a busy recording career throughout the 1980s with hits such as *Eat It* and *Like a Surgeon."*

His musical targets shifted from artists such as Madonna and Michael Jackson to Nirvana and Coolio in the 1990s.

"Pop culture changes and today's music is not any less deserving [of parody]," Yankovic said.

Writing his songs is "the least favorite part of the job," he said.

"I write at home from midnight to 6 a.m. when it's very peaceful. When I'm in the writing mode I'm not real fun to be around," he said with a laugh.

One thing Yankovic has learned since he started his career is that "everyone in the world has thought of a song parody."

"People come up to me and say, 'Eat It! I thought of Eat It'," he said chuckling.

To avoid copyright and ownership issues, Yankovic politely declines suggestions for new material and points people to follow his example and submit their recording to Dr. Demento.

A hit from his new album is *The Saga Begins,* which tells the story of *Star Wars: The Phantom Menace.* What amazed Yankovic's fans is the album on which the song appears debuted just weeks after the movie opened.

Yankovic explained that he began working on the song in December of 1998. Looking for a tune for his lyrics, he chose Don McLean's 1970 hit *American Pie.*

"It's a good classic song which began with the words 'long, long time ago' like the first Star Wars film," he said.

He tried to get George Lucas to allow him to see a script or an advance screening, but was turned down. So, he consulted story synopses on unofficial Star Wars websites. The lyrics Yankovic said were based on "Internet rumors."

He then held the release of the album until he had seen the film himself to make sure his story matched the film.

Besides his recordings, Yankovic has become well known for his clever music videos and many appearances on television. He had a short-lived children's show on CBS, in which he had one of his musical heroes, Stan Freberg, as a costar.

He also wrote and starred in the 1989 movie *UHF,* and he would like to do more movies. However he's aware that the enormous amount of work it takes to write a script does not ensure the film would ever go into production, and he's rather put that kind of effort into a project that would have a better chance of becoming a reality such as an album.

Yankovic started directing his own music videos several years ago to great acclaim. Rolling Stone magazine named his *Smells Like Nirvana* video to its "Top 100 Music Videos of All Time," and now Yankovic has directed the videos for other bands such as The Black Crowes, Hanson and The Jon Spencer Blues Explosion. He also created the opening sequence for the Leslie Nielsen comedy *Spy Hard.*

"I enjoy directing," Yankovic said. "I never thought I would."

Yankovic and his band have been on the road since June of last year and the current tour isn't scheduled to stop until this October. "The tours seem to be get getting longer and longer," said Yankovic. Judging from the comments on the Yankovic website (www.weirdal.com) from fans who've seen this show, Yankovic's efforts are appreciated.

JOSEPH CITRO

2004

My friend Joe Citro has earned the nickname the "Bard of the Bizarre" for his many books on the odd stories and histories of New England. One of my favorite activities is to join Joe on a road trip to see some of the strangeness he has discovered for myself. He teamed up with our mutual friend Stephen R. Bissette for one of his projects.

***

Most New Englanders became very aware of one regional curse this year – Babe Ruth's curse that prevented the Boston Red Sox from winning a world series - and author Joseph Citro takes credit for its lifting.

Citro, the writer described as "New England's Bard of the Bizarre," said that he-was sure his recounting of the Curse of the Bambino in his new book *Cursed in New England: Stories of Damned Yankees* was the reason the Red Sox were able to go all the way this year.

Of course, he was saying it with a laugh. Citro has collected ghost stories from the region as well as other odd historical notes in books such as *Passing Strange, Green Mountain Ghosts, Ghouls and Unsolved Mysteries* and

The Vermont Ghost Guide. His last book, written with Diane Foulds, *Curious New England,* was a travel guide to some of the odder attractions in the six-state area.

"Curses," though, had come up in his research for other books and he realized that no one, until now, had collected them.

He admits that, unlike ghost stories, they are "harder to unearth."

He added, "They are harder to believe in. Ghosts are all around us."

And yet Citro discovered that people have a tendency to believe in curses. In his introduction he tells the story of "Black Agnes," a statue found as part of a grave in Montpelier, Vermont. The locals believe that the statue depicts the Virgin Mary and that if one sits in the lap of the sculpture in the light of the full moon, one will risk having seven years bad luck that may end in a premature death.

Citro noted there is only anecdotal evidence supporting the curse and discovered in his research that not only is there no corroboration of the claim, but that the statue is not even one of the Holy Mother.

Regardless of that information, Citro admitted that he wouldn't sit in the lap of the statue.

"The notion of curses is so terrifying that we push it into our subconscious," he said. "A curse is really a prayer seeking the assistance of a higher power, whether that is of God, Satan or a demon. It's a willful action."

Throughout his book Citro recounts curses that range from colonial times to the 20th Century. Some he supports with hard evidence while with others he allows the reader to make up his or her mind.

Citro reluctantly added a chapter at his editor's urging about the curse on the Kennedy family. He didn't want to descend into the territory of the tabloids, but he admits that, as he researched the chapter, he become more intrigued with what happened to the family.

When Joseph Kennedy, the family patriarch, was returning to the United States from Great Britain on the eve of the Second World War, he apparently complained to the authorities on the ocean liner about a group of Jewish passengers who were praying. Their service offended Kennedy and apparently Rabbi Israel Jacobson laid a curse on Kennedy and his male offspring.

Citro said that, whether or not one believes in curses, the family history of the Kennedys certainly would give a person reason to pause.

His favorite story involves the string of death and destruction in Naples, Maine, where a pair of brothers brought a statue they stole from a Chinese temple in the late 1890s. According to the story, one of the monks at the temple placed a curse on them; and whether or not this is true, one can't dispute the history of the property there that was built with money that was discovered inside the statue.

Year after year, the owners of the land initially bought by one of the corrupt brothers have met terrible fates. What makes the story so compelling is that, in a tiny museum in Naples, the statue – all seven feet of it in glimmering gold plate – sits today.

"There's tangible evidence," said Citro, who explained that, despite the statue's value, it sits largely unprotected in a small building.

"No one would steal it. The curse is protecting it," he said.

"It takes two to make a curse, one person to make it and the other to believe in the other's authority," Citro said.

For more information on Cursed in New England log onto www.GlobePequot.com. or to www.josephacitro.com.

2005

Two western Massachusetts attractions are featured in the new book *Weird New England,* written by Vermont's "Bard of the Bizarre" Joseph Citro.

Citro has made a career of investigating and collecting the odd and unexplained stories of the six New England states in previous books such as *Curious New England, The Vermont Ghost Guide, Passing Strange* and others.

"If I didn't do this book, someone else would have done it based on my research," he said. Citro welcomed doing the project, though, as the book's emphasis on photos gave him the chance to illustrate many of the pieces with contemporary and archival material.

The way he learned of the assignment was just a little ... weird. Citro had been asked to do an interview for an article on "Weird New Jersey" for the *Boston Globe*. Authors Mark Moran and Mark Sceurman had just made up their minds prior to Citro's call to them to offer him the chance to write the Weird New England book.

"It was highly coincidental and synchronistic," Citro said.

The book features chapters ranging from roadside museums to Big Foot sightings to prehistoric stone structures and little-remembered moments in New England history.

Citro toured western Massachusetts earlier this year with this reporter as his guide. We visited several different locations of singular attractions, including Nash's Dino-Land in Granby and the Titanic Museum in Indian Orchard. Both of those stories made it into the book's final cut.

Citro had visited Dino-Land when he was "a little kid," and said he was "glad to see it was still there." The late Carleton Nash, who received national publicity for it, founded the dinosaur footprint quarry. His son Cornell now operates the quarry and museum.

The book's editors did cut some of Citro's material from the final version, including a chapter on an abandoned research facility in Vermont near the Canadian border. Citro said that in the 1960s the facility was used to develop a "super gun" a 500 foot-long cannon that would have shot satellites into space, rather than using rockets."

Visiting the lab is like "walking onto the set of [the James Bond film] *Dr. No,* he said.

Researching the book wasn't without risks, either. Although Citro has yet to have a paranormal experience during his career writing about the unexplained, he did take two serious falls when photographing two of the locations in the book. He attributed the mishaps to uneven ground, not to the unknown.

One would think that after writing his latest book, Citro is done mining the odd stories and history of New England. But he's not.

"New England is a gold mine," he said. "I'm learning new stuff all the time."

For instance, Citro said he's planning to investigate a story given to him by a man who is finding stone effigies on his remote rural property. What they are and where they are coming from are just a little of what Citro hopes to find out.

"New England still hasn't given up its mysteries," he said.

For more information on "Weird New England," log onto www.bn.com.

JOSEPH CITRO & STEPHEN R. BISSETTE

2009

We know there are bears, deer and moose living in the forests and mountains of Vermont. We know there are trout and turtles in the streams and lakes.

But did you know about big hairy ape-men, indestructible bucks and large, unknown aquatic animals?

By many accounts there are beasts spoken about in whispers in the state known for fall foliage, maple syrup and dairy products. A new book, *The Vermont Monster Guide* (University Press of new England, $18.95), written by Joseph A.

Citro and illustrated by Stephen R. Bissette, gives readers an encyclopedic look at the things that go bump in the night - and in the daytime as well.

The two native Vermonters have collaborated on several projects, most recently *The Vermont Ghost Guide*. Both men spoke to me in telephone conversations last week.

Citro is well known and celebrated as a collector and chronicler of the bizarre in such books as *Weird New England, Curious New England* and *Passing Strange*. Especially during October, Citro is in demand as a speaker about the odd footnotes of New England history.

Bissette is a veteran comic book artist, known for his work in such books as *Swamp Thing* and *Tyrant* as well as his cutting edge horror anthology *Taboo*. He is now a faculty member at the Center for Cartoon Studies in White River Junction, Vt., and continues an active career as an illustrator.

Both men agreed this book was a "fun project" and readily admitted some of the monster stories were more credible than others.

Bissette noted the story about a mystery mammal that looked like a miniature fur-covered stegosaurus was probably an injured fisher cat seen by someone who had never seen the elusive predator, a member of the weasel family.

Citro said if you created a continuum of credibility some of the monsters, such as "the sidehill cronchers" – a cross between a wild boar and a deer – would be at the ridiculous end, while others such as Champie, the lake monster of Lake Champlain, would be at the other end at real or almost real.

Catamounts or mountain lions are included in the book and Citro knows they are real, as he has seen one in a daylight sighting. Vermont wildlife

Joseph Citro

Stephen R. Bissette

officials claim the species has yet not returned to the state, with the last cougar shot in 1881.

"They're passing through the state to reach the tax free shopping malls of New Hampshire," Citro said with a laugh. He theorized state officials might not want to admit their presence as another endangered species might make land development more difficult.

Bissette said that he has never seen anything in the wilds that has made him stop and ponder. The only "monster" listed in the book that both men have seen is the remains dredged from the Connecticut River displayed with Barnum-esque panache at the Main Street Museum in White River Junction, Vt., that suspiciously looked like a skeleton of a horse.

Citro said this book relied on a lot of research, stories culled from newspaper accounts as well as eyewitnesses, some of whom he interviewed.

Bissette said his challenge, as the illustrator, was to be as faithful as he could to descriptions of the various beasts. In the story of a foot-long caterpillar, he had a colored drawing by the person who saw it as source material.

For Citro's accounts of Vermonters who've seen aliens and UFOs, Bissette was able to use original drawings as the basis of his illustrations.

In another accounts, he had to use some creative license. In one story, in which a winged, feathered serpent was seen, he said, "There were five or six ways of picturing it."

Bissette said their new book is the "kind of book we grew up on" – such as "Stranger than Science," collections of stories of the unknown.

For Citro, his favorite monsters to write about were the two with the most documentation: Champie and Bigfoot. He explained a recent video shot at Lake Champlain has certainly raised additional questions about what is living in the lake. A scientific study that showed something living in the lake was using sonar in the same way as dolphins and whales.

Champie and whatever has been spotted at Lake Memphremagog for years are the two most credible of Vermont's many monsters, Citro said.

Although he has done research into the oddities of New England for years, Citro admitted he was surprised to find the number of monster stories from his home state.

"It's the reason I stay inside," he said with a chuckle.

RACHEL MADDOW

Rachel Maddow

2004

Sometimes, an interviewer can conduct a conversation with someone at the beginning of his or her career. It can be a gratifying experience to see how a talent earns recognition.

The only shining star that came out of the ill-fated Air America network was a woman whose home is not too far away from mine in Western Massachusetts: Rachel Maddow.

I was fortunate enough to speak with her at the beginning of her career and as a former liberal radio talk show host, I was impressed with how she prepared for a show and her willingness to present compelling material. She doesn't go for the cheap shot.

***

Look out Limbaugh. Look out O'Reilly. In an industry dominated by conservative white males, there's a new talk radio personality on the air who is shaking up the public perception of the medium.

Air America's Rachel Maddow is a woman, a liberal and a lesbian. Her show *Unfiltered* is among the Air America programs that is making an impression among listeners long thought unreachable by talk radio – young people ages twenty-four to thirty-four – according to recent ratings.

And Maddow is one of us.

She made the leap to a national show heard in 33 markets across the nation from stints on the Valley's WRNX and WRSI.

Now, Maddow is broadcasting with co-hosts comedian Lizz Winstead and rapper, author and commentator Chuck D every weekend from 9 a.m. to noon.

Air America launched its broadcasting efforts earlier this year and promptly ran into trouble. There were problems with financing and difficulties with finding stations that would take on the shows.

And the shows themselves had problems as well.

Michael Harrison, publisher of *Talkers* Magazine, the trade publication for the industry, said the fledgling network "learned many lessons in [its first] 160 days."

Not everyone knew what they were doing on the air, added Harrison, who said that veteran host Randi Rhodes was an exception. Comics Al Franken and Janeanne Garofalo had to learn how to do talk radio, Harrison asserted.

But now things have changed. The shows have become more polished. The finances have been straightened out and the number of stations has increased.

The network offers 12 shows, mostly during weekdays, but several on the weekend as well. The network just added a station in San Francisco, California and now has 33 stations. It estimates the shows have two million listeners on the Internet.

The conventional wisdom by many people outside of the talk radio industry was that "liberal" talk could not attract an audience, according to Harrison.

He is quick to point out, though, that shows featuring liberal perspectives have long been part of the talk scene, and the publicity created by Air America has focused a lot of attention on talk radio. Talk radio is not just political radio, and he considers Howard Stern an example of a talk host who has strong ratings among young people.

Among the political shows, though, what Air America has accomplished is unique – the shows have attracted listeners ages twenty-four to thirty-four. Harrison called Air America a "phenomenon" that is "huge" and creating a "big buzz." He cautioned, though, that despite the network's upward movement, it shouldn't be deemed a success at this time. Success for Harrison is tied to longevity.

David Rubin, Air America's Director of Marketing and Promotion, said that in New York City, the network has reached the number two slot among the talk stations. Other markets have success stories as well.

And the success so far has attracted more advertisers and partnership with radio conglomerate Clear Channel, which has partnered with Air America in some cities.

The view from the 41st floor of 3 Park Avenue in New York, the home of Air America, is spectacular, but it's wasted on the three producers of the *Unfiltered* show. In a control room that seems little more than the size of a closet, the three producers are glued to their computer monitors. They send messages to Maddow and Winstead through an internal e-mail program, cruise news sites on the Web for breaking stories, and set up the telephone guests.

"Unfiltered," unlike Rush Limbaugh's or Bill O'Reilly's programs, is less about the hosts and much more about guests, issues and callers. There is a highly coordinated stream of activity in which telephone guests are called. The producers encourage them during commercial breaks and thank them at the end of the segment.

A young woman in charge of the guests who are live in the studio shows a similar efficiency. They are ushered in and out with courtesy and precision.

As the control room fills up with various people, I decide to wait for Maddow in the hallway. During a newsbreak, she comes out holding a sheaf of paper, plops down onto the floor, and starts reading and scribbling. She's oblivious to all of the people who pass her by. Once the break is over she leaps up and heads back to her microphone.

Maddow and Winstead face each other in the studio – Chuck D isn't there on the day I visit – and the two have developed a style in which they maintain a conversational tone without stepping on each other's lines.

Despite the constant monitoring of the time, instructions from the engineer, and messages from the producers, both women show little sign of stress.

Their studio is decorated with props and photos for the Al Franken show. That show follows them at noon and is televised at 11:30 p.m. each weekday evening on the Sundance Channel. Franken is a long-time *Saturday Night Live* writer and performer who has developed a new career as a political pundit. The producers and Rubin warned me that at noon sharp, the Franken crew rolls into the studio in order to get set up for the dual broadcast.

They're right. At 11:50 a.m., the hallway is filled with technicians carrying cameras and other equipment. Franken comes into an adjoining studio to record promos. Unlike everyone else who dresses very casually, Franken is in a suit – after all he is on television.

He's the only suit I spot at the place.

At noon, I manage to dodge the parade of technicians invading the studio and sit down with Maddow.

Maddow is a young woman with an easy smile and a voice built for radio –expressive, friendly but with enough authority to demand your attention. She brings a different background to talk radio that is dominated by former deejays, reporters and self-appointed pundits.

She is a Rhodes scholar who earned a doctorate from Oxford University in politics and did considerably research work on the spread of HIV/AIDS among prison populations.

Maddow is pleased that Air America and *Unfiltered* is attracting more than just liberal listeners.

"Now that we're on the air, we're realizing we don't just have a liberal audience. We have an appeal for talk radio listeners that is beyond our natural political constituency because we're doing good, funny, entertaining talk radio," she said.

There are now additional professional demands created by the move from the western Massachusetts radio market to a national one and Maddow revealed her way of coping.

"I try not to think about it," she said with a laugh. "I'm still thinking about my work in the same way."

The real differences are in the activities that actually have little to do with broadcasting, such as "going to launch parties for your colleagues' books."

She added, "That didn't happen before! My colleagues were great but they weren't having launch parties at hotels."

She said she still gets up early and "reads like a house on fire." She then gives her all while on the air and starts the process over again. Maddow displayed her daily notebook – a soft loose-leaf binder filled with notes. She prepares most of her own notes every day – she admits she's a little "controlling" about research – and she proudly noted that she touched on each subject in the notebook.

With the stream of guests, preparation is necessary. Former Secretary of State Madeline Albright, Pennsylvania Congressman John Murtha, a long line of reporters and writers from around the country and singer Michelle Shocked were a few of the recent guests.

Maddow explained that the format of the show is the "product of us trying to do an ensemble show." There isn't a "captain of the ship," she said. The staff decided that the best approach was to present the day's news and get three perspectives.

Maddow said she likes to "connect the dots" between stories and do analysis while Lizz Winstead brings her "huge comedic talent" to the table. Chuck D has the "citizen of the world" viewpoint.

"He's an international celebrity with opinions you don't expect from a rapper," she added. "He's a very, very interesting Renaissance kind of guy."

She added, "Hopefully we have something for everybody."

Maddow does feel some pressure to succeed, as "every hour Air America is on the air is so precious." She added there has been a lot of "heavy lifting" to get the network to the place it is now. And while she was anxious about the fate of the networks before the ratings were released, she isn't now.

Would Maddow like a television broadcast like Al Franken? On one level, she said it would be "great," but she's also happy just relying on her voice and not having to worry about what she's wearing.

And does Maddow miss anything from her days here in the Valley?

"I really miss the 'nuts and bolts' like snow days and real local announcements. That kind of stuff is just fun. I really do miss it," she said.

2005

At 8:30 a.m., Rachel Maddow's workday is done and she admits that she is ready for bed.

Maddow, the former Pioneer Valley radio personality who left the area to co-host the nationally syndicated talk program *Unfiltered* on Air America, has a new program that started in mid-April, *The Rachel Maddow Show*. It airs from 5 to 6 a.m. and Maddow admits the transition has been a challenge.

"You know I'm not yet adjusted at all. I'm completely out of my mind and I could go to bed right now," she said with a laugh in a recent telephone interview.

Unfiltered was replaced by former television shock host Jerry Springer's new talk program and Maddow was given a new show and a new time slot.

She described it as being "the front page for Air America." It is the first show of the day offered on the progressive talk network's schedule and the format is heavy on news reporting and analysis.

Originally, Maddow thought she could arrive at the studio at 3 a.m. to prepare the show, but discovered that she had to arrive at work about 12:15 a.m. to get ready for the program.

She explained that the newspapers on the East Coast put their editions online at midnight so she prepares 11 to 16 stories for her broadcast. She gathers sound bites from major stories as well. She said the work she is doing for her new program is "more highly structure" than for *Unfiltered*.

Maddow's style is to mix straight news reporting along with commentary.

"We've got a good show for your day: a sudden growth of a spine, which is good news, in unexpected quarters of the Democratic Party," Maddow announced in the opening of her May 5, 2005 program.

At this point, she is not scheduling guests, but is concentrating on a "rapid fire template" for "people who care about news."

The only element of *Unfiltered* that carried over to the new show is the commentary on the news by comedian Kent Jones.

Maddow said that low ratings were not the cause for *Unfiltered's* demise, rather it was Springer's availability as a talk show host and his selection of the 9 a.m. to noon *Unfiltered* time slot that caused the cancellation.

Maddow explained that many affiliate stations immediately picked up the Springer show in order to capitalize on his television notoriety. Springer's radio show is nothing like his television show. Instead it is a serious liberal talk show.

"I don't have any regrets," Maddow said. "It was easy to sell the Springer show and I'm really happy to have my own show."

Unfiltered was co-hosted by Maddow, comedian Liz Winstead, and rapper Chuck D and featured numerous interviews with newsmakers, authors and commentators each day.

Saying that the show had an "incredibly loyal" fan base, Maddow added, "The people who liked us, really liked us."

She noted that the show's format of having three hosts was different than most talk radio.

"We had an ensemble that was very diverse: a straight black rapper, a feminist comedian and an unknown lesbian activist. We did a great job," she said.

She said she is grateful for the opportunity to continue with the network, but she still hasn't figured out if she should maintain her work week sleeping schedule through the weekend.

***

The Springer show didn't catch on. Maddow went on to her acclaimed show at MSNBC and Springer resumed his television show.

LEONARD NIMOY

2004

I caught some flack from co-workers and friends over the following interview. I was told I should have asked some questions about *Star Trek*. After all I was speaking to "Mr. Spock."

My feeling is that I could not have asked a question that Leonard Nimoy hasn't heard 1,000 times before. Besides I knew that he didn't want to talk about the iconic television series, but about his photography. I didn't want to waste the limited time I had with him.

Since this interview, Nimoy has done some acting work in commercials, voice-overs on *The Big Bang Theory* and as the star of the Bruno Mars music video *The Lazy Song*. He reprised the role of Spock in the two J.J. Abrams rebootings of the *Star Trek* franchise. In 2014, he announced he was suffering from chronic obstructive pulmonary disease.

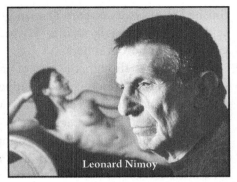

Leonard Nimoy

***

Leonard Nimoy is a man who understands artistic transitions.

The man who became a pop culture icon with his characterization of Mr. Spock from the first *Star Trek* series went from successful acting career to a successful directing career. He recorded albums of music and spoken verse and published two volumes of poetry. Now, he is practicing a form of art that has enthralled him since childhood: photography.

An exhibit of his work from is book *The Shekhina Project* is featured at R. Michelson Galleries at 132 Main St., Northampton, Massachusetts, from now until the end of the month.

When I asked Nimoy during a telephone interview conducted a few days before the exhibit opened if he consciously made the decision going from collaborative art forms to one that allowed him complete control, he burst out laughing and said, "I think, yes."

As an actor, he was at the relative mercy of writers, directors, producers and editors. As a director *Star Trek IV: The Voyage Home, Three Men and a Baby,* among others, he had to contend with studio execs and marketing campaigns that could affect the success of a film.

As a photographer, though, he now has a "totally self-reliant creative process."

"It's a wonderful thing," he said. "I get an idea in the morning. I can execute it that day and have the final version that night."

If he could write as well as direct a movie, he said, that might give him some of the same kind of satisfaction he receives from photography.

"This is much more immediate gratification," he said.

Nimoy started his love affair with photography at 13 years of age when he set up his own darkroom in his home. So great was his interest in photography that he considered leaving acting in the early 1970s to pursue it. He had finished three years of *Star Trek* and two seasons of *Mission Impossible* and he said he was "financially stable." He took classes at UCLA and followed around commercial photographers.

He said, though, the idea of having a career photographing products or models for advertisements didn't appeal to him and he remained an actor.

He has basically retired from acting anddirecting and photography has once again taken center stage.

The Shekhina Project is a photo essay first published in 2002 to both appreciative reviews and criticism that his work was offensive to some Orthodox Jews.

Nimoy, who is Jewish, explained that as a child of eight attending an Orthodox service he was told to cover his eyes during a prayer. He peeked and saw the men of the kohanim – descendants of the priestly class – chanting loudly and passionately. He never forgot the moment and years later learned that the reason one doesn't look up during the prayer is that the Shekhina or the feminine aspect of God then enters the sanctuary. Humans could not tolerate the "radiance of divinity" and could be blinded or die.

Nimoy chose to interpret Shekhina with a series of nude studies. Some people have seen his work as insulting, but Nimoy disagrees with that assessment.

"The body is a beautiful thing," he said. "There is a long history of sex and sensuality in the religion." He added, that "really at the root of it is a male dominated religion. Men pray and women can't participate. This book gives a powerful female figure."

Nimoy is proud that his work has been purchased by several museums and he was also pleased to be asked to exhibit his work at the Michelson Galleries. He combined his appearance at the Galleries last week with one at the National Yiddish Book Center in Amherst.

When I asked about his next project I felt a little guilty. After all, I explained the question sounds like the typical "what's your next movie" query that all interviewers ask an actor or director. As a performer and filmmaker, Nimoy has heard the question many times before, but now it's like asking a painter what his or her next work will be.

Nimoy was accommodating, though, and he does have an idea for a new book. He has purchased a countdown clock programmed to show that he has a little over 5,000 days to live – a number he derived from insurance industries statistics. His concept "doesn't yet have enough definition or shape" but he knows it would mark the passage the rest of his life in photographs.

When asked if he misses acting, his response is much more definitive. "No, I don't miss it at all. I did it for 50 years."

ALICE COOPER

2004

This interview is a classic example of a performer undertaking a media tour. Cooper's publicist set up a 10-minute time for me. He called me a few moments before the time, reminded me I had 10 minutes and then introduced me to Alice.

He was friendly, but very down to business and at the end of the 10 minutes, the publicist came back on the line, told me I was done and Cooper said goodbye before going on to the next journalist.

Currently Cooper keeps busy with a syndicated radio show.

***

It's been 35 years since Alice Cooper first burst onto the American music scene and it hasn't been the same since.

Cooper was the first to get widespread recognition for staging concerts that were almost as much theater as music and for creating an on-stage persona. He also understood that the spirit of rock that repulsed so many parents was also shared by horror films, and melded elements of the two together.

Yet through the changes of musical trends – and his own rise to pop music icon – Cooper has maintained his roots and his mascara. He is coming to the Hippodrome in Springfield on Sept 25 to support his new album *The Eyes of Alice Cooper.*

Cooper may be in Staples commercials, but he's still rocking.

He took time from the road to speak me and the veteran star said that one of the reasons he is still touring is because of the work ethic that he shares with his peers.

"[David] Bowie, Elton [John] and Rod Stewart – everyone is still working," Cooper said. "We're old pros. We done everything, seen everything and still are making some of the best albums we're ever made,"

Despite the length of his career, Cooper said that he certainly hasn't "outgrown the rock and roll sensibility." He still gets excited when the first chord is played at a performance,

"This is rock and roll. Get all those guitars on nine. This is Alice Cooper," he said with a laugh.

The Eyes of Alice Cooper is the result of an idea to go "anti-tech," he explained. With the advent of manufactured boy bands and the diva of the month, Cooper wanted to return to basics. "You can fake anything in the recording studio. That's the difference between old school and new school. You know how to play and how to run a stage."

Cooper said his idea was to play 13 new songs live and pick the best cut. He wasn't going to layer additional instrumental tracks or new vocals onto the songs. He and his band recorded a song a day and then he picked the best cut.

"It put all the pressure on the band and all the pressure on the writing," he said, "It sounds like 1960s garage rock."

Cooper has done plenty of experimentation before. A number of his albums and stage shows have had themes or story lines. He even teamed with writer Neil Gaiman and artist Michael Zulli on a comic book project. He's very proud of this new effort, though.

"It's the most honest album I've done," he said with enthusiasm. A sample of the album can be heard on www.alicecooper.com.

Cooper isn't concerned that his album won't get radio play, because he said that today's radio formats aren't geared towards "classic rockers." About the only "classic" group that gets air time, he said, is Aerosmith.

"I make records for my fans. I make them happy," he said. "The charts don't mean anything anymore."

Cooper is also enthusiastic about his stage persona's growing acceptance into the mainstream. He received a star on the Hollywood Walk of Fame last year and enjoyed appearing in the Staples commercial now airing.

He noted that 15 years ago there wasn't a single product that wanted Alice Cooper for a spokesman, but now the character has "become as much as an icon as [late horror star] Vincent Price."

He said, "I like putting Alice where he doesn't belong. He's the ultimate fish out of water."

CAROL CLEVELAND

2005

Sometimes timing doesn't work out so well. The availability of Carol Cleveland didn't jive with my newspaper deadlines so I put her interview on the newspaper's website. She wasn't pleased when I told her as she had hoped the article would spur her local fans to come to a local pop culture convention to see her. As an ardent *Monty Python* fan, I was just a little miffed she seemed to blame me for the lack of traffic at her table – so much for attempting a good deed.

***

If you don't know the name Carol Cleveland, just ask a fan of the highly influential comedy group Monty Python.

Cleveland was the beautiful young actress who was clearly up for anything in the name of comedy that John Cleese, Terry Jones, Terry Gilliam, Michael Palin, Eric Idle and the late Graham Chapman could dish out.

She appeared in most of the original television shows and all of the Python films.

Cleveland said, "The guys [the Pythons] are always amazed at the continuing popularity of Python."

Monty Python's Flying Circus is regularly seen on the cable channel BBC America in this country, but in its native Great Britain it is seldom seen, Cleveland said.

The Broadway musical *Spamalot,* based on the Python film *Monty Python and The Holy Grail,* is a hit and Cleveland attended the opening earlier this year. All the Pythons were at opening night and Cleveland said, "all the guys were overwhelmed" by the positive reception the new show received.

Cleveland was never officially a Python in the legal sense of the partnership, but she always has been in the eyes of the fans. Her close identification with the group has had its ups and downs.

"It has been, in a way, a bit of a ball and chain," she said.

She added that she has long been "fighting off" the role of the Python "glamour girl."

Active in British television drama at the beginning of her career and currently busy with various stage productions, Cleveland said, "People don't remember those things. Python just sticks out."

British by birth, but raised in Texas and southern California, Cleveland was active in the pageant scene before her family moved back to Great Britain. Winning titles such as "Miss California Navy" gave her a taste of show business and she was accepted into the Royal Academy of Dramatic Arts in London. Fellow students at the time included Sir Anthony Hopkins, Ian McShane currently starring in HBO's *Deadwood,* and David Warner.

McShane, Cleveland noted with a sigh, was her first true love.

Cleveland never intended to become a classical actor, although she enjoyed watching productions of Shakespeare, but she worked toward being an "all around actress."

"I didn't see myself as a comedian," she said.

After graduating she appeared in a number of television dramas, including shows that were popular imports to this country such as *The Saint* with Roger Moore and *The Avengers* with Patrick McNee.

She also was a busy model at the time and was one of the first Playboy Bunnies at the London Playboy Club.

Because she was busy appearing on programs on the BBC, her name was suggested when the Python troupe realized they could play women in certain roles, but not sexy ones and get the comic effect they needed.

Cleveland recalled that she knew of the Pythons because of the individual cast members' work prior to that show and she was "a bit in awe."

"I was just a high school girl from America," she said.

Cleveland had done work as a "glamour stooge" in previous comedy shows, but, on the Python show, she was able to be more than just a prop.

Cleveland said that Palin described her as being "happy to send herself up" and that she came across in the comic sketches as a real character.

The Pythons quickly took to her and fought for her to remain with the show at the end of the first season.

She never contributed ideas to the show, something she regrets now. She said that, by the end of the third season, she knows the Pythons would have received them well.

Although the shows have a loose, almost ad-lib feeling to them, Cleveland said they were tightly scripted and there was no improvisation. The impromptu atmosphere was created, she explained, because the troupe did not rehearse the material as many times as the casts of other televisions shows.

Cleveland now spends much of her professional time on stage and performed earlier this year in *Five Blue Haired Ladies Sitting on a Green Park Bench* in this country after winning raves for the show in Great Britain.

She has also written her own show, *Pom Poms Up,* which she described as a "semi-autobiographical, melodious, slightly outrageous look at the glamour business."

With her background in beauty pageants, one of her titles she recalled with a laugh was "Miss Paddington Shopping Queen," and her extensive modeling and acting careers, Cleveland knows a lot about the professional beauty business.

Young casting directors may not know what Cleveland has done, though, and she has received advice from friends that perhaps she should look more her age in order to obtain roles more easily.

They have told her that she should "grow into her age."

"Nor do I intend to," she said with a laugh. "I don't look my age and I don't act it. I still resemble myself."

Casting directors don't know what they are missing.

GEORGE BARRIS

2005

Forget *Monster Garage* and *Pimp My Ride.* If you want old school car customizing you have to go to the source – George Barris, "King of the Kustomizers."

If you don't know his name, you'll know his work. Among the 10,000 cars Barris has designed over his career is the Batmobile from the 1965 television series, General Lee from *The Dukes of Hazard,* the time machine Delorean of the *Back to the Future* films, and the Munster-mobile from *The Munsters."*

Barris is no nostalgic act, though. His company did the cars for *The Fast and The Furious* and *XXX.* He's currently working on a revised *Knight Rider* KITT for a new Adam Sandler movie *Benchwarmer* and some 400 Hot Wheels cars for a movie based on the popular toy.

Barris said that people from "age six to 60 still want to drive the Batmobile."

Barris began his career in customizing in the early 1940s, but started really gaining attention in the 1950s with the hot rod craze. He achieved

The legendary George Barris Batmobile

prominence when he produced a car for the 1958 film *High School Confidential.*

With car customizing magazines fueling the popular interest in altering cars, Barris found himself more and more influential. *Motor Trend* wrote that Barris's cars had changed the conventional wisdom of design among American auto companies.

Movie and television producers for special vehicles were increasingly seeking Barris's services:

" The cars were also stars. We did stunts with them. We made them look beautiful," he said.

Barris said that the creative process involves producers, directors, art directors and even the star of the production sitting with him and determining not only the look, but also the ability of a car.

"David Hasselhoff (*Knight Rider*) was very knowledgeable about cars," Barris recalled. "It's a very big team effort," he added.

And the effort is not just to build one car, he explained.

"Whenever you do a film you build more than one car. You can't stop to repair a car. You have to have a spare car or two or three," he said.

Some cars are built for specific stunts; others are designed to be sent out on tour for publicity purposes.

For instance, the *Knight Rider* television series had 15 KITTS. There were 12 cars for the original *Starsky and Hutch* series and 30 General Lees for *The Dukes of Hazard.*

Barris was one of the customizers who worked on the new *Herbie the Love Bug* movie in which there were 52 VW Bugs.

The trend to provide car thrills in films through computer-generated animation doesn't impress Barris. He contends the public wants to see real vehicles.

So far, the most difficult job Barris had was a pursuit version of KITT for *Knight Rider.* He said the producers wanted the car to do a multitude of effects that required quite a number of hydraulic systems.

"It was a fun project to do," he said.

And, although that was the most difficult job, does he have a favorite car? Barris said that would be like picking a favorite child.

"I've done 10,000 cars and they all have played a different part in my life," he said.

BEN GAZZARA

2005

Ben Gazzara was the real thing: an acting legend. His performance in the play *Nobody Doesn't Like Yogi* was riveting and I'm not a baseball fan at all. His performance was even more amazing considering his bout with mouth cancer.

He hosted a book signing of his memoirs during the run of the play and I got to meet him face to face, which is a rarity for me. He was a classy and genuinely cool guy, who passed away in 2012.

***

For acting legend Ben Gazzara the most attractive aspect of the one-man play *Nobody Doesn't Like Yogi* was the play itself.

"It's the material, always the material," Gazzara said during a telephone conversation from his home in New York City. "It made me cry. It made me laugh."

Gazzara knows "material." An actor's actor, the seventy-five year-old Gazzara originated the role of "Brick" in *A Cat on a Hot Tin Roof,* one of his many Broadway appearances. He had a highly successful television show in the 1960s and has appeared in dozens of movies, among the most recent the controversial three-hour film, *Dogville.*

And if you think a play about Yogi Berra, the Baseball Hall of Famer known for his unique use of the English language, would be just a series of one-liners, think again.

"It's about family, dignity and honor," Gazzara said.

Although the play had a substantial run in New York City and Gazzara received a 2004 Drama Desk Award nomination in the category of "Outstanding Solo Performance," he said that Berra has not seen the play. He suspects that Berra doesn't want to live through the ups and downs of his life and career once again.

Gazzara said he knows that Berra must approve of the play, though, as he sent many of his friends to see it.

He said that he was not intimidated by playing a well-known person and quoted an acting instructor to explain: "You're not stuck with a character. The character is stuck with you."

The way to create a characterization is to use your imagination, and to be honest, he said.

Gazzara doesn't look much like Berra, and said he initially considered wearing "a phony nose and. ears," but decided against it.

"I work from the inside out," he explained and added that people have come back stage after the performance to tell him that he looked just like Berra.

"That makes me proud," he said.

What also makes him proud is that fact that he can perform in a show such as *Nobody Doesn't Like Yogi* after cancer surgery. He said that his voice was a little rougher than usual because a recent run of performances left him with laryngitis. He underwent a seven-hour operation for cancer in his mouth and another seven hours of re-constructive surgery. A regimen of radiation affected his salivary glands, making speaking at length a challenge.

But Gazzara has made a dramatic comeback with the taxing role.

Gazzara, who is a three-time Tony Award nominee, doesn't prefer working on stage over movies. His only concern has been the quality of the project. His films have included Otto Preminger's *Anatomy of a Murder,"* the Coen Brother's *The Big Lebowski,* David Mamet's *The Spanish Prisoner* and Peter Bogdanovich's *They All Laughed,* but Gazzara is quick to name a favorite director: the late John Cassavetes.

Gazzara appeared in several Cassavetes films such as *Husbands* with Peter Falk and said the director was "a genius."

"He created an atmosphere in which to excel. You could do no wrong, he was a magician," Gazzara said. "Most directors don't like actors because they don't understand the process. They don't know how to help us."

Although a film such as *Husbands* looks spontaneous and improvised, Gazzara said that the cast rehearsed three to four weeks to "give it the sense of being done in the moment." Only one scene had been made up while the cameras were rolling.

Gazzara tried directing and said he enjoyed the experience. He directed several episodes of *Columbo* starring his old friend Peter Falk and did one feature film, the story of which is told in his recently-released memoir *In the Moment.*

Gazzara has had a career of being in both prestigious art house films and drive-in movies also and has appeared in his share of "schlock."

"Those have been 'pay the rent' pictures," he said with a laugh. He said that if he had waited for "terrific material" he would have only made a film once every four years.

"An actor has to act. If he doesn't, he's not an actor," he added.

One of his lesser efforts, *Road House* starring Patrick Swayze, has become a hit on home video and television.

"It's come back to haunt me," he said with a chuckle. Gazzara played the film's villain.

He spent many years of his career working in Europe where he said he was able to work on films better than those offered him in America in a place he loved. He worked so much in Europe that he bought a home in Italy.

His present tour with the play is only seven cities and Gazzara said that once he is through he will spend the summer in "my house, my paradise" in Italy.

In the meantime, the veteran actor is enjoying his current role.

"I'm having a wonderful time," he said.

RAY BRADBURY

2006

I had the opportunity of interviewing Ray Bradbury about our city of Springfield choosing his book *Fahrenheit 451* for a "One city, One book" program.

I was happy to see the library had made the decision to select the novel and asked if any effort had been made to contact Bradbury about commenting on the selection or coming to the city. The answer in both cases was "No" and I thought at the time this was a squandered opportunity.

Bradbury, who died in 2013, was one of this country's great men of letters and I thought I should try to interview him in conjunction with the library's program. I contacted his publicist at his publisher who gave me Bradbury's home number and told me when he liked to talk to people.

I called and instantly recognized his voice. It was amazingly easy.

Bradbury was great to chat with and if I had more time I would have branched into other subjects.

A fan of fantasy, science fiction and horror since childhood, I did ask him about his reactions to director Peter Jackson's *King Kong* and he said, "Ten minutes into the picture I began crying because I knew Kong was in the hands of a lover."

He believed the Academy snubbed *Kong* and that it should have been nominated for "Best Picture."

At the time of the interview, Bradbury was seeking a deal to make a new film based on *The Martian Chronicles* and was hoping that Jackson to direct it.

***

Ray Bradbury didn't have censorship on his mind when he wrote the novel. In a telephone interview from his Los Angeles home, Bradbury said that an incident with a police officer and his love of libraries provided the inspiration for the novel.

Bradbury recounted an incident in 1949 in which a police officer questioned why he and a friend were walking through a fairly deserted area after a meal. They were doing nothing more suspicious than walking on a sidewalk.

The incident led to the short story *The Pedestrian,* and he said, "*The Pedestrian* got me started," he said.

A year later, he added, he "took the character out for a walk." The revisiting led to his writing of *Fahrenheit 451,* first as a short story and later as a novel. The novel took him just nine days to complete.

Bradbury described himself as a "library educated person." He never attended college, but went two to three times a week to a library from his childhood through his late twenties to read and learn.

He said that "it broke my heart" to learn that the ancient library of Alexandria in Egypt had been burned three times – twice on purpose, and once by accident. He also spoke of his horror of how the Nazis burned books that they viewed as harmful to their regime.

"You can't touch libraries," he said.

"*Fahrenheit 451*" was published in 1953, a time in which there was growing fear about the menace posed by the Soviet Union. Bradbury said, though, at the time he wrote the novel there wasn't any threat of censorship. He said the earliest casualties of the Red Scare were people in the motion picture industry who were blacklisted for alleged Communist ties.

"They were easy marks," he said.

Bradbury maintained that a society such as the one described in "*Fahrenheit 451*" could never happen in the United States today.

"We've got to consider we have a very healthy society," he said.

He said that censorship would be "impossible" because all aspects of society are watching one another.

Speaking on the 1966 film adaptation of "*Fahrenheit 451,*" Bradbury said he was "80 percent pleased" with the movie directed by Francois Truffaut. His main complaint is that the famed French director cast British actress Julie Christie in two roles, which Bradbury believed confused audiences.

Although he had written screenplays – one of his most notable was adapting Herman Melville's *Moby Dick* for director John Huston – Bradbury was not involved with the script of "*Fahrenheit 451.*" He said that Truffaut's first script "was so bad he couldn't get any one to star in it."

Oskar Werner, who had starred in Truffaut's *Jules and Jim,* forced the director to re-write it. Werner played the lead role of Montag the fireman.

Bradbury revealed there is a new movie version of the novel in the works with a script by Frank Darabont, the director of *The Shawshank Redemption.* He said there are talks going on with Mel Gibson to produce the film.

Bradbury is one of this country's most popular writers – there are over five million copies of "*Fahrenheit 451*" alone currently in print – and among his 30 novels are *The Martian Chronicles, The Illustrated Man, Something Wicked this Way Comes* and *Dandelion Wine.* He has also written 600 short stories.

He has been active in making movies himself. He was nominated for an Academy Award for his animated film *Icarus Montgolfier Wright* and received an Emmy for his script for *The Halloween Tree.*

Besides scripting *Moby Dick,* Bradbury wrote the 64 scripts for his own television series *Ray Bradbury Theater.* He said that he writes his books in such style that they are easy to adapt.

He recounted that director Sam Peckinpah wanted to film one of his books. When Bradbury asked how Peckinpah would adapt the novel, Peckinpah responded that he would "tear pages out of the book and stuff them into the camera."

In 2000, he received the National Book Foundation Medal for Distinguished Contribution to American Letters.

Out of everything he has written does he have a favorite?

"All of my books are my children and I love them all," he said.

"I've had a jolly time, a great life," the 85-year-old writer added.

RICHARD SHER

2006

Generally I like a lot of the stuff on NPR because they're trying to use radio to its fullest. *Car Talk, Wait Wait Don't Tell Me, Market Place, This American Life,* and *Fresh Air* are pretty compelling listening.

Says You! is another good show and it came to our area for a local taping.

***

When this writer asked the producer of the National Public Radio quiz show *Says You!* if the program was inspired by the classic quiz shows of the 1950s and '60s such as *What's My Line?* Richard Sher laughed.

"I see it as outright theft," Sher said. "As my father said, 'If you steal, always steal quality.'"

Described as a "game of words and whimsy, bluff and bluster," *Says You!* has its panelists trying to come up with definitions of words, answer riddles and bluff each other. On the *Says You!* web site (www.wgbh.org/radio/saysyou/) is a daily riddle that is typical of the show's challenges. A current one is "Even though it's all showbiz, no 'Oscar,' 'Emmy,' or 'Tony' winner would ever have a shot at a 'Patsy' award. Why?"

Sher said the older generation of quiz shows featured educated witty people who came into your living room. After coming up with the idea for the game during a round of "Trivial Pursuit," he realized he could devise a game in which it was less important to know an answer than to like the answer you have.

Sher is the president and founder of Pipit & Finch, a marketing and media development company, with clients such as CBS/Westinghouse; Hearst Broadcasting; RISO, Inc.; and IBM.

He said that he recorded a pilot for the show and made an appointment with the programming executive at WGBH in Boston. To Sher's amazement, the executive listened to the entire show and eight months later the program was on the air.

"It was the easiest show to bring on the air," Sher said. "Why? I don't know. Maybe people like this kind of stuff."

Sher had little trouble finding panelists because "these were people in my living room. They are friends of long-standing."

Sher will be joined by public radio personality Tony Kahn; television producer and writer Arnie Reisman; *Ladies Home Journal* columnist and WBZ-TV consumer reporter Paula Lyons; public television executive Francine Achbar; actor Tom Kemp; and columnist/critic Carolyn Faye Fox.

Sher had never intended to be the on-air host, but took the role out of necessity.

Known for taping in locations around Boston, Sher said that this year the show is going to Ohio in October and the west coast in the spring.

Another big change for the show is that it will be produced in half-hour and hour versions. Sher is going to syndicate the show himself and wants to offer public radio stations an option.

"This is going to be a big year for us," he said.

GARY HALLGREN

2006

A cartoonist and illustrator, whose legal battle with the Walt Disney Studios helped define just how far parody could go, is now making his home and career in Western Massachusetts.

Gary Hallgren was one of the "Air Pirates," a group of underground cartoonists who produced a series of comic books in 1971 featuring Mickey Mouse and other Disney characters doing definitely non-Disney activities.

A prolonged lawsuit was eventually decided in Disney's favor, but the cartoonist and illustrator didn't allow the case to affect his career. He has been commissioned by publications such as *The New York Times, Forbes, Men's Health, The Wall Street Journal, MAD* magazine and *Entertainment Weekly,* among others, for illustrations. He draws much of the syndicated comic strip *Shylock Fox.*

And he has even done freelance work for the Disney Studios.

Currently he is working on the illustrations for a series of five books on health. To this date, *You: The Owner's Manual* and *You: the Smart Patient* have

been published and Hallgren recently finished a series of illustrations for a third book.

Publishers Weekly noted Hallgren's illustrations in its review of *You: The Owner's Manual,* and said, "The book has an entertaining feel: friendly elves guide readers through illustrations of the body and cartoons feature alien creatures that enter the body and cause illness. The humor is irreverent (e.g., muscle cells surrounding dead heart tissue start fighting with each other, like Jerry Springer's guests, instead of supporting each other, like Oprah's."

Artist Gary Hallgren in his studio.
Photo by G. Michael Dobbs

Settling in Massachusetts to live was "coming home to roost, so to speak." Hallgren lives in Granby with his wife, a native of South Hadley, and daughter, and has his studio in Holyoke at Open Square.

His studio – which Hallgren described as the "best studio I've ever had" – reflects Hallgren's interests and career.

There is eye candy on every wall. A print of a cover of a comic by Robert Crumb hangs on one wall. Hallgren said that in the heady days of the early 1970s no one could have envisioned that artists such as Crumb would have become as popular as they have.

A poster heralding a concert by the rock band of which Hallgren was a member is near his computer as are vintage ads for Studebaker cars.

Hallgren is a life-long Studebaker fan – "always was and always will" – and has restored a Studebaker truck. He is currently working on restoring a Skyhawk.

Hallgren said that he was a fan of newspaper comic strips when growing up and published his first cartoon in his high school newspaper. He noted that some of the acknowledged masters of comic art, including George Herriman (*Krazy Kat*), George McManus (*Bringing up Father*) Chic Young (*Blondie*) and Carl Barks (*Donald Duck* comics), are among his influences.

A set of book shelves is loaded with art books and collections of comic strips and on the walls are paintings that are Hallgren's takes on vintage comic characters.

In one painting, Dagwood's dog Daisy is seen tearing a mouse apart. The caption reads, "Dagwood, come quick Daisy's caught a mouse."

The rodent in question resembles Mickey Mouse.

Another painting shows a close-up Dick Tracy and his assistant Sam Catchem with the words "Bulletin!! Bullet in!!"

The one Hallgren displays in the window of the studio shows Blondie and Dagwood in bed asleep. Blondie is dreaming of Mr. Beasley, the letter carrier, while Dagwood has Betty Boop on his mind.

These vintage characters may not be familiar to younger people today, but Hallgren said. "They have been in my brain since I was a little kid."

While copyright laws prohibit him from reproducing these canvases, he is allowed to create singular works.

He said that he enjoys playing with these icons of popular culture.

He graduated from Washington State University where he studied painting and design. After graduation he trained as a sign painter.

Hallgren had his own sign painting business when he first met Dan O'Neill, then the creator of *Odd Bodkins,* a successful syndicated comic strip, at a rock concert in Washington in 1970.

Hallgren recalls that O'Neill was drawing comic strips about the rock concert from the media tent set up at the concert.

"I was impressed that an 'over-ground' artist was at the rock festival," he said.

O'Neill was impressed with the lettering Hallgren had done on a side of a van and wanted to meet the artist. Hallgren said that he had been thinking about trying to break into the undergrounds but had no idea where to start.

When O'Neill invited him to California to start up a studio and take on the Disney Studios, Hallgren said, "It sounded like a plan."

Artists Bobby London, Ted Richards and Shary Flenniken joined Hallgren and O'Neill.

And with the publication of three comic books that used Disney characters to lampoon their own image and contemporary politics, Hallgren said, "We did do what he [O'Neill] said. We were focused enough to make it a semi-reality."

The Disney Studios did sue them for copyright infringement and the case was not resolved until 1980. The court decision helped clarify the limits of parody and use of copyrighted characters.

Hallgren said, "Knowing what I know now, I would have handled things differently." And yet he added, "I would do it all again."

He is still in touch with Flenniken and with O'Neill and said there was an effort to put together a reunion project, but it proved not to be financially worthwhile.

Hallgren has long wanted to have a comic strip of his own, and has come close on several occasions to closing a syndication deal. He was in the running for taking over *Nancy* and had proposed a comic strip based on the *Eloise* series of children's books.

He was considered for both assignments based in part on his ability to copy the style of other artists.

In several illustrations for magazines such as *Entertainment Weekly*, he showed his skill at capturing various styles in illustrations on the animation industry.

Hallgren was interested in working in animation and was approached to come to Los Angeles to work at Games Animation, the studio then producing the *Ren & Stimpy* cartoons. Hallgren was hoping to become a background painter – he was a fan of the show – but instead he was seen fulfilling a role of "a minder," Hallgren said.

He was seen as an older artist who could be a role model to the younger ones and manage them to make sure they made their deadlines.

That wasn't for him, he explained.

When asked if he had a favorite project, Hallgren paused and then mentioned a magazine cover. When told this reporter hadn't seen it, he walked across the studio and brought back three leather art portfolios to a table.

Inside were hundreds of pieces of art, mostly by Hallgren but also originals by O'Neill and others.

Hallgren never found the cover illustration, but a quick look through the pages of the portfolios was like taking a whirlwind tour of the artist's life with illustrations from major mainstream magazines, art for video boxes, and original pages from Hallgren's underground comics.

Hallgren has had a busy and successful career in illustration since 1979 and he is concerned about the future of illustration, as more and more art directors have turned to the use of stock photography to accompany articles, instead of commissioning original illustrations.

Unlike many other artists today, he still works in traditional artistic methods and does not use a computer to aid in drawing or coloring a project.

He isn't a Luddite, though, and he would like to "get a presence going" on the Internet.

He is considering launching a website, though, to showcase his years of work. His plan is to post a new item each day.

"If I'm a cult figure at all, I'm a very tiny one," he said with a smile. "I'd like to get a little bigger one."

SHANNON WHEELER

2006

One of my favorite cartoonists, I ran Wheeler's *Too Much Coffee Man* in one of our newspapers. I'm sure it probably confounded some people, which is exactly what I wanted to happen.

***

Wearing a skin-tight suit with the letters "TMCM" emblazoned on the chest, and a headpiece or head shaped liked a coffee mug, one might assume that *Too Much Coffee Man* is a superhero of sorts.

Despite the costume and the large coffee mug head, *Too Much Coffee Man* doesn't have any super powers and he doesn't fight super villains. He muddles through life like most of us do, questioning just why he is here and what's going on.

Too Much Coffee Man is the star of a weekly syndicated comic strip by Portland, Ore., cartoonist Shannon Wheeler. Wheeler's new collection, *How to be Happy: Too Much Coffee Man* is now available through book stores and Wheeler's website www.tmcm.com

The current collection is sarcastically described as a self-help book, but in reality Wheeler's cartoons take a biting look at human behavior, American society and Bush Administration politics.

Wheeler explained he has been writing and drawing the *Too Much Coffee Man* strip for over ten years.

"I'm built to do it," he said with a laugh.

Originally presented in a mini-comic format an eight-page format, Wheeler admitted that his creation was far less a parody of superheroes and was far more the result of a search for something that would appeal to people who hang out in coffee shops.

Although many of his cartoons are very political, Wheeler, who grew up in Berkeley, Calif., doesn't consider himself as political as the residents of his hometown. He is a self-described "news junkie."

He said that by following the news every day, he gets angry and that the anger leads to astonishment. He expects to rise up in protest and start a revolution, he added.

"It's the best soap opera around," he said with a laugh.

Don't expect a lot of caricatures of the president and senators in his strips, though. Wheeler uses more subtle visual representations, such as a little boy with over-sized hands to represent George W. Bush.

Wheeler's strips frequently cause a reader to question himself. Among his favorite themes are rampant consumerism and how Christmas can depress people.

When asked if he hates Christmas, Wheeler laughed.

"I actually enjoy it," he said. What he doesn't like is the "inordinate pressure to consume" the holiday brings with it.

"My family was not all that materialistic. It wasn't a major consumer holiday for us," he added.

Too Much Coffee Man has been joined over the years by a number of regular supporting characters including Espresso Guy, a curmudgeon who has a demitasse cup strapped to his head. Wheeler said that many people pressured him to create a "Too Much Tea Guy" and "Too Much Hershey Man." He said they just didn't understand what he was doing.

So, he brought in Espresso Guy "just to shut people up," and the character has worked out well as a foil to *Too Much Coffee Man.*

One strip has Espresso Guy coming up with the ultimate moneymaking scam he has copyrighted the copyright symbol: ©.

"Now when someone uses a © they have to pay me a royalty," he declared.

In response, *Too Much Coffee Man* said, "I flip between hating him and wishing I had thought of it first."

Wheeler said that one of his main inspirations has been underground cartoonist Gilbert Shelton, the creator of the "Fabulous Furry Freak Brothers." Shelton's artistic sensibility of blending political commentary with humor was one lesson Wheeler learned from him.

Another was selling the same material two to three times. Originally, Wheeler put his characters in comic books. For the past few years, he has syndicated his strip into newspapers and then released collections.

Wheeler also started a magazine, which collected other comic strips, essays and articles on popular culture and coffee.

When Wheeler started publishing his comics, there were a number of distributors that serviced comic book shops. Today there is one major distributor and Wheeler has diversified to make sure all of his eggs are not in one basket.

He said that the comic book market, especially for novices, is "real tough."

"I see other people starting out and it's hard," he added.

Fans can read *Too Much Coffee Man* on his website, if a newspaper in their area doesn't carry it. And Wheeler's magazine, which is available in bookstores, also carries the strip.

His website also features a number of *Too Much Coffee Man* products, from tee shirts to a lunch box.

Wheeler has put the magazine on hiatus while he returns to comic books with two non-Coffee Man projects, but he will start it back up at some point as he enjoyed working with his contributors.

Although Wheeler has made *Too Much Coffee Man* available to different audiences, there's one who probably never sees it: television audiences. Wheeler said that companies wanting to make an animated version of his strip have approached him.

Each one has offered a treatment in which *Too Much Coffee Man* uses coffee like Popeye used spinach. That's not what the strip is about.

"It [an offer] has come and gone three times," he said.

Maybe those guys have been drinking too much espresso.

JOHN SEBASTIAN

2007

John Sebastian may not be the first person who comes to mind when thinking about the blues, but the man known for his pop hits such as *Do You Believe in Magic?* with the Lovin' Spoonful has quite a history with the blues.

In a telephone interview, Sebastian said he was listening to the blues before it became fashionable.

Growing up in Greenwich Village in New York City, music was a key part of his upbringing, he explained. His father, also named John, was a classical harmonica player who also played the blues. His mother was a writer of radio dramas.

Being around musicians such as Mississippi John Hurt and Lightnin' Sam Hopkins had a profound effect on the young Sebastian. He recalled carrying Hopkins' guitar case around for a year and half.

"My father said to me, 'As I watched you watch Sam Hopkins leave here, I saw you leave home,'" he said.

He said that part of his growing up were frequent trips uptown and visiting musicians in their homes. Famed record producer John Hammond's release of near mythic bluesman Robert Johnson's recordings was also a "pivot point" for Sebastian.

Although his greatest fame came with Lovin' Spoonful hits such as *Summer in the City, Did You Ever Have to Make Up Your Mind* and *Nashville Cats,* Sebastian has been a busy performer. He scored a solo hit with his theme song for the venerable sitcom *Welcome Back Kotter,* and has made albums that have reflected his interest in root music.

Although he is happy to play Lovin' Spoonful music today, Sebastian has been busy with his jug band the J Band since 1993. Jug bands feature a musician playing a jug and the music reflects country blues roots.

His jug band had included the late Fritz Richmond, the man who gave the Lovin' Spoonful its name. Sebastian remembered that Richmond said the group's music was "Chuck Berry meets Mississippi John Hurt."

Sebastian said his sets vary from audience to audience.

"I know who they are after five minutes. I know who my peeps are," he said.

And he enjoys performing in Massachusetts where he has maintained a large fan base.

"I'm certainly not the first person someone thinks of in the world of modern blues, but I've benefited from the great men who came before me," he said.

KEVIN MURPHY

2007

Mystery Science Theater 3000 remains one of the great achievements in television, in my opinion. I was thrilled to have an opportunity to speak to one of its architects.

***

Kevin Murphy admitted with a laugh that he has "an odd peculiar talent."

Murphy is one of a handful of people who have carved out a true niche career in show business by making fun of bad movies first as a writer and cast member on the late and much lamented television series *Mystery Science Theater 3000* and now as part of *The Film Crew.*

Murphy, who was puppeteer behind Tom Servo on *Mystery Science,* has reunited with fellow cast members Mike Nelson and Bill Corbett on a new project, *The Film Crew.* The premise is that Murphy, Corbett and Nelson are three working class Joes hired by eccentric billionaire Bob Honcho to provide commentary tracks on movies that have never before been given a commentary track.

The Film Crew DVDs continue the career Murphy started in 1988 when he started working on *Mystery Science,* then a local program on an independent UHF station.

"That's a dang long time to be making fun of movies," he said.

Three films that have been given *The Film Crew* treatment so far include: *Hollywood After Dark,* a disastrous cross between a serious drama, a caper crime film and an exploitation film with strippers starring Rue McClanahan; *Killers from Space,* a science fiction film featuring Peter Graves, features alien invaders with, literally, ping-pong balls for eyes and scene after scene of stock footage; and the newest release, *Wild Women from Wongo,* a 1958 film about ugly and good-looking cave people worshipping alligators and trying to find love or something close to it.

The three films have been released on DVD by Shout Factory and a fourth film, a Steve Reeves sword and sandal epic, will be released later this year.

Murphy described *Wongo* as a film that was supposed to be "a caveman sex romp" and should appeal to anyone who grew up thinking "Betty Rubble was hot."

"*Wongo* is a train wreck, yet in another way is wistful," he added.

Murphy explained the new premise allows the emphasis to be placed on the commentary or "riff." *Mystery Science* was about a guy marooned on a space station by an evil scientist who wanted to torture him by forcing him to watch bad movies. The former series required a team of six to 10 writers not only coming up with the commentaries but also with the gag-laden framing sequences.

He described the premise of the new show as a "paper thin fiction."

For the new incarnation, Murphy, Corbett and Nelson each write a third of the script. Murphy lives in the Minneapolis, Minn., area, Nelson is now on the west coast and Corbett has been busy commuting to Los Angeles where he has co-written the script for the new Eddie Murphy film *Starship Dave.*

They then do a re-write as a group, rehearse it and shoot the framing sequence and commentary in a studio in Minneapolis.

Murphy said the writing process works so well he dared anyone to try to tell where one writer ended and another begins.

Murphy said the area is a "great town" for film production the *Mystery Science* shows were all produced there.

"Nobody needs to go to Hollywood to produce stuff," he said.

The films themselves come from Sinister Cinema, a company that sells movies that are in the public domain. Murphy said each film must go through a process to make sure it's not under copyright before production begins.

He said the best films are "earnest but inept," have an audible sound-track and "the camera's in focus."

Murphy had been producing commercials for KTMA in 1988 when comedian Joel Hodgson had the idea of a movie program in which the host of the film stays with the audience through the duration of film.

His involvement with the show until the end of its run in 1999 was "stunning."

"How many people get to work on a TV show that much of their career?" he asked.

Murphy has done other things, though. His book *A Year at the Movies: One Man's Film Going Odyssey* was a critically acclaimed recounting of his going to a movie every day of 2001. During that time he went to theaters in several countries, tried to exist one week on concession food and even sneaked his

Thanksgiving dinner into one theater.

He said the result of the exercise was "I think I have more patience now [with movies]. One thing I never do is to walk out [of a film]."

He said it's more difficult to sit through a bad independent film than a mainstream Hollywood offering because the Hollywood films "coat the stomach with a layer of slickness."

He said seeing that many films in a year allowed him to "expand my cinematic palette." Another result was that he grew to like the theater experience less and less in this country. He noted with expectation that an up-coming vacation to Italy will include a trip to a theater there with a considerably better environment than that of American multi-plexes.

Murphy, Nelson and Corbett are also expanding their critical talents to www.rifftrax.com where their fans can download commentaries for current films for replay on their computers or MP3 players.

Murphy said making fun of movies such as *The Lord of the Rings* and *300* is "a different beast."

"It's a little scarier, but fun," he said. He added the group actually likes some of the films they lampoon.

And with hundreds of films under his belt, what was the one that induced the most headaches for Murphy?

Murphy said that *Mystery Science* favorite *Manos the Hand of Fate* was difficult because "nothing happens in the film."

The Vermont-made science fiction feature *Time Chaser* was unusual in that it was the only film the filmmakers actually wanted the *Mystery Science* crew to demolish.

The most challenging film for Murphy, though, was *Red Zone Cuba,* a 1966 bargain basement drama about three ex-convicts who get involved with the Bay of Pigs Invasion.

The film "looked horrible" and director, star and writer Coleman Francis was a "horrible man," Murphy said with conviction.

He noted the team cut out a rape scene from the film.

"There are snuff films that are more refined," he noted.

"I needed to take a shower [after working on that film]," he said.

LISA WILLIAMS

2008

Lisa Williams does something this reporter has never seen on television shows featuring mediums or clairvoyants. Oh, sure, on her Lifetime program *Lisa Williams, Life Among the Dead,* she performs readings for people, but she will also just walk up to a person on the street or at a mall and give them a message from someone who has passed.

The result can be both moving and shocking for the person receiving the unexpected message. Her catch phrase question is "Do you want to know everything?"

Williams said attending a live appearance such as this one could be "an emotional rollercoaster."

"They [the audience members] are hoping to be picked," she explained. "It's just an overwhelming experience."

Although members of the audience don't get up on stage, Williams comes to the person to whom she is being led by a sprit she sees. She often stays with that person five to 10 minutes relating a message from the deceased.

Williams said she has always been able to see spirits and realized something was different after her grandmother died, but she still kept seeing her around the house.

Her ability certainly has met with skepticism, which she said she doesn't mind. One of her biggest critics is her own father who "doesn't believe what I do."

Williams doesn't judge other people's beliefs and asks that others don't judge her views.

She said she would walk right up to a stranger and tell them things that are being passed on by a dead relative or friend. She said sometimes the messages clarify something and sometimes they are items the person needs to hear.

Generally people today are more open to what she and other mediums do and she credits the success of fellow medium John Edwards, who "really opened the pathway."

"I really do love that people are more open-minded. They're just accepting it," she said.

Explaining the interest in communicating with the dead, Williams said, "People need some sort of belief."

She believes what she does ties into the Christian faith and has spent time with ministers discussing what she does and thinks sometimes the difference is in semantics.

"They call it 'God' and I call it 'Spirit,'" she said.

SUZANNE STREMPEK SHEA

2008

Going to church for most people is part of a weekly schedule, but for local author Suzanne Strempek Shea, her year of experiencing 50 different Christian churches across the country truly was an adventure.

Strempek Shea's new book, *Sundays in America: A Yearlong Road trip in Search of Christian Faith* examines the differences and the commonalities Christians share in this country.

She is well known for her highly acclaimed novels such as *Selling the Lite of Heaven* and *Hoopi Shoopi Donna* as well as her non-fiction that includes *Songs From a Lead Lined Room* and *Shelf Life*. She spoke after a signing at Edwards Books in downtown Springfield. The interview was interrupted several times by people wanting to meet Strempek Shea, whose books have created a loyal audience not only here in Western Massachusetts, but across the country.

She said her initial idea for the book came from watching the funeral of Pope John Paul II on television. She couldn't help but notice the passion and the reverence mourners had for the pope and she started wondering how someone chooses a religion. Do other faiths have leaders like the pope?

Raised Catholic, she recalled she was discouraged from attending other Christian churches as a youth. She said she wondered, "Who are my Christian neighbors?"

It took a year for the concept of the book to be finalized, but on Easter in 2006, her husband Tom Shea, a newspaper columnist, and she boarded an Amtrak train for New York City and attended services at New Mount Zion Church in Harlem.

She selected that church because she wanted an experience very different than her own and said she was impressed with the two-and-a-half hour service filled with music, dance and spontaneous reactions from the congregation.

That started her tour that brought her as far as Hawaii where she attended an open-aired Episcopal service.

"Everywhere I went, with one exception, I was greeted warmly," she said.

Strempek Shea didn't tell the church's ministers she was coming and didn't announce what she was doing. She arrived at each church and attended services just as another member of a congregation.

"I just went with a notebook," she recalled.

She used up her frequent flyer miles and "mooched off friends" to make the tour possible. She said with a smile that she would look to see where there was a special on a flight on Southwest Airlines and then figure out a church to go to in that city.

Suzanne Strempek Shea
Photo by Michael Gordon

Some of her choices had to do with a holiday. She traveled to Bethlehem, Pa., to attend Christmas Eve services and on Halloween she went to a Spiritualist Church.

Although she initially thought to include other faiths, she and her editors believed that could be a little unwieldy. Instead, she stuck to Christian denominations, but she had plenty of material since there are 2,000 Christian denominations in this country alone and 34,000 worldwide.

The road trips, which she usually took alone, weren't daunting to her.

"As a reporter it's exciting to enter a community you know nothing about," she said.

Her conclusion: Christian churches are more alike than not.

One of her favorite experiences was attending Sunday services at the church where President Jimmy Carter is a member. Carter teaches Sunday school there and Strempek Shea said that people attending his part of the service are searched before they're allowed to go in. Carter's daughter Amy's fourth grade teacher introduced the audience to what behavior and questions are acceptable and which aren't before the former president starts speaking.

She was impressed with Carter's plain speaking and humanity during his part of the service, and explained that Carter helped found the church when his previous pastor refused to admit an African-American into the congregation.

The author enjoys being able to switch back and forth from fiction to non-fiction and is currently working on a novel about a dog.

"I like changing gears in that way," she said.

MICK FOLEY

2008

I've been a fan of professional wrestling for years and when a regional promoter starting presenting shows locally I sought opportunities to speak with these athletes and entertainers.

***

Mick Foley is apologetic that his son, who is loudly enjoying Disney.com, might interrupt this telephone interview.

Some might think it's ironic that one of the toughest men in professional wrestling is a dedicated father of three, but Foley is pretty much retired from competing and is happy spending more time at home than on the road.

"My family is one of my main focuses," he said.

Foley said he is currently doing only one or two wrestling shows a year and his most recent was an appearance at Madison Square Garden.

"It's [a casual schedule of appearances] a goal to work toward," he said.

"I've never done the math involved, but I think I've done more of them [matches] in buildings like the Knights of Columbus than in Madison Square Garden," Foley said.

Wrestling historian Tony Burke and wrestling legend and best-selling author Mick Foley. Photo by G. Michael Dobbs

He doesn't really miss wrestling full time. "I feel absolutely good about what I've accomplished," he said.

A wrestling fan as a teen, he wrestled on his high school team with classmate comic Kevin James before he entered the field professionally in 1986.

He backed away from competition in 2000 and has appeared as a commentator and personality in the ring more than as a wrestler. He and his long-time employers, World Wrestling Entertainment, parted ways last month and Foley said he was looking forward to his new association with Total Nonstop Action Wrestling on the Spike television channel.

He said he is "sleeping easier at night" staying out of the ring.

Besides outrageous characters, Foley was known for his do-anything attitude in the ring, which made for memorable moments for fans and a lot of injuries for him. He said that he has sore joints and pain in his back and neck, but that he actually feels better today than he did 10 years ago.

"I was never under the illusion this [career] wouldn't come with a price tag," he explained.

In a form of entertainment that demands both athletic ability as well as portraying a character, Foley's personas were known for their outrageousness. Cactus Jack was capable of dishing out considerable violence; Dude Love was a throwback hippie; and Mankind wore a Hannibal Lector style mask and had an ally in a sock puppet known as "Mr. Socko."

Foley said that Mankind, perhaps his most popular incarnation, came about in 1999 when most of the other wrestlers were portraying characters that were either "cool good guys or cool bad guys." Foley wanted to do someone different and Mankind who lived in a boiler room and talked to a rat was different. Eventually mankind became more comical.

"I was lucky," Foley said about the creation of his characters. "Other guys were restrained. I was given free reign for a number of years and allowed to make alterations."

Foley said he never considered himself a "leading man" wrestler, but rather a "character actor."

Foley has written three memoirs, three children's books and two novels. Some of his books have been on the New York Times Bestseller List. He said he started his writing career in 1999 when he read what the ghostwriter assigned to his first book, *Have a Nice Day: A Tale of Blood and Sweatsocks,* had written and he thought he could do better.

He said he enjoys writing and that readers like his conversational style.

One might wonder why a man who has built up a huge fan base and has skill portraying characters wouldn't take those assets to the movie screen such as his one-time tag team partner Dwayne "The Rock" Johnson. Foley explained while he likes acting, he didn't want to come off the road to take more time away from his family.

Today he said he is able to make his own work schedule, spend time with his family and do volunteer work.

SEAN PATRICK FLANERY

2008

It might be daunting for some actors to be cast in a role made famous by another performer, but for Sean Patrick Flanery, the star of *The Young Indiana Jones Chronicles* there wasn't a lot of pressure.

Flanery said there was a "little leeway" in his characterization because his role revealed the elements that were "all of the things that created the Harrison Ford character we all know and love."

Flanery had the chance to portray events such as Indy's first kiss and the first time he took a life, he said.

The third volume of *The Young Indiana Jones Chronicles* will be released April 29 on DVD. The series, which was originally broadcast in 1992 and 1993, is currently being shown on The History Channel.

What made the series unique was placing the Jones character either as a boy of 10 or as a young man in the middle of real historical events or meeting historical figures. Pancho Villa, Lawrence of Arabia, Louis Armstrong and Sigmund Freud were among the real people who shaped the life of the fictional archeologist.

And for people who might think history is boring, the films have the same kind of rousing adventure as the big screen Harrison Ford outings.

The DVD release of the stories, which run close to two hours long, is accompanied by documentaries that highlight the historical events and people.

Flanery said he is "super, super proud" of his work on the series. Although he said he doesn't have a lot of access to the show's fans, he's been told the shows have been well received by new audiences.

When asked if he was spoiled by the series with its high production values, Flannery said, "It did and it didn't."

Because the series was something no one had ever tried before, he really did expect other television shows to be similar to the experience. He appreciated the chance to work with the writing and directing talent that was attracted to the show. The roster included noted directors such as Nicolas Roeg, Mike Newell and Terry Jones.

Flanery has been very busy with both film and television work and he said his time on *The Young Indiana Jones Chronicles* also taught him not to prefer one medium to another. "Young Indy is a great example of why I don't care," he said.

A very busy actor, he had a re-occurring role in the television series *The Dead Zone,* as well as guest appearances in hit shows such as *C.S.I.* and *Numb3rs.*

On the sets of *The Young Indiana Jones Chronicles,* Flanery began his own interest as a filmmaker. He made his first film using "short ends" – the leftover film stock – while starring in the series. He has made four other short films since then.

Right now, Flanery is waiting to hear whether or not his first feature film, *Sunshine Superman,* will be able to go into production due to a looming strike by the Screen Actors Guild. The film is described at its Web site as "a grand love story that can only happen in that vortex in one's life when they are neither too young to reason, nor too old to dream."

Although many actors turn to directing as part of an evolution of their career, Flanery is actually going a bit backward. He actually wanted to write and direct, rather than act. He explained a friend suggested him for a part and he was accepted. Since then "I haven't not had a job."

His window for the shooting of the film is tight as he is going to begin filming the sequel to the cult hit *Boondock Saints* on Aug. 25. He admitted feeling "a mixture of desire and trepidation" toward the sequel and compared it to coming back from "the perfect exit" at a date because "the girl is so beautiful you just have to see her again."

JON BAUMAN

2009

Listening to Jon Bauman speak during an interview, there was no indication that since 1969 the musician, singer, actor and activist was actually the Brooklyn-toned "Bowzer" the long-time front man for the celebrated rock revival group Sha Na Na until the end of the conversation.

That's when in his best Brooklynese accent he said good-bye with his signature line "Grease for peace."

If this conversation has been on a videophone there is little doubt Bauman would have flexed his arms and reared back his head as Bowzer has done since 1970.

Bauman credited Sha Na Na, which started as an a capella singing group at Columbia University, as being the sparkplug for the revival of classic rock 'n' roll from the 1950s and early 1960s. Now decades later, Bauman is keeping that flame alive for people who

Jon Bauman as Bowzer

remember the era and for those just discovering it with "Bowzer's Rock-n-Roll Party."

The show featured Bauman's back-up band, the Stingrays, as well as Rocky and the Rollers, Charlie Thomas's Drifters and Shirley Allston Reeve, formerly lead singer of the Shirelles.

Bauman said the show is really designed for people to dance through it.

He said with a laugh, "We probably have more show than we have time for it."

"Show" is very important to Bauman, who said that Sha Na Na actually had a profound influence on contemporary rock 'n' roll. Before the group's hit television show in the 1980s, Sha Na Na was "a very hip underground act," he said.

"We were all about the show," he explained.

Most rockers at the time simply got on stage and performed their latest recordings.

"There wasn't much 'show' in live performances ... it was an era of wonderful music, but little showmanship," he said.

He recalled a 1971 performance in the Winterland Theater in San Francisco, Calif., when the group opened for Jefferson Airplane. After the evening, Bauman said Jefferson Airplane told their agents never to book them with Sha Na Na.

"The opening act ran away with the show," he said.

He said Sha Na Na "felt a kinship with Alice Cooper and David Bowie" who also embraced their own brand of theatricality.

Sha Na Na helped break the ground for movies such as *American Graffiti* and television shows such as *Happy Days* and *Laverne and Shirley*, Bauman asserted. The success of those television shows and movies made their own syndicated show possible.

Bauman left the group in the mid-1980s and has been successful as an actor, television host and producer. He currently does 65 to 70 live shows a year.

A magna cum laude graduate from Columbia University, Bauman has had interests other than performing. He has also been very active in the Truth in Music Association. Bauman has successfully lobbied for legislation in 33 states that prohibits bands from promoting themselves fraudulently as being a classic rock act.

"Consumers pay good money for a phony show," he said.

He explained the greatest problems have been in the Northeast in the past and that Massachusetts has been active in enforcing this legislation.

He noted that at his performances today, he now greets people who watched the Sha Na Na television show as children who are now bringing their own children to his live shows. He has heard more than once that bedtime for these children of the 1980s was often defined as when he closed the show with his "Grease for peace" line.

Bauman said, "I really still enjoy doing this. It's vital. It's upbeat and it keeps you young."

ROWDY RODDY PIPER

2009

Scheduled to speak to me about a local wrestling appearance, Piper stood me up. Hey, it happens. I had a time set for this interview and his call was not forthcoming. I took my wife to Cracker Barrel for dinner and that's when he called. He was very apologetic and gracious and I was glad I had my notebook ready. Interviews can happen at any time!

***

Rowdy Roddy Piper has spent his career in professional wrestling as one of the baddest of the bad boys, but on the phone, he is a gentleman with an easy laugh. He is even apologetic for calling in late for an interview.

Western Massachusetts is no new territory for the wrestling star, who said New England venues "are some of my favorite places – even where they hate me."

Piper is the only professional wrestler who appeared at the first Wrestlemania and at the 25th event. He admitted that even though at age 55 he still wrestles, he wasn't happy with his performance at the recent Wrestlemania.

Having been inducted into five wrestling halls of fame, Piper explained he is at a point in his career where he is interested in "giving back to my fans." He said he has had a "wonderful life" with his wife of 27 years, two children and four grandchildren because of the support from wrestling fans.

He said he comes to wrestling shows today with "a whole lot of heart" for his fans and noted, "I've never cut off an autograph line."

At the local show, Piper will conduct his Piper's Pit interview show, his signature event that graced many WWF and WWE television shows in the 1980s and '90s. He said he came up with the idea for an interview segment - that would inevitably lead to some sort of mayhem - while sitting in a bar in St. Louis, Mo.

His first guest was wrestler Frank Williams and he admitted that the first time, "I didn't know what I was going to say."

"I thought [the interview show] would be fun," he added. The first Piper's Pit is on YouTube at www.youtube.com/watch?v=zW8-zPSWibU.

He even invited this reporter to join him in Piper's Pit, but warned him with a laugh to make a fast exit when the wrestlers show up.

Piper is also well known for his appearances outside of the ring. His starring role in the 1988 science fiction film *They Live* marked the "first time a wrestler starred in a major motion picture from a major studio."

He said that shooting that film was difficult, as he had to learn that "wrestling is explosive and acting is implosive."

He said his status as a professional wrestler meant that acceptance from the motion picture community was slow.

"It was difficult to adhere to the rules Hollywood imposes," Piper said.

They Live proved to be very successful and while Piper didn't develop into being a mainstream action star, he has appeared in numerous television shows and movies since then. Two of his new movies, *Clear Lake* and *Fancypants,* are currently being completed.

He said there is interest in a remake of *They Live* and John Carpenter, the film's director, contacted Piper to see if he would be interested in being involved.

"I'm really proud that I opened up the door for other people," Piper said.

PETER LAIRD & KEVIN EASTMAN

2009

My work-related reason to go to the New York Comic-Con in 2009 was to do a story on Mirage Studios of Northampton and on the 25th anniversary of the Teenage Mutant Ninja Turtles (TMNT). That story follows below.

I knew Peter Laird, the co-creator of the Turtles at The University of Massachusetts back in the dim dark days of the 1970s and I bought his first comic book project *Barbarian Fantasy*. Later when he and Kevin Eastman started the Turtles I was re-acquainted through my friends Stanley Wiater and Stephen R. Bissette. I put together a show of original art at the Wistariahurst Museum in Holyoke, Massachusetts just before their highly popular first animated cartoon series hit in the late 1980s and hosted the guys at a signing at the theater in South Hadley I managed when the first movie came out in 1990.

I then wound up working for Eastman at his Tundra publishing experiment doing publicity for Rick Veitch's *Brat Pack*, Mark Martin's *20 Nude Dancers*, Bernie Mireault's *The Jam* and Bissette's *Taboo* projects.

I don't pretend to call myself "friends" with either guy – never have actually – but their story is a fascinating and typically American tale of what happens to two everyday guys whose creation catches lightning in a bottle.

***

If there is one rule in pop culture it's that relatively few books, movies, comic books or songs make the transition from phenomena to icon, but one group of characters born and raised in Western Massachusetts have made the leap.

The Teenage Mutant Ninja Turtles, created 25 years ago by artists and writers Peter Laird and Kevin Eastman, have a multi-generational fan base as seen at the New York Comicon conducted this past weekend at the Jacob Javitts Center in New York City. Fans in their twenties and thirties lined up with their children at two different areas at the convention to meet Laird, Eastman and the other artists of Northampton-based Mirage Studios.

And although the two creators are not active collaborators on the Turtles comic books, cartoons series or movies any longer – Eastman is the owner and publisher of *Heavy Metal* magazine – they both expressed amazement – and gratitude – about the popularity of their characters.

"We never thought it would last beyond the first issue," Eastman said after finishing a signing.

"It's been a blast," he added.

Laird said he never thought the success of the Turtles would be so long lasting.

"I was telling someone here that in the first issue of the Turtles, we killed off our main villain and people ask us about that and I say 'We had no idea.' We did that first issue thinking that would be it. There wasn't going to be a second issue," he said.

The long-term success of the Turtles has been "a complete surprise," Laird said.

In 1984 when the Turtles made their debut, the distribution models of the comic book industry allowed for independents such as Eastman and Laird to get their publications into the market place, but 25 years later it is more difficult.

Part of the problem is there has been an increase in both black and white and color comic books and "the market is only so big," Laird said.

Now, comics also compete with a number of other entertainment choices, such as free content on the Internet.

"I think that is one thing that has cut into the sale of comic books," he said.

Laird also believes that people "have only so much time in each person's life and they have to allocate that time, a kind of triage thing."

Laird and Eastman's independent comic grew into one of the greatest success stories in licensing and merchandising history. The comic books series spawned several successful television series, three live-action films, an animated feature film and dozens and dozens of licensed products.

Laird said the highpoint of all of this creative output has been the comic books he did with Eastman.

"That was probably the most creatively fertile periods of my life," Laird said. "If we had never had the big licensing success I would have been happy. Because with the comics, Kevin and I were finally doing something we loved doing, we had complete control over it and we were making decent money. The first couple of issues brought in more money than I had made in a year as an illustrator and it was doing something we just loved to do."

There is a new movie in the works, but because the deal hasn't been set Laird declined to speak about it in depth. He did say that his hopes are to use revised computer animated Turtle characters created for the last film and integrate them into live action.

The fact the Turtles have now two generations of fans is "really humbling" to Laird, who said that while the first cartoon series wasn't among his favorite Turtle spin-offs it did expose the characters to a huge audience "that we could never have reached with the comics."

"Kevin and I would often think about what happened with the Turtles and marvel at it. It was something we never planned. That's the thing. If you sit down and try to plan something like this, it rarely works. Our thing was we did this thing completely out of fun. We put a lot of passion it in. It came directly from our souls if you will," Laird said.

"I've never understood why it did [touch a nerve with fans], but maybe that's part of it," he added.

Eastman's career, while not focused on the Turtles, is still very much rooted in comics as the publisher of *Heavy Metal*. Since buying the magazine in 1990, he secured the long-delayed home video release of the first *Heavy Metal* film, developed one animated feature film based on the magazine and now is in pre-production of another feature film.

This new film involves some Hollywood A-list heavy weights, including director David Fincher, the director of the current hit *The Curious Case of Benjamin Button*, Zack Snyder, director of *300*, and Gore Verbinski, the director of the *Pirates of the Caribbean* series. The animated film will have eight segments, Eastman said, with an over-arching storyline to connect them.

Although a largely computer animated film, Eastman said each segment will have its own distinctive style and look.

Eastman thanked the Turtle fans for "25 amazing years" which gave him and Laird "an amazing life."

***

Shortly after these conversations, Laird, who owned the Turtles solely, sold the property to Viacom for a reported $60 million. Eastman is working on a new series of Turtle comics and has sold *Heavy Metal*, although he remains as the editor.

DAVID PAKMAN

2010

In the basement studios of 103.3 FM in the Florence, Massachusetts, Community Center, David Pakman is bantering with Glenn Miller, a candidate for the Senate from Missouri who is running on the platform "It's the Jews."

The longtime anti-Semite and convicted felon doesn't seem taken aback when Pakman tells Miller that he is Jewish,

"Do you hate me?" Pakman asked.

"I hate all Jews," Miller replied without hesitation.

David Pakman in his studio in Northampton, Massachusetts in 2010. Photo by G. Michael Dobbs

The interview may have given exposure to Miller's racist fringe candidacy, but it drew more positive attention to Pakman's show. He saw a noticeable increase in traffic to his Web site and more people interested in hearing his podcast.

For Pakman, 26, the interview with Miller is just one in a long list he has conducted for his weekly talk radio program now heard and seen on over 75 radio and television stations. The show's "reach" is seven million people.

Recently, he conducted interviews with Massachusetts Governor Deval Patrick, former Governor Jesse Ventura, Congressmen Barney Frank and Dennis Kucinich and Richard Clarke, author of the new book *Cyber War*.

Pakman's show has received press coverage in both traditional and Web-based media and has even has had a clip played on Howard Stern's show.

As an undergraduate at the University of Massachusetts Amherst, Pakman started a local version of *Midweek Politics*, a show that had been heard over WXOJ, a Pacifica radio affiliate. Although Pakman admitted the early shows weren't very polished, they were good enough that they were carried on the non-profit Pacifica stations.

"I started reading news [on the show]," he said. "It was really bad, but I started growing slowly, slowly getting better with guests."

Pakman continued doing the show while he was earning a master's in business administration at Bentley College and is now focusing his effort on growing the show.

Speaking before and during the taping of the show, Pakman attributed the professional sound of the show to his producer Louis Motamedi, who joined the show in 2007. During the show, Pakman discusses current issues with Motamedi, who closely watches the clock as well as cueing up audio clips.

Two video cameras are aimed at the two men, so Pakman's brother Nathan can assemble a video version of the show that will be distributed to public access channels for broadcast and for distribution on YouTube.

Pakman is following a different business model for his radio show, one that utilizes the Web as well as social networking. He prepares one version of the show for non-profit stations without any commercials and another with commercial breaks.

"It's a little bit of a challenge," he admitted.

Not only does he sell commercial sponsorships to the show, but listeners can buy a membership to his show for $4 a month that gives them material not heard on the air.

During the show, Pakman refers to several pages of notes. He said he spends over an hour a day finding audio and video material for the one-hour show.

He used to broadcast live and take calls, but discontinued that format when he added the video component to the show. Instead, he encourages people to send him e-mail, of which he reads a selection on each show. People can call a recorded line to leave comments as well.

Pakman does a "live to tape" format, which means he records his show as if it were being broadcast live. He doesn't stop the recording to correct any mistakes.

Unlike most talk radio shows, Pakman's hour is a progressive one that a few years ago it would have been called "liberal." He added he has lost several stations for being too progressive.

His goal is to expand the show to twice a week and then go daily. This year he intends to build a network of 100 stations. He said he would consider a syndication deal if it was offered him.

At one point in the interview with Miller, the candidate told Pakman that "the whole world would be better off if Hitler had succeeded" and that "Hitler was a great man . . . the most lied about man in history."

Pakman didn't flinch once at Miller's outrageous statements. At times he had to suppress his laughter. He clearly understood what he was creating was good talk radio.

HACKSAW JIM DUGGAN

2010

Hacksaw Jim Duggan has beaten the odds. He has been in professional wrestling for 30 years – not an easy profession – and he has survived kidney cancer.

Talk with him for five minutes and despite the challenges of his life and profession, he is still enthusiastic about it.

Duggan – who recently ended his long career in World Wrestling Entertainment (WWE) – said he is looking forward to working in independent promotions such as this one.

"It's a whole lot of fun," he said in a telephone interview.

Duggan, known for his huge personality and the sizable length of a 2-by-4 inch stud he carries into the ring, said the smaller promotions offer wrestling entertainment with an emphasis on what is going on in the ring, instead of a soap opera back-story.

He added that he is concerned about some elements of the national wrestling programs that are not family-friendly, while shows put on by regional promoters are still good family entertainment.

Duggan, born in 1954, played football for Southern Methodist University and then turned pro with the Atlantic Falcons. A knee injury ended his football career and he was recruited into professional wrestling by Fritz Von Erich.

He wrestled in regional promotions until he was signed by the World Wrestling Federation (WWF) – the WWE's predecessor – in 1987.

He said the biggest change he has seen through his career is the shift from 10 to 12 regional wrestling promotions across the country to one: the WWE.

Working for the WWF and WWE has brought Duggan to every state in this country, every province in Canada and 25 countries.

"It's crazy, the reach of the WWE," he said.

While the attention paid him through a WWE contract has been beneficial, he noted that when he started, there were a lot more people wrestling because of the number of regional promotions.

The competition to be part of the WWE has increased. He noted there are only about 100 wrestlers signed to the WWE, as opposed to 1,500 people playing in the National Football League.

He explained, "There's no set formula to make it in the WWE." He added that wrestlers with different styles and personas have found success.

Athletic ability is only part of what's needed, as he said a professional wrestler has to know how to talk as well.

So how did he acquire his trademark 2-by-4? Early in his career, Duggan said when professional wrestling hadn't yet evolved into "sports entertainment," the fans could be a bit dangerous.

He wondered about some sort of additional protection and fellow wrestler Bruiser Brody said to him, "whatever you carry [into the ring] make sure it is something you can use," Duggan recalled.

Duggan chose a section of a 2-by-4, which he said could be used in a rowdy crowd to "part the Red Sea."

While wrestling can both be lucrative and appealing, Duggan said being a wrestler is "hard on your family" because of the amount of time wrestlers are away. Many people have had "trouble with the road," he said.

He added for all of the shows in big venues, such as Madison Square Garden in New York City, many more are in small towns throughout the country.

The highpoint in his career was wrestling the late Andre the Giant at Madison Square Garden. He called it a "super thrill."

"There was only one Andre the Giant," he said.

STEPHEN LANG

2013

Actor Stephen Lang may be familiar to millions of movie fans as the villainous military man in *Avatar,* but the stage and screen vet drew positive reviews well before the blockbuster film with his one-man show *Beyond Glory.*

Lang is once again performing the show – he hasn't undertaken it since 2007 – in a tour.

Lang explained the genesis of the show.

"I had a basketball buddy who was the managing editor of *Parade* magazine, Larry Smith, who gave me an uncorrected copy [of his book *Beyond Glory*]," he said.

Smith's book tells the stories of Medal of Honor winners and Lang was transfixed by what he read.

"I heard the voices so clearly," he recalled.

With Smith's permission, Lang took one chapter and started "to shape it into a bouillon cube of theater."

He adapted the chapter and then began developing the play at the renowned Actor's Studio in New York City. Lang said he would work on one character and then add another until he reached the point of telling the stories of eight of the men.

He completed the work in May 2003, and in March 2004 he produced and performed it at a theater in Arlington, Virginia – the start of 400 performances he gave through 2007.

That run included producing the play on Broadway, which yielded positive reviews.

Christopher Isherwood praised the play in his New York Times review, saying, "With his chiseled physique, commanding square jaw and sharp buzz cut, Mr. Lang might almost seem carved from a block of granite. But he individualizes each of the eight portraits here with precision and economy, a new man by a subtle adjustment of posture that alters his physical presence, evoking a new personality through the coloring of his voice."

Lang readily admitted that becoming eight different characters on stage was "a challenge to revisit."

He added the men's stories are "as timely as they are timeless."

Part of that challenge is being on the stage alone.

"So much of acting has to do with listening [to fellow performers]," Lang said. "You create an energy between them."

In a show such as this one, he explained, "It all falls on your shoulders. You are more aware of your relationship with the audience."

An actor, Lang said, "never wants your 'acting' to show." In this play, the audience sees Lang change characters before them in "a very quicksilver way."

Unlike so many Broadway extravaganzas *Beyond Glory* is "a lean show in its way – the characters are so rich," he said.

Lang has spent much of his career in the theater – he was nominated for a Tony for his work in *The Speed of Darkness* – but he has been in many films and television shows. He enjoys both film and theater and said, "I love working. I love a good part. Both in their own way deliver so much fulfillment for an actor."

In theater, Lang said there is "an immediate response from the audience. You get to do the A to Z of a story … it gets richer and deeper in repetition."

With film, an actor "can go into a world only imagined on stage."

He added, "I feel fortunate to have crossed over those frontiers."

With a steady stream of film work in the past few years, Lang said, "I haven't done a play in five years and it was time to carve out time to do one."

When asked if he predicted the kind of box office success *Avatar* received when he read the script, Lang said, "I knew it was a great story. I knew it was a terrific role. I knew it was as ambitious as can be. I never doubted James Cameron's ability to transfer it to the screen, but no one predicted the global phenomena."

Lang's portrayal of the villainous Col. Miles Quaritch in the film was memorable, but Lang said he has suffered from typecasting.

"I've done a lot of military guys. I do get offered my share ... I don't mind if I'm being thought of [for such] roles as long as I get the opportunity to do others."

He cited his new film, *A Good Marriage,* in which he co-stars with Joan Allen. He plays a "broken down detective."

He added, " I couldn't ask for someone further than a fierce military guy."

VICKI LAWRENCE

2013

Lawrence was another pro: extremely down-to-earth and a fun interview.

***

Vicki Lawrence is having a busy day. She's juggling media interviews, waiting for the piano tuner and talking over her barking dog, but she is clearly enjoying the fact that her long-running sit-com *Mama's Family* is finally coming out on DVD.

Lawrence followed up her many years as a cast member on *The Carol Burnett Show* with a spin-off of the popular *The Family* sketches. *Mama's Family* ran for two seasons on NBC and then an additional four years in first-run syndication.

Lawrence explained that when she was taping interview segments for the bonus features for the DVD release of *The Carol Burnett Show* she would ask executives from Time Life video if *Mama's Family* could also be released.

"They said it was never going to happen," Lawrence recalled. She said she received "the whole lecture" about how difficult it can be to secure the legal clearances to make such a release possible.

She added, though, "Unbeknownst to me, they were fishing around."

Obtaining the rights to the music in the show proved to be a task, but the DVD producers "kept trudging ahead," Lawrence said.

The result: every episode is now on DVD, available by the season or in one single set.

Lawrence was happy to see the kind of extras the DVD producers added, including the 1982 made-for-television movie *Eunice,* based on the Burnett sketches that garnered an Emmy nomination for Lawrence.

It was that movie that Burnett "looked me in the eyes" and told her she needed to do a spin-off as Thelma Harper, the matriarch of the show, Lawrence recalled.

Mama's Family, set in the Southern community of Raytown, tells the story of a somewhat dysfunctional family. Lawrence said, "It's still pretty funny to laugh at."

The character of "Mama" was a plainspoken one dealing with her extended family who had come to live with her.

She explained, "Raytown was a funny little bubble ... guest stars would come on the show and ask if it was a period piece and I'd say, 'No, this is modern times.'"

"The Family" sketches on the Burnett show mixed laughs with pathos and at times they were "heartbreaking," she said,

"Within the confines of the Burnett show that works," Lawrence said. "They were like little playlets."

When approached to do the spin-off, despite having played the role for years, Lawrence said, "My struggle was to find 'Mama.'"

She said, "It didn't feel funny. It didn't feel right."

Lawrence noted that during all the time she played the character there hadn't been one time she had smiled.

One of her Burnett co-stars, Harvey Korman, provided valuable advice to her as the sit-com was being planned. She said that Korman told her, "You are her. Anything you can do, she can do."

She added, "That gave me the responsibility to set her free."

Mama's Family came to being without even shooting a pilot, Lawrence explained. The show's producer, Joe Hamilton, sold the idea to Grant Tinker, the head of NBC in 1982 while the men were playing golf.

The writers assigned to the project had to come up with a version of the characters that were similar, yet different. Although Korman was involved with the first two seasons of the show, Burnett was not.

Both Rue McClanahan and Betty White were co-stars on the show.

The show was broadcast on NBC for two years and then cancelled due to slumping ratings. That didn't kill it though.

Lawrence said that with the first-run syndication deal, they could re-make the show without network interference. NBC had insisted on two teeage characters – two normal kids in the middle of people with a dysfunctional back story" – but they were removed.

"We re-cast, re-thought and re-tooled [the show]," Lawrence explained. "It was very liberating."

Lawrence noted that both McClanahan's and White's characters also had to be written out as both actresses had been cast on *The Golden Girls.*

The syndication producers at Telepictures "didn't meddle like the suits at the network," Lawrence said, and allowed the show's staff to make it as they saw fit.

"First time syndication was a very new thing," Lawrence said. "It was like working in a vacuum. We were doing our own thing and having an awfully good time doing it."

What made the production of the show easier is that she had brought over many of the staff with whom she had worked for years from the Burnett show, she said.

"It was very comforting and familiar," she added.

The show became the highest rated syndicated show on television.

Although she said with a laugh she could have gone on playing the character, the show ended in 1990, but has been re-broadcast on several cable channels including a nine year run on TBS.

Lawrence said that she was "definitely" typecast as "Mama" in some people's eyes.

"It's problematical, but it's an iconic, wonderful character," she added. Lawrence does tour with a "two-woman" stage show – her and "Mama."

She has appeared on many television programs since that time and most recently had a recurring role as Miley Cyrus's grandmother on *Hanna Montana.*

A mother of two, Lawrence said her experience as "Mama" has an influence on her own parenting style. "It makes you think twice before you shoot your mouth off."

She admitted with a laugh, "In general I agree more with 'Mama' as I get older."

RICHIE HAVENS

2002

Havens died in 2013. His film *Catch My Soul* has been considered "lost" for decades, but a print has emerged and in 2013 Tom Mayer wrote about it in a revealing essay on-line at www.theunmutual.co.uk/catch-mysoul2.htm.

***

In an industry obsessed with classifying artists, singer/songwriter Richie Havens has prospered for almost 40 years without a specific label.

"That's why my first album was called *Mixed Bag*," Havens said with a laugh.

"My music comes from a lot of different places. It's been that way for a long time," he added.

If you can't pigeonhole the singer/songwriter as a folksinger or an R&B artist, you can accurately describe him as an observer.

Havens explained that he started his musical career in New York's Greenwich Village in the 1960s after a stint as a sidewalk artist drawing people's portraits. He not only listened to the performers in the Village, but also to what people was talking about as he sketched.

The experience gave him an "objective view" on life, which helped form his music.

Although he had a musical background as both a doo-wop and gospel singer, Havens took several years before breaking into the exploding musical scene of the 1960s.

Havens started touring in 1967 and achieved fame several years later at Woodstock as the seminal music festival's opening act. His performance of "Freedom," based on the spiritual "Motherless Child," was included in the documentary film Woodstock.

Haven's appeal wasn't just to the counter-culture. He also made appearances on television programs such as *The Ed Sullivan Show* and *The Tonight Show Starring Johnny Carson.* On the latter program, the audience was so enthusiastic that Carson asked Havens to return the following night. In the show's long history, the only other guest booked back to back based on such an overwhelming audience response was Barbra Streisand.

Now, more than 30 years, countless performances and many albums later, Havens still lives by his habit of observation. Whether in a big city or a small town, Havens likes to sit in a place where the residents gather and listen.

Through his listening, he concluded, "We are still becoming America."

Havens also appeared as an actor, with his debut in the 1974 movie *Catch My Soul,* a musical adaptation of Shakespeare's *Othello,* with Havens in the lead role. The rock opera has never appeared on video, something that Havens hopes to change.

Although Havens has acted in other roles, his first time was very daunting.

"I got talked into playing Othello. It was difficult," he said. "I was scared to death."

Havens has a new album, *Wishing Well,* which the artist is distributing himself in this country, Canada and Japan, a task which does not daunt him. Like many other performers who are not pleased with the lack of resources offered to non-mainstream artist, Havens has turned to the Internet for marketing assistance. The new album is being sold on his website (www.richiehavens.com) and on Amazon.com.

His website also carries many of his previous albums.

Havens wrote a book in 1999, *They Can't Hide Us Anymore* (Harper Collins), recounting the Greenwich Village music scene, Woodstock, and his career to that date.

Unlike many of his contemporaries, though, Havens is no nostalgia act.

With his distinctive, passionate voice, he is reaching new fans.

"I'm very blessed that I'm still doing what I'm doing," Havens said. "It's more than a living. I am living."

JUICE NEWTON

2002

One night, she'll work with Willie Nelson. At another show, she'll headline with Huey Lewis.

Singer Juice Newton continues to successfully straddle both the worlds of country and pop in her personal appearances and recordings.

"It's really fun," she said.

Newton, whose many hits include *Angel in the Morning, Love's Been a Little bit Hard on Me* and *Queen of Hearts,* has quite a resume. She has sold 150 million albums so far in her career and won a Grammy for "Best Pop Female Artist" and a Country Music Association Award for "New Female Vocalist." Billboard, the Bible of the music industry, dubbed her "Artist of the Year."

Angel in the Morning was recently covered by hip-hop artist Shaggy and Newton thought "it was really cool. It was so, so contemporary."

Although Newton made the decision years ago to raise a family, she kept on performing and recording, she explained

"We've kept working with a large record label although at a lower level," she said.

Touring 100 days year didn't seem to this reporter as "working at a lower level," and Newton admitted that the schedule is "a lot more than a lot of people [do]."

Her touring gives Newton the chance to interact with her fans and to perform at a variety of venues. She spoke to me from the Iowa State Fair - one of the largest in the nation - where she would appear before thousands of people. One of her next gigs, though, was a dinner club in Florida that seats 300 people.

"Working at a lower level," means working as an independent and Newton explained there are both advantages and disadvantages following that road.

Newton explained that for instance a large record label has "the resources to get [a song] out to the public."

Being an independent, though means the freedom of making your own decision.

Her latest album, *Every Road Leads Back to You* illustrates the point. Recorded live in concert Newton mixes new material – both with a pop and country feel – with some of her many hits. The result is an intimate recording that showcases Newton's outstanding musicianship.

The album is available on compact disc and on DVD as a live concert. For more information, log onto www.juicenewton.com.

Unlike too many musical acts today, Newton is concerned only about the music. There are no pyrotechnics at her shows. She feels that today's recording technology – which can easily alter a singer's voice – has produced a group of performers who may look good and move well on stage, but can't sing.

While that may give the edge to some more photogenic, but musically less talented entertainers, Newton said these people have a much tougher time having a long career.

"The record companies are so willing to toss [new talent] today," she said.

Newton dropped out of the music scene in the 1990s to be a full time mom, and joked, "I exchanged one grueling schedule for another grueling schedule."

She returned to recording and touring though because she "missed the energy level. I missed the creativity. I liked the singing."

The singing and the playing are what Newton's performances are all about and regardless if she is in an arena or a club the emphasis is on the music.

"Big or little, we do the job," she said with a laugh.

THE COMEDIANS

My first efforts in interviewing comedians came about when I was a local talk show host from 1982 to 1987 at WREB in Holyoke, Massachusetts. A 500-watt daytime AM station, WREB was among the first stations in that part of the state to adopt the talk format. Talk was still relatively exotic at a time when AM radio was king and music was the dominant format.

I had received the job based on two merits: I had been a frequent guest on my friend George Murphy's talk show speaking about the films of the 1930s and '40s and I was a newspaper reporter. I had no training in radio and received next to no advice or guidance about how to produce a show.

I soon realized that I wasn't cut out to assume some sort of persona to either inspire love or hatred from the audience – a talk radio device that is still used today. I decided that I should simply be myself and wanted to have a show that was hopefully entertaining and interesting to the audience.

To achieve this, I prepared material for conversation everyday and booked a lot of interviews: local officials, people involved in presenting some sort of local activity or event and celebrities either passing through the area or looking for some press to publicize something.

Several of those interviews are in this book, but many are not as the tapes for those shows are missing.

Among the comics I spoke with at that time were Emo Philips and Yakov Smirnoff who quickly illustrated the difference between interviewing a comic for radio and for print. Radio is a performance venue well suited for most stand-up comics whose voice and words are their medium. Gags often don't translate as well in print – the timing and inflection are missing or difficult to convey.

So while I've had some good conversations with comics for print, the ones I interviewed for radio were largely stand-up sets with me as the audience.

Philips has a highly eccentric persona and his interview was equally different. He actually had a friend at a piano for the interview who provided a musical accompaniment to his jokes. Smirnoff basically did part of his stage routine – the Russian who escaped the Soviet Union for the brave new world of the United States – and was very funny.

On the other hand, Lois Bromfield took a different approach to being on my talk show – she didn't make one joke. She spoke about her life as a comic and later thanked me for not requiring her to be "on."

Journalists have to take advantage of what's in their circulation area as story generators: museums, colleges, businesses, music and comedy venues. Since I have a comedy club that brings in national acts I've made a point to build up a relationship with the producers and speak to as many of the comics that I can.

While many of the comedians I've interviewed for print have been funny during our conversations, nearly all of them have provided observations into their process for writing and their life, which I find even more interesting.

I've had the opportunity of doing more than one interview with several comedians, which has also provided greater insights into their careers.

I've been surprised by some of the interviews – not in the least was with a guy whose signature persona as a neurotic frequently irritated me: Richard Lewis. Lewis turned out to be a great interview.

***

RICHARD LEWIS

2000

Richard Lewis says he feels good.

Well at least as good as the famously neurotic comedian can feel.

Lewis, the man who has made audiences laugh by baring his soul on stage predicted people would see "one happy dysfunctional guy."

The veteran comic found that writing a memoir, which will be published later this year, has helped his stand-up career.

"I pity the editor because it's 558 pages," he said with a laugh.

Writing about both his professional and personal life, including his successful battle against alcoholism has been "cathartic" for Lewis.

"I've been rigorously honest when writing and I've tried to upgrade my honesty on stage," he explained. "I've been more fearless than ever."

Honesty is a cornerstone of Lewis's comedy. Unlike other comics with carefully honed routines, Lewis "works without a net." His life is his material and he said he never is sure what he is going to do until he walks onto the stage.

Lewis recounted a conversation in which fellow comic Jay Leno asked him why he was so nervous before every show. Lewis told Leno his anxiety came from now knowing exactly what he was going to talk about.

His audiences are not surprised when Lewis hilariously details his fear and obsessions. No dark secret of Lewis's life seems to have been spared from being fodder for his comedy.

"My onstage persona is me," he said.

His approach has worked well for over 20 years and his success as a stand-up comic has enabled him to branch out into other entertainment ventures.

Lewis starred for four years with Jamie Lee Curtis in the sitcom "Anything but Love;" has had a string of HBO specials and had both comic and dramatic roles in a number of movies.

Lewis has a reoccurring role in Larry David's new HBO series. David, co-creator of *Seinfeld,* has been friends with Lewis since the comic was 12 years-old and Lewis is "thrilled" to be working with his childhood friend.

Lewis said that a comedy album would probably come out of his current cross-country tour.

No matter what other project Lewis undertakes, performing in front of live audiences is still his number one priority.

"I love looking an audience in the eye and making them laugh," he said.

JIM BREUER

2000

I did not prepare as well as I should for this interview with Jim Breuer and I mistakenly believed he was still on *Saturday Night Live.* The comic good-naturedly roasted me for a few minutes. I deserved it. I've spoken with him three more times and have never made an error like that again.

***

Veteran stand-up comic Jim Breuer caught this writer flat-footed when he corrected my assumption that he is still a cast member of *Saturday Night Live.*

Breuer, who gained fame on the television institution for his impersonation of actor Joe Pesci and his "Goat Boy" character, hasn't been on the show for two years. He good-naturedly chided me for my faulty research, but admitted a lot of people are confused about that thanks to reruns of the show.

Breuer doesn't miss SNL "not even a blink," and has kept busy with a starring role in the cult movie Half Baked and a supporting performance in the movie *Dick*. He has a cameo in the up-coming drama *Once in The Life*. His half-hour comedy special, part of the Pulp Comic series, is currently running on the Comedy Central cable channel.

"Performing on *Saturday Night Live* was the easiest part," Breuer said. He said the real struggle was in the performers and writers competing with one another to get material on the air.

Breuer has made numerous television appearances doing his stand-up act and acting in shows such as *Home Improvement,* and recently shot a pilot for his own situation comedy in which he plays a substitute teacher. He will find out if a network picks it up later this month.

He isn't too concerned if the show is passed by because he isn't a fan of the medium.

"TV is not where my head is at. TV is too uncreative," he said. "The people involved get in the way of things."

His ambition is to continue his film career and to produce the works of other comics. He said there are many outstanding comic talents that haven't received the attention they deserve.

He still loves performing live and said his success has "enabled me to take more chances."

Breuer's natural sleepy-eyed look is the grist of a long-running part of his stand-up routine in which he says police officers always believe he is under the influence of something. Breuer said that he hasn't been pulled over lately; his eyes still get a reaction from audiences.

"I go on stage and I hear them buzzing 'Oh my God, he's high!'

2005

Jim Breuer is on satellite radio with a daily show and he loves it.

"It's a guilty pleasure," he said.

Jim Breuer Unleashed is heard every day on Sirius Satellite Channel 147 from 4 to 6 p.m.

Breuer said the radio job has been a "one year goof." He started the show last November.

"By far it's my favorite thing I've ever done," he exclaimed.

Breuer, who started as a stand-up comic, has been a regular on *Saturday*

Night Live and appeared in films (*Half-Baked*). But he loves his radio show because it allows him to be more of a storyteller.

It's also "paid therapy," he said, as he is able to sit down with two high school friends and a fellow comic and discuss whatever they like in the manner that they like.

Be forewarned: they don't mince words. There's no censorship on satellite radio.

Breuer said the four friends "leave their egos at the door" and talk about things so they "can get on with their lives." He said that one friend is a musician, while another works at an airport.

"I love it. We heal a lot of people," Breuer explained. He said that once a listener hears how messed up their lives are, listeners' lives seems better. He added the show features "tofu and sandals wisdom" along with blistering comedy.

Listening to excerpts of the show on Breuer's web site www.breuerun-leashed.com the show sounds like a Breuer version of TV's *The View,* only with a lot of gags, guests, such as comic Dave Attell and musician Vince Neil, and calls from listeners.

Rather than the daily show impeding his stand-up career, Breuer said that he has been creating new material through the daily shows.

"I'm the best at my game," he said. The show has "opened so many doors creatively."

Breuer, who still tours with a band, doesn't miss television and is now planning direct-to-DVD releases of his work, such as *Hardcore,* his first DVD. His contract for the radio show ends in November and he would love to extend it if he could. He's considering assembling an audio CD that would collect the best moments of the first year.

For now, though, Breuer said, "I really do like making people feel better."

2009

Log onto Jim Breuer's Web site and you'll see a commercial for his new comedy DVD starring his young son. When I ask him about it, the comedian – known for his rock 'n' roll comedy, his years on *Saturday Night Live* and movies like *Half-Baked* let loose with his distinctive cackle.

The commercial, like his act and the latest phase of career, is all about family. The comedian, noted for how his naturally half-closed eyes made him look constantly stoned, now presents a non-cursing family-friendly show.

What's the reaction from his fans? His lengthy comedy tour has been sold out 90 percent of the time, Breuer said.

"It's been a phenomenal year – a great tour," he said.

Breuer said that his comedy reflects where he is in his life and family is foremost.

He did a daily show over satellite radio for several years and now does it weekly –so he could be with his three children and so he could develop an off-stage persona.

"I'm rebuilding a whole career," he explained.

Technology has allowed him to stay in touch with his eleven, eight and five year olds while on the road. "Thanks to Skype ... they have a lot more understanding. They get what Daddy does," he said.

The radio show also allowed him to stay near his parents. Part of the result of this experience is not just his stand-up act, but also a situation comedy for television he is currently developing. Breuer's concept is built around a "sandwich guy," someone in his forties who not only has children but has his parents living with him as well.

Breuer said that he has been described as a "Bill Cosby with a Metallica shirt."

"That sums up the show," he added.

He said his comedic goal isn't for audiences to say, "That was nice" at the end of the show. "I want you to leave saying 'That's the hardest I laughed in 20 years,'" he said.

Breuer said he now has several generations coming to shows, with people his age bringing parents and children.

Part of his current act is a reaction to the "everything sucks generation." He said he is tired of comics who present a litany of dislikes.

"There's way too much [of it] dominating comedy," he asserted. "We don't need comedy about what's awful with marriage, kids and family."

Instead, what audiences need is some "good laughter," Breuer said.

2012

Jim Breuer is part of a new trend in stand-up comedy by taking direct control of producing and distributing his own DVDs and comedy specials.

He said that he loves the independence.

"I like to be hands on," he said.

Named one of Comedy Central's "100 Greatest Stand-Ups of All Time," Breuer was a regular on *Saturday Night Live* in the mid-1990s and has appeared in the films *Dick, Titan A.E.* and *Beer League.* His most recent movie was *Zookeeper.*

Besides his TV work on *Saturday Night Live,* he has appeared on *Late Night with Conan O'Brien, The Daily Show with Jon Stewart, The Late Late Show with Craig Ferguson, Jimmy Kimmel Live* and *The Marriage Ref.*

To call Breuer a busy guy is an understatement. Besides touring, he produces his own videos for his YouTube channel; his book, *I'm Not High: (But I've Got a Lot of Crazy Stories about Life as a Goat Boy, a Dad, and a Spiritual Warrior)* went to paperback last year; he shot a new comedy special; and he just came back from a tour in Germany.

A project special to him is *The Jim Breuer Road Journals,* a four-hour DVD, which documented a 2008 comedy tour on which he took along his then 85-year-old father. Although it is funny, it "really touches people," he said.

His new comedy special is designed for viewers from "8 to 80," he said. A comic who really has never worked with "blue" material, Breuer likes to describe himself as "Bill Cosby with a Metallica shirt."

Although he has "cursed a little" in his act, Breuer said that staying away from adult material "challenges me to write better."

His act is "100 percent family story telling" that deals with his wife, children and elderly parents.

He admires fellow comedian Louis CK who made show business headlines by his announcement he would sell tickets to his current tour only through his website.

"He's the 'Money Ball' of comedians," Breuer said.

Although he enjoys the independent route he has taken with his career, Breuer readily admitted he wouldn't mind his own television show.

"My management has tried hard," he explained. "The process is so exhausting."

Breuer added, "I would be a liar if I said I wouldn't mind making $50,000 a day working Monday through Friday."

His YouTube channel has dozens of videos and Breuer said, "It's a great medium."

Breuer is also well known for his love of heavy metal rock and roll and how he has integrated that into his act. He said he is interested in staging the act as an Off-Broadway play, which he would then take on tour.

He added that this year would be the last one in which he performs in comedy clubs. He is more interested playing in theaters and other venues – even churches – that do not serve alcohol.

"I would love people to come to see me in a healthy, safer environment," Breuer said.

DAVE ATTELL

2003

Dave Attell is more than a popular comedian. He is a guide to times and places where few people dare to tread.

Attell is our Virgil to the underworld of the late night. He does on a regular basis what many only hope to do – stay up all night and explore bars, clubs and whatever else is open at 3 a.m.

Attell is the creator and host of *Insomniac,* Comedy Central's only "reality" show. Forget about those horned-out brats on *The Real World* or the lies of *Joe Millionaire, Insomniac* presents an unvarnished view of the world that is always amusing, sometimes shocking, and, for some of us, unsettlingly like our memories of college years.

The premise of the show is pretty simple. Attell takes us on a late night tour of a city in which he's performing a stand-up gig. When he gets offstage after his last set, he hits the streets with his crew to see what's happening.

Attell is out there for the viewers, popping shots with locals, tucking a few bucks at a strip club, taking in a late night rodeo or stock car race, and talking to people on their way to another bar or to a place to eat.

And Attell always makes sure to tag along with someone whose job entails staying up all night.

You never really know from show to show and city to city just what Attell will be doing. For instance, in New Orleans, he spent part of a night tagging along with a unit of the Sheriff's Department shooting nutria – a 20-pound South American rat that is raising havoc in the local waterways – from the back of a pick-up truck. He squeezed off a few rounds himself.

The program is an underground travelogue for cities such as New York, Chicago, Boston, Montreal, Houston, and Little Rock.

If you've seen Attell's stand-up you know his twisted sense of humor. If you haven't, here are a couple of examples:

• "I'm not into jogging. It's just that joggers are the ones who find the dead body. You never find a dead body sitting at home eating ice cream watching porno. Do you?"

• "I fly all the time. In fact I have a name in the airport: 'random bag check.' The security guard goes 'Maybe you should look less threatening when you fly.' Less threatening? What am I supposed to do? Walk around holding a balloon and a Hello Kitty lunchbox?"

His stand-up act is featured on a new CD, *Skanks for the Memories* on Comedy Central Records and available on the network's website, www.comedycentral.com. This writer finds Attell's material hilarious, but it is designed for adults.

With his wit and his ability to make friends quickly, Attell has become the nation's most accomplished night crawler.

Of course, it doesn't hurt that he doesn't mind indulging in a few libations wherever he goes.

Unlike too many other reality shows, Insomniac "isn't about celebrities. It's mostly about bars and people having a night on the town," Attell explained.

The show's been so successful that Attell just wrapped up taping the fourth season and Comedy Central has just released *The Best of Insomnia with Dave Attell Uncensored: Volume One* on DVD.

Attell said he approached Comedy Central with the premise. A night owl and party guy, Attell wanted to show a bit of what life on the road can be for a stand-up comedian.

Dave Attell

Comedy Central liked the show because it would give the cable network a reality show and because "it's really, really cheap," explained Attell.

"It's not scripted. There's no makeup and hair," said Attell. One might think by watching the show that Attell is out cruising the streets and the bars with just a soundman and a camera operator, but he said there's actually far more people out there with him.

His executive producers have scouted out a city beforehand, knowing which bars and clubs would welcome Attell and his crew and which would not. They also come along with Attell smoothing the way. Plus a number of production assistants are on hand to get signed release forms for the folks who appear on camera.

"We rarely get someone who doesn't want to be on camera," Attell noted.

Amazingly enough, Attell's crew doesn't automatically include a security detail. He said that in some of the smaller cities, local officials have provided him with a police escort – something which comes in handy when Attell goes into a bar and 200 people all want to buy him a shot.

"You can get killed with kindness," he said.

When this writer expressed concern about the amount of alcohol Attell consumes on camera, he expressed thanks and explained the partying he does for the show is far more than he does in his private life.

"I'm 37 and I'm way too old to do this kind of thing," he admitted, and added that he doesn't drive during the production of the show.

And he doesn't want to encourage people to drink to excess. Each show is taped over a three-night period after two days of research and set-up, and Attell said that the smaller cities have frequently been the most fun for him. Production can start as early as 8 p.m. and will last until dawn.

"It takes more time than I thought it would," he said.

"From the beginning I wanted to do that - to get out of New York City and Los Angeles," he added.

He said smaller towns usually are more accommodating to the show than larger cities, which generally have more restrictions.

The most difficult shows have been in New Orleans and Las Vegas, where there is no last call at bars.

"You just keep going," he said.

For the purposes of the show, he likes a 4 a.m. last call, such as New York City's final chance to buy a drink.

Attell is enjoying the show and the freedom the format allows.

Unlike many stand-up comedians, Attell does not aspire to have a situation comedy.

"I've been a stand-up comedian for 16 years and I've written for television. I'm not an actor, though. Everyone thinks you have to be in a movie or a sitcom. I enjoy being on the road. Stand-up is the primary thing for me," he explained.

"I don't think I'm missing anything. I care about making good money, good shows and being my own guy. I'm really happy," he added.

And on behalf of all of those folks who start to pass out before the 11 p.m. news is finished, we appreciate the chance to live the late nightlife, even if it's vicariously through *Insomniac*.

2004

Comedian Dave Attell sounds just a little beat on the telephone, but you can't blame him as he just got back from Japan where he hosted a one-hour *Insomniac* special set in the Land of the Rising Sun.

The stand-up comic has found television fame by doing what comes naturally to him – performing at a club and then nightcrawling through a town.

Speaking of Japan, Attell said it was "wild, a great experience." It was also an easier place to film an episode of his program than back home.

If you've not seen *Insomniac*, you've missed not only one of the most consistently amusing shows on Comedy Central, but also one of the most honest "reality" shows on the tube.

Attell interviews people on the streets, checks out local nightspots, and hangs with people who have to work all night. The show has covered cities such as New York, Boston, Atlanta, Boise, among others, and has gone to Montreal, London and Amsterdam as well.

Many of us, who have abandoned an active nightlife due to advancing age or common sense, live vicariously through Attell and his late night travels.

The show has had a run of 40 half-hour shows over four seasons.

Unfortunately, it has become the victim of its own success, though, as Attell said it has become more and more difficult for him and his crew to go through city streets and visit bars without being mobbed.

He said that toward the end of the run of the half-hour show "a lot of time was talking to people about the show instead of shooting the show."

Although he quickly added that it was very rare to find someone who treated him poorly, and that he appreciated his fans, he and his crew spent a lot of time getting away from the throngs of people who would gather around them.

Initially, people didn't know too much about the show, but as it became more successful, people on-camera became more self-aware, he said.

So the format has been changed to an hour-long special and Attell has shot one in Brazil at Carnival and another in Japan.

He said Brazil was a "really good place to do the show. We had better access to events and there weren't so many drunken frat boys."

The only problem overseas is the language barrier, and Attell had to have a translator. Although he noted that he found a great number of Americans in both of the foreign locations.

One thing Attell also likes about the new format is carrying his all-night activities into the following day when you can stumble across some wild events, such as being on the beach in Brazil or attending a fertility festival in Japan.

"Not everything happens at night," he noted.

Despite all of the television activity (Attell is one of the phone practical jokers on *Crank Yankers* and is a regular on *The Daily Show with Jon Stewart*) he still maintains a schedule of stand-up appearances. He recently completed a tour with fellow comic Lewis Black.

"I love working with him," he said.

At a recent appearance at the University of Connecticut, Attell had to contend with a rowdy St. Patrick's Day crowd, but it was all in a day's work.

"I like a wild crowd. I feed off the energy," he added

While he doesn't mind an occasional call from the audience, he said that people sending up shots to the stage throws off his timing.

Speaking of shots, when asked to recall some of the worst challenging drinks he has encountered through *Insomniac* he quickly recalled "Red-headed Slut" – a cranberry juice drink – and "Blood," an English drink that tasted, well, like blood,

"There were some weird things in it," Attell said with considerable understatement

2005

Dave Attell may not be shooting his hit show *Insomniac* any longer, but he's keeping very busy.

Attell's most recent Comedy Central special allowed him to feature three up-and-coming comedians performing live, and pretty much uncensored, in Las Vegas. The feature-length comedy concert film was the first for the cable network and it featured Attell and fellow comics Sean Rouse, Greg Giraldo and Dane Cook.

Attell has also produced a DVD of a live stand-up performance that he is selling on his web site (www.daveattell.com) and Comedy Central will be releasing Dave Attell's Insomniac Tour Presents Sean Rouse, Greg Giraldo And Dane Cook on DVD in time for the holidays.

"I'm always on the road," Attell said. "I'm excited to come back. It's always fun working in Massachusetts."

Attell said that he does miss some aspects of *Insomniac*. The show featured Attell in a different city cruising the streets and meeting people after he performed at a local club. Part reality show, part twisted travelogue, *Insomniac* revealed what happens in America after dark.

Attell admitted that filming the show meant an increase in his alcohol consumption. Pushing the age of 40 and being in a bar with frat boys, he said, was "weird."

What he really liked about the show was the freedom he had with Comedy Central.

"They give you the leeway to do your own thing," he said.

The new comedy special combines *Insomniac's* format of the comics interacting unrehearsed with themselves and others with a concert film.

Attell explained he was looking for a project that would allow him to be the host and present fellow comics.

"It was cool to bring out other guys," he added.

While the number of people performing comedy remains strong, Attell said there is a new dynamic happening: family friendly shows.

Due to a new wave of political correctness, Attell said some clubs wouldn't give a chance to certain comedians.

He said that many clubs are looking for comics who are "squeaky clean." While the change has not affected him much. His reputation for filling clubs with people who enjoy his no-holds-barred comedy is secure, but new comics have a rougher time establishing themselves.

He explained that many club owners don't want to book someone who hasn't been on television and want an act that won't offend audiences.

"It's bad," Attell said. "Comics in clubs are supposed to be edgier and raw. I've seen it everywhere."

It's not just comedy clubs in the South or Midwest, he explained, but also in New York as well.

"That's just not right. I really don't understand it," he said.

What's up next for Attell? He said he loves working in Las Vegas and would like to host a variety show from Sin City.

Naturally for Attell, it would be an edgy variety show.

2009

Comedy can be hard work. Just ask Dave Attell.

The veteran comedian said that the taping of his new comedy special, *Dave Attell: Captain Miserable,* was a bit of a challenge.

"They weren't my crowd at all," Attell said.

The special was seen on Comedy Central and it is now available on DVD.

Originally taped a year ago for HBO, Attell said Comedy Central had obtained the rights to the show and then delayed broadcasting it.

The show had some classic edgy Attell observations ranging from potential commercials for Jägermeister to performing for American troops in the Middle East.

Attell said the special was taped in a theater instead of his favored environment, a club, and had a "very politically correct" audience.

"When you do a show for a network, you're a hired hand," Attell explained. At this taping, "people weren't rolling with me. It was like going uphill."

Attell's fans know to expect the unexpected from the comic but when he launched into a joke about pedophiles, he had to change gears.

Because of the delay in broadcast, Attell said some of the material was older than he would have liked.

"[Some jokes] made me cringe," he said.

Although he said he doesn't censor himself for Comedy Central – "you know what to say and what you can't" – Attell added, "I try not to edit myself unless I absolutely have to."

There was one political joke in the special, which Attell pointed out as his lone topical gag. He has resisted putting political material into his shows, as those jokes aren't as "evergreen" as others.

He noted, though, "everyone is talking about politics now, [it's] like sports."

He tours a lot, something he called both a "blessing and a curse," and people still recognize him from his show *Insomniac,* despite it being off the air since 2004. He would like to reach a point in a couple of years where he can get off the road as much.

When he is home in New York City, he's "constantly thinking of new stuff."

"It comes together in the clubs," he explained.

Attell is working on a new CD. His first recording, *Skanks for the*

Memories, was a hit and he's planning to do another.

"That's the thing that's constantly there," he said.

Skanks for the Memories came out before the dominance of iTunes and other Web-based distribution of recordings, a technology Attell called "interesting."

"People say they love your CD and they stole it [off the Internet]. It's a compliment, but a crime," he said. "I tell them 'You owe me a $1.'"

Despite the economy, Attell said there are still a lot of comedy venues and a night at a comedy club is a "pretty good bet" as a show can provide "four hours of conversation" afterwards.

2012

If you have been to one of his shows or watched his act on cable, you know that comedian Dave Attell will take you to some pretty edgy places, so his television series, *Dave's Old Porn* will not be for everyone.

His show is entering its second season on Showtime and Attell described it as "basically 'Mystery Science Theater 3000' with retro porn." Instead of having hand puppets riff on bad movies, though, Attell invites fellow comics and some of the performers from the movies made 30 years ago to comment on clips from films.

Some of the comics on the second season of the show include Artie Lange, Kathy Griffin, Joe Rogan, Marc Maron and Andy Dick. He noted that convincing current adult performers to appear on the show is easy, but landing the "legends is trickier."

"They really are like heroes to me," Attell said. "They were important at a lonely time in my life."

Attell came up with the idea for the show several years ago and produced a pilot for another network, which ultimately passed on it.

He added the show is all unscripted. Although he watches the clips before, he and his guest comics don't plan quips for what they see.

He described the show as "jokes, porn and fun" and added with understatement, "It's not a deep discussion show."

"It's a tribute to some amazing work," Attell explained.

He selects the films – some from his own collection – buys the rights for the scenes they use and then tapes about an hour's worth of remarks with the guests, which are edited to a half-hour program. Attell is involved in the editing as well.

"I'm having a good time doing it," he added. "This is the perfect project to do in these politically correct times."

Although Attell has been busy with the production of the new season, he has a busy schedule of stand-up planned.

"I've got a lot of weekends coming up," he said.

He enjoys getting on stage and crafting new material, but he has noticed that many audiences "want more of a performance [of familiar material]."

Attell said, "Comedy is not made that way."

He's also involved with the *Anti-Social Comedy Tour* co-starring Jim Norton, Artie Lange and Amy Schumer. "It's no 'Blue Collar Comedy Tour,'" Attell said, stressing it was definitely for adults only.

"It's a nice colonic for the soul," he said with a laugh.

Between technology and social media, being a comic today has some interesting twists and turns. Attell said a young comic might be able to have a video that goes viral and sell out a venue, but doesn't yet have the comic skills to satisfy a live audience.

The ever-increasing presence of cell phones is also a trend comics don't like as audiences use them during a performance, he noted.

While fellow comic Louis C.K. is a hero to Attell for avoiding ticketing agencies and selling tickets to his recent tour exclusively through his own website, he admitted that being on Facebook, creating videos and posting to Twitter is a lot of work.

"It's [comedy] becoming more self-promotion than just stand-up," he said.

Attell doesn't fault young people today for being so plugged in.

He noted that if he had had the Internet when he was younger, "I wouldn't have left my room."

MIKE EPPS

2005

Mike Epps said that he "can't get away from [comedy.]"

While his career has been busy with film appearances, he said that performing on stage is like "therapy for me."

"I can talk about my problems and they are not problems anymore," he said.

After coming from a background of stand-up comedy, Epps became known to film audiences as "Day-Day" in *Next Friday* and *Friday After Next* with Ice Cube. He also appeared with Ice Cube in *All About the Benjamins*.

Epps was seen earlier this year in the Ed Norton role of the remake of

The Honeymooners, a film that he said "wasn't a movie I wanted to do. It was a movie to do."

He did admit that he had watched a little of the original television series and said that *The Honeymooners* remake was a "feel good" movie.

Mike Epps

Upon reflection he added, "It's cool."

His new film *Roll Bounce* is due out soon, he said. It's a roller skating movie set in the 1980s and stars Bow Wow. He said his role in the film is to supply the "comedy relief."

He said the older he becomes, the more he appreciates film making, and that he didn't care for the start and stop of movie production when he was younger.

"I can dissect it and appreciate it," he said.

He is currently working on a new half-hour show for HBO. When he made the statement, someone in the background asked "You've got a show for HBO?"

"I've got it popping, baby," Epps said in reply.

Epps said it is more difficult for young people to break into comedy today than when he did over a decade ago.

"Comedy is like the NBA or the NFL. You're up against 144 people," he said.

"Comedy should have a draft," he added with a laugh.

For Epps, though, he was "born into this shit."

"I have no choice to be good at it," he said. "I do it for survival."

CAROLINE RHEA

2005

Caroline Rhea was enthusiastic about returning to perform at the Comedy Connection at the Hu Ke Lau in Chicopee.

"I love saying 'Hu Ke Lau Chicopee,'" she said with a laugh during a telephone interview last week, "It sounds like someone sneezed."

Rhea is currently host of the second season of the NBC reality show, *The Biggest Loser* and HBO recently began airing her new stand-up comedy special. She is now touring comedy clubs.

Her recent television gigs complement her previous credits a long run as "Aunt Hilda" on the hit sit-com *Sabrina the Teenage Witch,* a returning role on *Hollywood Squares,* a stint as one of Drew Carey's girlfriends on his show and her own talk show.

"I've been lucky," she said of her career, but admitted that of her credits, she loves performing stand-up the most.

"It's the place where I feel most comfortable," she said. Rhea has been on stage making people laugh for 16 years.

The freedom of being in front of a live audience means that Rhea doesn't have to worry about being edited or censoring herself. Although not known for a raunchy or political style of humor, she noted that when doing radio interviews that she has to be careful, as many stations are now very sensitive to offending listeners.

Her act is basically her life, she explained and she tries to keep it as current as possible. Twenty to 30 percent of it, though, is improvisation.

"I have hours of material. I'm a windbag," she added.

"The Biggest Loser" is a project that Rhea enjoys. She is the host of the show, supervising the weigh-ins and giving out assignments.

"It's like being inside a soap opera," she said.

What intrigues her about the show is the amount of empathy it generates for the participants who are trying to make a significant transition in their lives. She believes that the show has heightened awareness of the issues of being overweight and she called the cast members "lovable characters" that are inspiring.

She also called her role in the show as a "great part-time job," as her involvement during the 14-week period to shoot the show allowed her to do other projects.

One kind of project Rhea said she would not do is take over for someone in an established show. She did that with Rosie O'Donnell's popular talk show.

"I would never replace anyone in anything [again]," she said.

Although she might have misgivings about the talk show that lasted one season, she said that she has fond memories of "sitting close to Pierce Brosnan" and having the chance to interview the late John Ritter and Christopher Reeve.

If she ever did another talk show, she would try to for a late night program, so her self-described "irreverent" brand of humor might find a more receptive audience.

EDDIE GRIFFIN

2005

Ask Eddie Griffin why he's been out of the country for much of the last two years and he has a quick answer: "That's where the movies are being shot."

The stand-up comic has two new films that will be released in the next few months. Griffin starred in the *Malcolm & Eddie* sitcom from 1996 through 2000 and has been in movies such as *Undercover Brother* and the *Deuce Bigelow* series (Griffin played the manager of the unlikely gigolo).

But don't expect a new *Deuce Bigelow* film among the new productions.

"We're done with that. We squeezed all of the blood out of that," he said with a laugh. "The vampires would have to go someplace else to feed."

Besides shooting the second *Deuce Bigelow* film in Amsterdam, Griffin also appeared in *Irish Jam,* a comedy set in Ireland that was shot in Cornwall, England.

"That was interesting," Griffin said with understatement.

In *Irish Jam,* Griffin plays an American who wins an Irish fishing village through a poetry contest. Besides the problem that he stole the lyrics from a rap album to win, he suffers a big case of culture shock. The film is scheduled for release next month.

Griffin plays a take-off of the Robert DeNiro role from *Meet The Fockers* in the film *Date Movie,* now in post-production, and provided the voice for Babe the Blue Ox in the animated pro-

Eddie Griffin

duction *Bunyan and Babe.* It was his first time doing voice work and Griffin declared, "It was fun."

He also made his directing debut with *N.T.V.,* which will be going straight to DVD. When asked what the "N" stands for he offered, "Nepotism? Narcissistic? Use your imagination."

He "had a ball" directing the film.

Griffin said he likes the freedom of performing in films over his experience with television. He explained that "suits who never told a joke on stage" were experts in comedy.

Griffin added that the attitude among television executives is "if the wheel is working, we must destroy it."

Still, Griffin said he doesn't really have a preference over the different parts of his career.

"I like all of it. It takes a whole lot of different slices to make a pie," he said.

Showtime subscribers will see Griffin as Sammy Davis, Junior, in an up-coming biography he made. In describing the film, Griffin launched into a perfect Sammy Davis impersonation.

He is currently working on a similar type of film on the life and career of Richard Pryor and talked about the project in Pryor's voice.

When he was told this writer has an autographed photo of comic and filmmaker Rudy Ray Moore on his office wall, Griffin instantly started reciting part of Moore's seminal routine, *The Signifying Monkey.*

"Everyone has professors," said Griffin. "Those are mine: Professor Davis, Professor Pryor and Professor Moore."

JUDY TENUTA

2006

I've interviewed a fair number of comedians who've appeared in our area, but no one has ever serenaded me before. But then, I've never talked to Judy Tenuta before.

Speaking from her California home at 8 a.m., Tenuta first told me that it wasn't too early for her to do an interview, because she has a lot of energy in the morning.

That proved to be an understatement.

After telling me that she was wearing her gold lamé leopard bikini, she told me to hang on while she fetched her accordion. Popping on her speakerphone, she launched into a song extolling the virtues of the club at which she was going to appear locally.

Judy Tenuta

I discovered that I wasn't going to get many in-depth answers about the nature of comedy. Whether it's on stage or over a telephone, Tenuta is a total entertainer.

Tenuta is a veteran on the national comedy scene whose act is part political commentary, part audience participation and part religious and social satire.

The comic can also be very politically incorrect. Talking with her proved to be a wild ride.

Sometimes she describes herself as a "petite flower." Other times, she calls herself a goddess and preaches the faith she invented herself: "Judyism."

She said she loves appearing in Massachusetts. She will also be at the Comedy Connection at Faneuil Hall in Boston and that it's been a while since she performed at the Hu Ke Lau.

"I love it. It's been five years since the last time and they were sweet enough to have two of the [Polynesian] dancers carry me on stage," she said. "I want them to do a fire dance around me."

She also likes the venue because the audience is "lit," by the time she arrives on stage, she said.

"We are all best friends by then," she added.

Tenuta is one of nine children of a Polish-Italian family from Chicago. She said her brothers were required to play musical instruments, but unlike them, she enjoyed the accordion.

When asked how much of her act is ad-libbed, Tenuta replied that she "makes it up right there."

"I do have certain things [planned] on a kind of mental outline, but you never know," she said.

Tenuta revealed she will be husband hunting while in Chicopee and Boston and she does have her eye on one New England celebrity.

"Quarterback Tom Brady needs to meet the goddess now. I expect him to be at Faneuil Hall for the goddess!" she said.

She will be asking or dragging various men on stage to audition as potential husbands. Among her requirements are the candidates "have to complete a sentence and should have a wallet."

He should also be "pretty cute," as she said, "The goddess is pretty cute." Candidates also should bring presents and flowers to increase their attractiveness.

One last word: Tenuta warned that candidates have to have a job.

"The goddess will not be supporting a pig," she added.

TRACY MORGAN

2007

Days before I was to do this interview Tracy Morgan was arrested for driving under the influence. It made some headlines, but I thought readers would rather hear more about a performer's experience in Emmy-winning television shows than in a courtroom. At the end of the conversation, he thanked me for being "a gentleman."

***

Tracy Morgan has done it all: movies, television and stand-up but he doesn't have a favorite.

"I love it, " he said. "It's all show business."

Morgan is a busy performer. He currently co-stars in the NBC sitcom *30 Rock* and was recently seen in the films *Little Man* and *Totally Awesome*. He also has provided voices for the up-coming film *Farce of the Penguins* and for the MTV series *Where My Dogs At.*

He appeared on *Saturday Night Live* (SNL) from 1996 to 2003 when he left to star in his own sit-com.

During his long stint on SNL, Morgan became well known for character that included "Brian Fellow, the host of "Safari Planet," and space adventurer "Astronaut Jones" as well as impersonating people such as Mike Tyson, Busta Rhymes, Maya Angelou and Samuel L. Jackson.

Acting on *30 Rock* is a change for Morgan after years of appearing before a live audience. He explained the show is filmed with a single camera, like a movie, and that a person has to have confidence in what they are doing since there is no audience to affirm whether or not they are being funny.

The new assignment has meant a shift in his schedule: no more late nights.

Unlike many stand-up comedians who have a love-hate relationship with television, Morgan said he loves it.

"It's a personal medium," he explained. "You can reach out and touch people."

He was an active writer on SNL, and still has a hand in what happens to his character on *30 Rock.*

"I helped develop the character," he said. "I let the writers know what he's thinking and who he is."

30 Rock is about the back-stage happenings at a SNL-like television show. His character, also named "Tracy," is a star on the fictional show.

"The guy's unstable," Morgan said. "He's an international superstar and a sweetheart, but when he's off his meds he's 'coo-coo for Cocoa Puffs.'"

Morgan said he has known some people like his character, but didn't base him on anyone specific.

Morgan said that comedy was part of his childhood.

"My uncle, father and all of my mother's family were funny," he said.

Growing up his comic heroes included Jackie Gleason, Redd Foxx, Lucile Ball and Carol Burnett. Martin Lawrence was also an influence on him as well as Chris Rock and Adam Sandler.

What's it like working with the people one admires?

"One word explains it: heaven," Morgan replied.

CHARLIE MURPHY

2007

There's plenty of acting siblings in show business today, including the Wayans, the Baldwins, the Cusacks, and the Gyllenhaals, and now the Murphys.

Only the prominence Charlie Murphy has seen in show business thanks to his appearances on *Chappelle's Show* hasn't been due to his famous brother Eddie, but to his own hard work.

And it hasn't come overnight, but after years of working in the industry.

Murphy has had small parts in big movies such the recent hit *Night at the Museum*," larger roles in low budget films, written scripts, performed voice-overs for animation and taken a stand-up act around the country.

He said that his career has been the result of "happy accidents."

"I've worked for it for 17 years," he said.

Charlie is the older brother of the two and started working in the industry first. His resemblance to his brother has actually been a hindrance as some casting directors used it as an excuse not to hire him. They didn't want people to think they hired an Eddie Murphy ringer, he explained.

"I had to force my way in," he added.

He was asked to try stand-up and despite his brother's reputation Charlie called Eddie "one of the last true kings of the game" he "summoned the cajones to show up."

He remembered the first time on stage was not as scary as every time since.

"The first time I had nothing to lose," he said. "Now every time you go out, you've got to deliver."

He loves the medium, though. Stand-up, he said, is "the most free" a performer can be.

"It's your thoughts, your creation," he said. "It means more because it's all you."

Although a large part of his act is

Charlie Murphy

improvisation, Murphy is constantly thinking of gags and routines.

"Twenty-four hours a day even when I sleep that light is on," he said.

Murphy said that being a stand-up comedian is like being a boxer and one has to train all year-round, not just before a big fight.

He has been busy with a number of film projects but he is especially excited about *The Perfect Holiday*. Gabrielle Union and Queen Latifah star in the holiday release about a young woman finding true love.

Murphy has a role, which "allowed me to breathe in the movie."

"A whole lot of range was shown," he said. "I'm not bragging."

DOM IRRERA

2007

Veteran comedian and actor Dom Irrera is looking forward to performing in Western Massachusetts again.

"I have friends in Springfield," Irrera said.

The Philadelphia native began his career in 1980 acting and performing stand-up and improvisational comedy. His big breaks came in 1986 when he appeared on *The Tonight Show Starring Johnny Carson,* and in 1987 when he was part of the line-up for an HBO Rodney Dangerfield comedy special.

Since then, Irrera has been nominated six times for an American Comedy Award and won two Cable ACE awards. Besides a string of comedy specials, Irrera's comedy series on sports, *Offsides,* was seen for four seasons on Comedy Central and he has appeared in numerous guest spots on television sitcoms.

Irrera is well known for his Italian ethnic humor, which comes naturally as he grew up in a three-generational Italian household.

"I always felt I was going to be a comedian," he said,

His favorite comic has been Woody Allen. Irrera has long admired Allen's writing style, although it hasn't influenced his own comedy that much.

He noted that no one has ever come up to him after a performance and said, "Man did you rip off Woody Allen with that goomba act of yours."

Ethnic humor has both its advantages and disadvantages, he said. If you stick to ethnic humor, you tend to maintain a core fan base, he explained.

A comic can broaden his or her base by performing less ethnically oriented material, Irrera said. He recalled meeting the son of the late comic and actor Red Buttons after a performance who told him his father wanted to talk with him. Irrera called him and Buttons said, "Don't paint yourself into a corner with that goomba act. Don't be an Italian comedian, be a comedian who happens to be Italian."

Irrera took the advice to heart, but he still does some Italian humor. "It does leave a lot of the audience out, especially the Persians," he added.

Irrera has built up a side career as a voice artist for animation. He is currently recording the voice of Duke the Dog for the up-coming series based on the animated feature *Barnyard.*

He has also performed voices on *Hey Arnold, Hercules,* and *Dr. Katz, Professional Therapist.*

He and his fellow cast members are given a script to perform, but are allowed to improvise, which is a lot of fun for Irrera.

Irrera has also appeared in a number of movies, the best known might be his funny bit as a chauffeur in *The Big Lebowski.* Irrera said he is a big fan of the Coen brothers who wrote and directed the shaggy dog tale starring Jeff Bridges and had no idea they had attended one of his performances.

A script came in the mail with a notation the Coens wanted him to play the role and Irrera was amazed to see they had used lines from his stand-up performance for the character.

He had no idea the film would achieve cult status and admitted the first time he saw it he didn't care for it. By the second viewing, though, he was a fan.

Irrera has had plenty of television experience on sitcoms, but he's in no rush to try to get his own.

"Beware of what you wish for," he said. "It's [sitcom work] a drag compared to stand-up."

Irrera isn't a snob. He readily admitted that he would accept a starring sitcom role if offered. "I'm not willing to go around pitching and pitching [a show]."

After more than 25 years in the business, Irrera stills enjoys the "immediate gratification" one gets from performing stand-up comedy.

WENDY LEIBMAN

2006

Wendy Leibman thinks her appearance in the film *The Aristocrats* and a recent appearance on *The Tonight Show with Jay Leno* "solidifies everything together" in her comedy career.

The woman who has the stealth delivery – her punch lines come in under the radar – said that she has known Penn Gillette, half of Penn and Teller, for years, and was among the first comics filmed for *The Aristocrats* four years ago.

The movie became an art house hit last year. The premise is having a lengthy list of comics recite their version of what has been dubbed in comedy circles as the world's dirtiest joke. The participants also discuss the nature of dirty jokes and free speech issues.

"I was honored to be part of comedy history," Leibman said. "I made myself laugh when I saw it."

Leibman said she is looking forward to a return to Massachusetts – "I have a fan in Chicopee" – and this is her eleventh year appearing in Massachusetts near Valentine's Day.

"I better start loving myself," she quipped. "That's one of my goals for 2006 loving myself and going shopping."

Leibman also hopes to record a comedy album shortly.

Although she had appeared on *The Tonight Show starring Johnny Carson*, Leibman said that the Leno appearance in January "made me feel bona fide. Jay could not have been nicer. It was really great."

She admitted to being a little nervous as she was on the same show as the American Idol judges, but she said they were all "sweet," and the infamous Simon Cowell was the nicest.

Although she said "that ship has sailed" when asked about starring in her own television series, Leibman and her husband, Jeffrey Sherman, have written and directed a short film which they hope to sell as a series. Sherman wrote the television movies *Au Pair* and *Au Pair II* and was a writer on the sitcom *Boy Meets World*.

The film stars Larisa Oleynik, a busy young actress perhaps best known for her Nickelodeon series *The Secret World of Alex Mack*.

If the film sells, Leibman will be wearing a new show business hat producer. In the meantime, though, she's looking forward to returning to the stage.

CARLOS ALAZRAQUI

2006

The deputies of *Reno 911!* are back – on television and on DVD.

The fourth season of the popular comic police show has started on

Comedy Central and the third season has just been released to DVD in a two-disc set.

If you've not seen the show, it's a clever and raucous parody of FOX's *Cops*. Set in Reno, documentary cameras follow around a group of sheriff deputies during both their professional and personal lives.

Led by the hot pants-wearing Lt. Jim Dangle (Thomas Lennon), the Reno squad includes the in- your -face Deputy Raineesha Williams (Niecy Nash), the flack-vest wearing Deputy Travis Junior (Robert Ben Garant), the deeply disturbed Deputy Trudy Weigel (Kerri Kenny), the amorous Deputy Clementine Johnson (Wendi McLendon-Covey)and ladies' man Deputy S. Jones (Cedric Yarbrough), the seasoned vet and bigot Deputy James Garcia (Carlos Alazraqui) and the rookie Deputy Cheresa Kimball (Mary Birdsong).

Very politically incorrect, *Reno 911* is a show that constantly surprises and sometimes shocks. Viewers are never quite sure how far a gag will be taken. One episode in the third season DVD, Dangle and Junior go undercover at a spa to follow a suspect there for a massage. The suspect takes off in his car and Dangle and Junior rush out of the door of the spa in hot pursuit with only their socks and shoes on. The spa locks its doors behind them and they have to make their way back eight miles to the station house.

The third season opens with episodes that show how the group got kicked off the force, served time in jail and then resumed their lives, but as civilians. There is some funny stuff here, especially with Dangle trying out for *American Idol* and Jones and Garcia relishing their new lives as mall cops.

The third season set also features two groups of extended outtakes, which show how the cast crafts the scene through trial and error. The cast provides commentaries on several episodes, which gives insight into the creative process.

What makes *Reno 911* unique in American television is that it's a sit-com that is almost all improvised. After four seasons cast member Carlos Alazraqui said in an interview that the cast is now a lot better at the acting challenge than during the show's first season.

He attributed the early success of the show to "dumb luck."

He explained how the show is shot. The cast is given a general description of a scene and then rehearses a short length of time developing some of the dialogue. If the director likes the lines, they start filming. Alazraqui estimated that the actors improvise 70 percent of the show.

The show is not shot in Reno, Alazraqui explained. It's filmed in the greater Los Angeles area. The sheriff's station is a real police station in Carson, Calif., and Alazraqui said the officers generally support the show.

"Ninety-five percent really love it," Alazraqui said.

He added that one officer in particular makes an effort to help them out by telling them about real life incidents that could be used for the comedy. He has told the cast that some of their antics are reflections of what has happened to cops in real life.

Alazraqui's character is frequently paired off with Yarbrough's Jones and that was because the two actors hit it off in the pilot. Alazraqui said the producers liked the physical contrast between the men as well as the fact that Garcia was an unapologetic bigot.

Alazraqui added, "The whole staff is racially prejudiced."

Alazraqui comes to the show from a stand-up comedy background and

Carlos Alazraqui in character as Deputy Garcia in "Reno 911!"

from a very active career as a voice artist in animation. If you've watched Nickelodeon in the past few years, you've heard him on shows such as *The Fairly Odd Parents* (as the evil Mr. Crocker), *Camp Lazlo* (Lazlo and Clem) and *Rocko's Modern Life* (as Rocko).

Rocko was his first animated role and he is again working with Rocko creator Joe Murray on his new show *Camp Lazlo*.

"I've come full circle with 'Camp Lazlo,'" he said.

You also heard him as the voice of the Taco Bell Chihuahua, a commercial campaign that is still remembered six years after it ended.

"That was a bizarre thing to land," Alazraqui said.

He's a cast member of the new animated film *Happy Feet* due for release in November, and plays a Latino penguin named Nestor. The voice cast also includes Robin Williams.

That feature film release will be following in January 2007 with the premiere of *Reno 911!: Miami.* Alazraqui explained that in the movie the Reno deputies travel to Miami to attend a law enforcement convention in Miami. They lack the proper credentials and are not allowed in.

But when a biohazard forces the quarantine of the officers in the convention hall, the Reno deputies take to the streets of Miami to keep the peace.

The film was shot in the same improv style, although Alazraqui said the cast had to pay much closer attention to creating dialogue and situation that matched the movie's plot.

Alazraqui still performs stand-up and he said he favors no one aspect of his career.

"It's so relative to the situation," he explained. "There is nothing like the live response [to stand-up] when they love you. I get paid to do goofy voices. That's another high."

"The benefits of a multi-pronged career is that I get to do different jobs," he said.

SOMMORE

2006

Sommore never thought she could do stand-up comedy despite her love for it.

Twelve years after she read a book on the subject and tried out on stage, she has appeared as one of the *Queens of Comedy,* been called "a force to be reckoned with in the new millennium" by Oprah Winfrey and won the Richard Pryor Comic of the Year Award.

Sommore said that after some initial efforts during open mic nights, she received her real training as comic as the emcee for a male strip revue. She recalled with a laugh that she had to appear before "300 women who weren't interested in anything I said."

Week after week though, she would try out material and include it in her 20-minute set until people started coming early just to see her.

She said her comedy is based on observation.

"I listen, I watch everything," she said.

And Joan Rivers and her aggressive say-anything style of comedy inspired her.

Unlike Rivers, whose stand-up included some severe self-deprecation, Sommore said that women comics who are attractive "have a fine line to walk."

The wrong choice of outfit could inspire remarks from male members of an audience that could make the female members a little upset, she said.

"I point out my flaws first," she said.

Women comics today still fight a battle about whether or not they are as funny as male comedians. Sommore recalled how she and other women would be introduced at open mic nights with an admonition that the audiences should go easy on them.

That's one reason she, Adele Givens, Laura Hayes and Mo'Nique toured as *The Queens of Comedy* in 2001 she wanted to show that women comics are the equals of men.

Sommore said she appreciates both working live on stage performing stand-up and acting in a sit-com or movie. She's appeared on *The Hughleys* and *The Parkers* and in the movies *Soul Plane* and *Friday After Next.*

She'd like to have a television comedy of her own and shot a pilot that wasn't successful. She added that she draws inspiration from the fact that Dave Chappelle had 13 pilots before having success with his Comedy Central show.

She said the challenge is to find a format to present "my voice, my true voice."

"It's not easy to do," she added.

She said it's frustrating as a comedian who writes her own material to perform a script that is supposedly funny, but isn't.

She also noted that success on television could come with a big paycheck that can be accompanied with a loss of creative freedom.

"Me, I'll take the money," she said with a hearty laugh.

Sommore is known for a hold-no-prisoners humor and said she "makes a distinct choice about the style I'm going to do.

"I curse to make a point, to enhance a joke," she said and added that she hosted an entire season of BET's *Comic View* show without using any questionable language.

What she likes to present is "the real raw truth."

"Sometimes we need a little severity," she said. "Life isn't all peaches and cream."

JOHN MELENDEZ

2006

John Melendez has a list of his greatest hits, but none of them involve music.

The Howard Stern alumni, who spent much of his 15 years with the "King of All Media" ambushing celebrities with outrageous questions, recalled how Raquel Welch punched him in the nose and how Sharon Stone's bodyguard "laid him out." Joan Rivers insulted his looks, but Melendez thought she was funny.

These days, though, Melendez doesn't have to worry about dodging punches. As the announcer on *The Tonight Show with Jay Leno,* Melendez gets to act in comedy sketches and go on the street as a correspondent.

Now he is touring as a stand-up comic.

He has been performing comedy for the last four years, something he has wanted to do since he was a child watching *The Carol Burnett Show* and *Saturday Night Live.*

Yet what held him back was being "terrified of getting on stage and bombing." That fear abated when Melendez realized his gig with Howard Stern required considerable courage and that he "had the nerves to ask a celebrity about bowel movements."

He has been writing jokes for years and has "always wanted to do [stand-up comedy.]"

Through therapy, Melendez has overcome his stutter and had to prove to NBC executives that he could do the announcing chores on *The Tonight Show* without a hitch. He was first offered a job as a correspondent on the show after he had completed his appearance in the reality show *I'm a Celebrity Get Me Out of Here.* He recalled lying on his cot and fantasizing about being on *The Tonight Show.*

Much to his amazement, when he returned from the show, there was an offer for him. He had to turn it down as he was "getting crap from Stern about being gone too long."

A second offer was also turned down, but Melendez accepted the third and last offer.

"It was time for me to go," he said. "There were no hard feelings. It was the right move to make."

He said that being on *The Tonight Show* is the "complete opposite of the show I was on before."

Melendez had started with Stern as an intern and spent 15 years on the show. He said he enjoyed doing the hit and run interviews of celebrities, although there came a point when many of his interview subjects played along with the gag, rather than be insulted.

"It was less interesting," he said.

He recalled disguising himself in order to catch people off guard, but he was still recognized.

Melendez said he had both "good times and bad times" on the Stern show and he was invited to be on the last broadcast before Stern made his move to satellite radio. He didn't attend because of a scheduling problem.

RALPHIE MAY

2006

For Ralphie May, it didn't matter that he didn't win the first season of *Last Comic Standing*. He said that his loss only made his fans "more vehement."

"They've stuck with me for 17 years," he said.

May has become well known through his appearances on *Last Comic Standing, The Late Late Show with Craig Kilborn, Jimmy Kimmell Liv* and *The Tonight Show with Jay Leno.*

May has recently released his second CD *Girth of the Nation,* which is also the subject of a special for Comedy Central.

May started his career in comedy at age 17 and recalled how he had to have his mother bring him to some of his appearances because he was too young to be in a bar by himself.

"It was an adventure," he said.

He said that it has taken him 14 years to make a living as a comic and the relatives who told him he should have gone to college aren't telling him that anymore.

At 17, he won a talent show that gave him a chance to open for the late Sam Kinison.

"He was a heck of a guy," May recalled. "He was very nice to me and showed me there are no boundaries [in comedy]."

May isn't concerned about boundaries and freedom of speech.

"I slam everybody," he said. "I have a major problem with political correctness."

May is concerned about the fallout from the highly publicized incident concerning the language used by actor Michael Richards in a stand-up performance.

"He's our Janet Jackson", he said, referring to the controversy over Jackson's Superbowl half-time performance that resulted in a Federal Communication Commission's crackdown on broadcasting standards.

Richards, he emphasized, is not a stand-up comedian, but rather "a crazy homeless man with money."

He also was critical of the Rev. Jesse Jackson becoming involved in the Richards issue. He said Jackson has been silent on the slow re-building of New Orleans after Hurricane Katrina and the erosion of voting rights of African-Americans.

He said that some people might believe that comedy "can't offend anyone, but comedy has always been about offending someone."

May said that like other stand-ups comics he wouldn't mind doing a situation comedy, but that it would have to be "really good, like 'Everybody Loves Raymond,' or 'Seinfeld,' or 'The Honeymooners.'"

He said he and his wife, fellow comic Lahna Turner, had considered starring in a reality show about their lives on the road. Besides *Last Comic Standing,* May has appeared on another reality show, *Celebrity Fit Club.*

He said ultimately he and his wife rejected the ideas because every couple that has had such a show has broken up and that he doesn't want to lose his wife "because she married me when I was fatter, broke and not famous at all."

"I'm extremely lucky," he added.

PAULA POUNDSTONE

2007

During a telephone interview there are the sounds of vacuuming and children in the background, but that's typical for working mother and comedian Paula Poundstone.

Poundstone, named one of the 100 greatest stars of comedy by Comedy Central, balances a performing career and being a mother of three children.

She is also a regular on *Wait! Wait! Don't Tell Me,* the weekly news quiz show heard on National Public Radio. When asked if she prepares for the show that will test her knowledge of the week's events she said, "Sadly, I do cram. But it does no good."

She didn't audition for the program, but was asked by the producers and has appeared for the past six years. Originally, she would go to a local NPR in Los Angeles and be connected electronically to her fellow contestants and host Peter Sagal. But now the show is taped live either on the road or in a theater in Chicago and Poundstone said, "It's definitely better."

"Before I was a ball player in a batting cage," she said. She added she likes actually seeing her fellow cast members.

The live tapings mean travel, though, and Poundstone said it can be difficult being both a parent and a touring comedian. Generally, she tries to be away from her home and family only an average of eight days a month.

And when she is home she focuses on her family duties.

"When I'm home, I'm really home," she explained.

Poundstone started her comedy career at age 19 in 1979 performing in Boston. She said she had no responsibilities at that age and "rode the wave of that time" a time that she called a "renaissance of stand-up comedy."

She said she had "no particular skill or talent" but was in "the right time and the right place."

"I went around the country learning and having fun, when it was fun," she said.

She credits Robin Williams for attracting attention to the new generation of comics and for allowing random thoughts and non-sequiturs to be part of the new comedy landscape.

Although her act is not known for profanity or adult material, Poundstone said "the stupidest thing" for a comic to worry about today is language.

"My goal is to entertain people. I don't want to say things that are mean," she said.

She added she doesn't deliberately want to insult people and that words are not as important as intent.

She admitted she is not as in tune with changes in stand-up comedy as some of her colleagues because many of her performances are at theaters rather than nightclubs. The advantage, she said, is that people really want to be at her shows and they're not drinking.

Today, there are fewer venues for aspiring comedians. She said that a recent club appearance she noticed several young comics who drove an hour and a half just to be able to appear a few minutes at an open mic night. She explained that in the 1980s and '90s, in a city such as San Francisco, she could do three open mics during one evening.

When asked if she had pursued the sitcom career route as so many other comics had done, Poundstone said with a laugh that she hadn't rejected sitcoms, they rejected her.

She said that her efforts to develop a sitcom hadn't made it as far as being a pilot. She said that when she first started exploring a career in television she didn't understand the language used by television executives.

This was apparent on the ABC variety show she did in 1993 that lasted three episodes. She recalled networks officials using phrase such as "We'll leave you alone." "We'll give you time to develop." and "We want something different."

She thought the show was an interesting experience that presented some "really great ideas."

She realized that there are "only a handful of people lucky enough [that] when an executive said those words they mean something."

After her cancellation she had lunch with another ABC executive who was interested in having Poundstone host a daytime program. She recalled she was uncertain over whether or not that would be a good move for her until the exec said, "We'll leave you alone."

"I've had a lot of good lunches out of show business," she said with a laugh, although she added she no longer discusses businesses over a meal.

Network execs aside, Poundstone said, "I love my job. I'm the luckiest comic in the world."

DAMON WAYANS

2007

So why is the star of the successful ABC sit-com *My Wife and Kids* as well as an alumnus of *In Living Color* and *Saturday Night Live* and the star or co-star in a dozen movies touring the country performing stand-up in small clubs?

Damon Wayans laughed and said, "I'm still in shock why I'm doing this."

He quickly explained, though, that of all of the things he has done in show business from acting to writing to directing nothing "gives me the same joy" as performing live and alone on stage.

He said there is no better way to test your skills and timing as a comedian than performing live.

His fame doesn't allow him to coast.

"You have a grace period of about five minutes. If you're not funny, they start yelling at you," he said. "You constantly have to prove yourself."

He said the stand-up tour was a "tune-up" for a television special he will be shooting. When asked what network it will be on, Wayans laughed, and said, "Whoever spends the most money."

Wayans is well known for pushing the comedy envelope. He recently was banned from The Laugh Factory in Los Angeles for three months for repeating the "n-word" on stage.

Wayans said that he apologizes to his audiences up-front.

"I will offend you tonight," he said.

For him, comedians are "the voice of the people."

"If you stop comedians from telling a joke, you stop the masses from expressing their point of view," he said.

Weighing in on the firing of Don Imus for saying "nappy headed hos" on his radio show, Wayans said that Imus shouldn't have been dismissed. He said he thought Imus was "speaking-matter-of-factly. I didn't feel any malice. He was trying to be cool."

Commenting on the love-hate relationship many comics have when they land a television sit-com, Wayans pulled no punches. "I love the money and I hate everything else."

Wayans is currently working on launching his own web site, www.wayouttv.com, which will feature new comedy shows designed for Internet audiences. He said he doesn't understand why the television networks aren't designing new programs for a web-based audience instead of developing new shows.

His site should be up June 1 and will feature a sketch comedy troupe. If a character does well, Wayans hopes to launch more shows.

Movies hold little interest for Wayans right now. He said unless you have written the film and "want to protect the baby," being an actor for hire isn't appealing.

"I don't want to play the third lead in a Charlie Sheen movie, if you know what I mean," Wayans said laughing. "That's nothing against Charlie Sheen."

He said he makes sure to connect with an audience on their terms. He doesn't get on stage and talk about his life as a star.

"I talk about stuff they can relate to," he said.

He knows that some fans have misconceptions about the life of a person in show business.

Believe or not he said, he does not spend every day waking up with four women in bed, followed by his butler delivering breakfast, then spending all day hanging with other celebrities and ending it with five women.

"Well, not every day," he added.

Instead he'll wake up at 3 a.m. with ideas that he is compelled to write down.

"I work hard. My brain is calloused," he said.

He said the people he knows who excel in their field are the ones who work the hardest.

He said his friend, basketball great Michael Jordan, was the first one in the gym and the last one to leave.

LARRY MILLER

2008

Comedian, actor and writer Larry Miller had a job the day he spoke with me: he was to provide the voice for a French-Canadian goose in the upcoming animated film *Alpha & Omega.*

The assignment was an example of Miller's far-reaching career in show business. He has been a top stand-up comedian for years, but he has been a busy character actor as well. His on-camera roles have been in such movies as *Pretty Woman* as the salesman who "sucks up" to Richard Gere and Julia Roberts; the two *Nutty Professor* movies in which he played the exasperated college dean; and the two *Princess Diaries* films.

He has worked in animated productions such as *Bee Movie,* and in one of this writer's favorite animated series, *Dilbert,* in which he was the evil pointy-haired boss.

Ask Miller what he likes to do best, though, and he says "all of it."

He considers himself like baseball great Lou Gehrig, "the luckiest man in the world," although after a beat Miller added, "Well, that didn't work out, come to think of it."

Miller attended Amherst College and after graduation in 1975, he said he decided he wanted to do "something as an entertainer." His subsequent career has been "frankly astonishing" to him. He started performing stand-up comedy in the mid-1970s in New York City where his friends included Jerry Seinfeld and Jay Leno.

"I should be horsewhipped if I wanted to change something," he said. "What a joy it is."

Despite over 20 years in show business, Miller is still thrilled by it.

"I had an acting job last week. I was thrilled to be on the set. I waved at the tour buses in Universal [when they passed the set]. I wanted to say to them 'I know why you're on that bus. I'd be on it, too.' It's cool."

Miller became well known for his routine called *The Five Stages of Drunkenness,* and he said that he might include it as part of his current act, which mostly will be new material. He admitted that while excessive drinking and its effects are "horrifying," he does find humor in it.

He said he tries to "write all the time." Miller has written a book titled *Spoiled Rotten America,* as well as opinion pieces for the "Huffington Post" on the Internet and the "Weekly Standard."

Writing for a stand-up routine is different than longer forms, he said, likening comedy writing to a still: "One drop comes out every 10 seconds." He said a friend of his said a good comic should put in an hour a day. And if you put in two hours, "you're really going to be a good comic, a monster."

He views himself as a professional who can follow a director's requests on a set or in a recording booth but also bring his own skills as a writer to a production.

The difference between theater, the movies and television is that theater is the actor's medium, while film is the medium for directors and television is controlled by the writer/producer, Miller said

Larry Miller

"Each captain is different and I follow what the captain wants," he explained.

He did say that being in a recording studio for five hours portraying a goose could be a little taxing.

"It's not tarring roofs, but I can get a little dizzy," he said.

2012

Larry Miller is a guy with a lot going on. He's not complaining, though. He loves it.

The stand-up comedian, actor and writer recently finished a role in a film, writes and records a weekly podcast and is a doting father. He has developed the creative vehicle that intrigues him perhaps more than any other of his show business endeavors: a one-man show.

Cocktails with Larry Miller: Little League, Adultery and Other Bad Ideas is coming to CityStage from March 21 through 24.

Miller said his one-man show "is something I will do the rest of my life."

He explained that while being alone on stage is nothing new for a veteran stand-up comic, "a one man show is different than stand-up. There are pieces [in it] that wouldn't function as stand-up."

The show combines several of Miller's interests: comedy, acting and music. He was a music major at Amherst College and the show features several original songs he has written as well as several parody songs.

His acting roles started with a smarmy salesman in *Pretty Woman,* and have included additional movies such as *The Princess Diaries, The Nutty Professor, Best in Show* and *The Mighty Wind* On television, he's had dramatic assignments such as an unrepentant wife killer on *Law & Order.*

Miller explained that having acted on stage, he knows that "once a play gets locked, even if it's a great play, it's locked in. You don't feel the need to grow."

Cocktails, though, allows him the ability to alter the material as he sees fit.

"I expect to live another 300 to 400 years and will continue to work on it," he quipped.

He added, "Walking out on stage and doing a lighting check [for 'Cocktails'], now that's a good place to be."

Miller said that he recently completed a role in a new film by director Michael Polish – best known for the film *The Astronaut Farmer* – and the day after he wrapped his footage he was performing *Cocktails* in Stowe, Vt. He then brought the show to a theater in Queens, N.Y.

He likes having a varied career like that, but he corrects this reporter when the word "fallback" is used to describe *Cocktails.*

"It's not a fallback," Miller said. "It's a fall-forward."

When asked about his writing regime, Miller said with his trademark timing "I'm desperately scratching for more time."

He said when he hears about an author going "to a cabin in the woods for a year and half to write," his reply is "Who does that?"

Miller explained he got up at 6 a.m. on the day of this interview so he could get an hour to write before he woke up his wife and children. Once breakfast, making lunches for his children and getting them to school was completed, Miller said he had the "great luxury" of writing from 9 a.m. to noon, although he said this time was punctuated by answering emails and taking phone calls.

"I'm not complaining. I love every minute of it," he added.

He also loves recording his weekly podcast, *This Week with Larry Miller,* which is available on iTunes. "There are no guests. It's just me telling stories," Miller explained.

He said he usually writes down 10 subjects and manages to talks about two of them in the half-hour recording.

Speaking of his career he said, "I was made to do this. I'm a story teller."

LAVELL CRAWFORD

2008

Lavell Crawford said that as a child he wanted to be a superhero specifically, Spiderman.

"There were plenty of spiders in my basement, but none of them were radioactive," he recalled with a laugh.

His career goals changed, though, when he listened to a Richard Pryor album for the first time.

"I thought it was incredible," he said.

Television audiences will recognize him from appearances on *The Tom Joyner Show, Steve Harvey's Big Time, BET's Comic View* and from the most recent season of *Last Comic Standing,* where he came in second in the comedy competition.

Crawford has been very busy with his first Comedy Central special debuting on Feb. 22 as well as the release of his CD *Takin' a Fat Break.* He also recently appeared on the cable television special, *Martin Lawrence Presents the First Amendment.*

When he spoke with me he was waiting for the limousine to arrive to bring him to a taping of Chelsea Handler's talk show, *Chelsea Lately.*

While in college his interest in comedy was strengthened when he saw Sinbad perform live. At first, Crawford thought his road as a performer was as a rapper, but he noticed that his rhymes were comedic and making people laugh.

Crawford said he was lucky to break into the industry in the early 1990s when comedy was booming. It took him five months of calling a local comedy club before they would give him a slot on an open mic night, but he was persistent.

"It was calling me," he said.

Crawford said that appearing on *Last Comic Standing* was a mixed blessing. He wanted to be in the final five comics because of the exposure it would give him, but the actual competition itself "was really bogus." The comics never learned of the percentages of audience approval.

"Television is a strange animal," he said. He noted that he and the other comics had to re-write their material to make sure it met the network's rules, but that dramatic shows are held to a different standard.

Crawford said the show was a "learning experience" for him and proved worth it as he is booked through December. He added that if the producers had wanted a more authentic reality show, they should have put the comics on the road and sent a camera crew to document them.

"They try to control it on television, but you can't control it on the road," he said. "Make it on the road, that's where all the drama starts."

The comic never censors himself, but his comedy is not laden with curses, the "n-word" or sexual references.

"I don't go overboard," he said.

Crawford would like to do everything in show business. He has written scripts; he is currently promoting and would like to get more acting roles.

Although Crawford formally writes his act, he said, "The stage is my notebook."

"I've written more jokes on stage than off," he said. He explained that he edits material as he works, subtracting and adding to a gag or routine depending upon the audience.

And Crawford explained how a comic has to be ready to exploit whatever happens before an audience. He explained that the Comedy Connection in Boston doesn't have a step onto the stage. The club was packed and Crawford said he was so excited he missed the stage and "fell on my face."

He didn't let that stop him once he was on stage; he did 40 minutes on his accident.

BOB MARLEY

2009

Bob Marley leads two lives. After touring comedy clubs for years, recording CDs and DVDs and making dozens of appearances on televisions shows, he has built a huge fan base for his comedy.

Marley, though, has other fans – people who know him from his supporting role in the cult classic movie *Boondock Saints* as the hapless Boston detective who is plagued by an FBI agent played by Willem Dafoe.

Now Marley fans will get a double scoop of the versatile performer this month. He will be touring comedy clubs and will be seen in *Boondock Saints: All Saints Day,* the sequel to the film, when it opens at the end of the month.

The Maine native spoke from his tour and said he was "really excited" about the release of the new film.

Marley started performing while in college in Maine. He then spent two years in Boston and then 11 years in Los Angeles. He moved back to his native Maine four years ago. He and his wife wanted their three children raised in their home state.

While his Maine accent emerges as he speaks faster during his act – confounding many non-New England audiences a bit – his humor is not based on region as much as it is a "fish out of water."

He observed to audiences in Los Angeles "there are more lanes on the highways here than in the bowling alley back home."

Although he never imagined himself as a comic who wrote material about his family, he said he now writes about his wife, his kids, his parents and himself.

He said that what he likes about New England is that despite differences in dialect, region or economic standing, the people all do about the same things: root for the Red Sox and Patriots, vacation at the beach and go to their mother's for supper.

He said that one audience member met him after a show in Denver and asked him, "Where are you from?" He called his Maine accent "a slow, dumbed-down version of a Boston accent, but not as angry."

Marley got the role of Det. Greenly in *Boondock Saints* through a friend of his who was in turn friends with Troy Duffy, the writer and director of the film. Marley read the script, was impressed and learned the lines for Greenly. He didn't hear anything more for three months and then was asked to audition at the director's home.

He impressed Duffy by performing the monologue he has at the beginning of the film from memory. He recalled Duffy saying, "Yup, you're the guy."

Marley had acted in some independent films, but never one with as big a budget as *Boondock Saints* or with a cast that included such veteran performers as Dafoe, Sean Patrick Flannery and the legendary Scottish comedian and actor Billy Connolly.

He said that while filming the first film in 1999 the cast "didn't have a full grasp on how big it was going to be."

Marley also praised Dafoe, the star of the first film, who he said could do a take nine times and in nine different ways.

Although the theatrical release of the film was marred by studio politics, the film attracted an appreciative audience through home video and Marley said the number of fans he's met over the years wearing "Saints" T-shirts and tattoos has amazed him.

With the second film, his character has more screen time and more back-story and while he enjoyed making the sequel – "We had a blast" – there was some pressure.

"All you thought about were the fans. You didn't want to let them down," he said.

As a comedian, Marley was impressed that Connolly was watching him work and becoming his friend.

Marley recounted, "I thought, 'There is no way Billy Connolly is standing in front of me and praising me.'"

He called Connolly "the salt of the earth" and "just humble" and recalled how the two couldn't make eye contact during a climatic barroom shoot-out scene. The set had been wired with hundreds of explosive squibs to simulate gunshots and both men were worried they would start laughing during the take causing the crew to re-wire the squibs.

"We would have been in big trouble," he said.

He was allowed to adlib some in the film and he said that acting in a dramatic part has less pressure because "you're not getting a laugh out of it."

Marley doesn't think of himself as an actor, though.

He described himself as "a guy who is in some movies."

BILL COSBY

2009

Bill Cosby has a reputation of being generous and cordial to people he likes and not so friendly to people who offend him. I was actually pretty nervous when I spoke to him, as I didn't want to say the wrong thing. His publicist told me when to call and when I asked how long I had, he replied, "You'll know when you're done."

Yikes!

Cosby scheduled the interview for 8:30 in the morning and he picked up promptly. When I told him I was a life-long fan of his – the truth as my parents played his comedy records – he told me the interview would go smoothly because of that. And it did.

The conversation went well but at one point it sounded like it was winding down. I said, "Well, Dr. Cosby, thanks for taking the time to speak with me." He replied, "What, I'm not done, you people from East Longmeadow are trying to rush me."

East Longmeadow, Massachusetts, is the home of the newspaper company for which I work and I told him in mock indignation I live in Springfield. Cosby has undertaken several charitable efforts in Springfield and he liked my comeback.

I actually got a laugh from him when he asked me if I had ever seen him on the University of Massachusetts campus in the 1970s when we were both there.

I said, "Dr. Cosby, I put you in the same category as the Loch Ness Monster and Big Foot. I believed you existed even though I never saw you."

Getting a laugh from one of the most influential comedians of the 20th Century? That made my day.

***

Since 1963 Bill Cosby has been making people laugh and the iconic comedian said that he has no intention of stopping anytime soon.

The most famous resident of Western Massachusetts will be appearing for two shows at Springfield's Symphony Hall on Oct. 16. Although known more in recent years as a social commentator and author, Cosby is dedicated to comedy.

His appearances here are part of a lengthy touring schedule that brings him from California to Massachusetts to Florida and Canada.

"I've been doing this [comedy] since 1963. That when I made the commitment," he said in an early morning telephone interview from his home in Shelburne. "It's important that this mind think things and I write them down and I can't help it."

"My wife says I'm being beamed," he added with a chuckle.

The man whose show business career has included Grammy-winning comedy albums, many successful television series and movies, as well as being a highly influential stand-up comedian, said his path toward being a comic came out of education.

He explained that he was "born again" when attending college not renewing his Christian faith, but rather "in terms of accepting education, of wanting it."

While at Temple University, he said he became serious about writing and read extensively. He also began listening to comedy albums and studied comedians such as Jonathan Winters, Elaine May and Mike Nichols, Shelly Berman and Don Adams.

It was while listening to the Mel Brooks and Carl Reiner album *The 2,000 Year Old Man* that Cosby said he realized, "you don't have to have a joke."

The story and the delivery were more important. He began to write and enjoyed it.

He said that while in his freshman remedial English class, the professor assigned the student to write about a first time experience. The class was full of members of the football team and Cosby said, "The football players wrote about their first touchdown, but I got beamed."

He wrote about the first time he pulled out a tooth as a child.

"There were no computers just a number two pencil and a legal pad," he said. "I had so much fun and I just wrote and wrote and wrote."

He found that he didn't mind revising his work.

"When you're born again, you don't mind going over it," he explained.

In his junior year of college, he said he "began to see things differently," and thought he could sell what he was writing.

In the early 1960s there were no clubs dedicated to comedy as there are today, and Cosby said he went around the nightclubs of Philadelphia. He explained the clubs would feature a singer and a comedian and he would try to sell his work to the comics, but no one bought any of his stories.

"One fellow read it and said, 'This is not funny.' I started to perform for him and he said, 'It's still not funny,'" Cosby recalled.

The manager of the Gilded Cage nightclub finally gave Cosby the chance to perform for 15 minutes.

"There were seven people in the room and they were spread out three, two and two," Cosby said.

The manager didn't care for his act, although the audience laughed and Cosby lost hope momentarily. "That night I took those pages and I threw them down the sewer, but when I woke up I was right back at them," he said.

Cosby said his career started taking off, though, with appearances in clubs in New York City. In 1963 he made his first comedy album, *Bill Cosby is a Very Funny Fellow, Right!* and was booked onto *The Tonight Show*.

He said his career was like a slide one could do on a kitchen floor wet with soap and water.

"There was no long suffering," he said.

After all these years of performing, Cosby said, "I still have those thoughts. I'm still being beamed. I still have things to say."

Cosby said that his material today provides a "night of comfort."

"I put a chair on the stage, I sit and talk and tell a story," he said, resulting in the audience and himself "feeling comfortable."

And now Cosby will enter a unique group that recognizes his contributions to American humor. On Oct. 26 he will be receiving the Mark Twain Prize for American Humor presented by The Kennedy Center.

The Twain Prize has been awarded for the past 11 years – Cosby will the twelfth recipient – and, according to the Kennedy Center Web site, "recognizes people who have had an impact on American society in ways similar to the distinguished 19th century novelist and essayist best known as Mark Twain. As a social commentator, satirist and creator of characters, Samuel Clemens was a fearless observer of society, who startled many while delighting and informing many more with his uncompromising perspective of social injustice and personal folly."

Although this description certainly fits Cosby's many accomplishments, the entertainer said that he had turned down the award three times.

He explained he had heard about the first award presentation for Richard Pryor in 1998 and that some of the young comedians who had been asked to perform in Pryor's honor had used profanity and the "n word" in their routines. Ironically Pryor had long stopped using the "n word" in his performances.

"There were many people there who were from the civil rights movement," Cosby said. "It was disgraceful and embarrassing. When they came to me I told them no."

Cosby is a 1998 recipient of the Kennedy Center Honors and said, "I was a friend of Teddy's. I met Bobby and I was a friend of Ethel's."

Cosby only consented to the award once he sat with the producer of the show who assured him he could approve the guests.

"As you know," he recalled talking to the Kennedy Center officials, "I want [my award] to represent who I am and the style, that would be jazz."

Acclaimed saxophonist Jimmy Heath will be among the guests as will be jazz great Wynton Marsalis.

Cosby said he wanted specific people to appear, such as Len Chandler, the folk singer and civil rights advocate who introduced Cosby as a young comic to Bob Dylan, when he was beginning his career.

Not only does the Twain prize's connection to the Kennedy family have meaning for Cosby, but Twain and his works do as well.

"Our mother read Mark Twain to us," Cosby said. For him and his brother James – who died at age six – Twain's works were a regular part of their childhood.

He said that Twain's importance rests in part in his style.

"You could finish fifth grade and the only thing keeping you from reading Twain's essay is the subject matter."

He called the recognition "wonderful."

TOM GREEN

2010

If you think of outrageous when you think of comedian Tom Green, you would be right. Green came to prominence with a program on MTV that emphasized a willingness to do almost anything to himself or his sidekicks for laughs – or shock.

Talking to Green reveals another side to the guy willing to put live mice in his mouth for an audience's amusement. He's a performer who is very serious about developing his stand-up act.

MTV picked Green up for his first show in 1999, after the performer had starred and produced his own show for the Canadian Broadcast Corporation, which was based on his long-running homemade show seen on cable access.

The success of the first MTV show led to subsequent shows and specials on the network as well as a string of movies, including the infamous *Freddy Got Fingered,* which Green directed and co-wrote.

Having started performing stand-up at age 15, Green has returned to the comedy format and has been touring for the past two years.

"I always wanted to do it again," he said of stand-up. Green stopped performing when he started his cable access television show.

He added he enjoys the writing process of developing jokes and stories.

"The real fun I have is crafting a joke with a lot of structure, but make them look unstructured," he explained.

Green does improvise on stage as well and uses stand-up for the expression of opinions on social issues.

After working on mainstream television and movies, Green appreciates the one-man quality of stand-up.

"What I love about stand-up is the complete freedom. There are no rules there," he said.

"With the television shows, we were challenging ourselves to smash the rules each week into smithereens," Green said.

Green was raised in the culture of skateboard and said that was the inspiration for the crazy physical stunts seen on his show. When asked if his show inspired MTV's *Jackass,* he said, "People ask me that [all the] time. I tell them to drawn their own conclusion."

While Green doesn't think MTV copied him, he said he has been told by *Jackass* cast members, such as Steve O, that they were inspired by him.

Green's success also led to movie roles in a number of films as well as his star turn in *Freddy Got Fingered,* a film that is now considered a cult movie.

He said that acting in someone else's film "takes a lot of pressure off" him and he "doesn't necessarily have to always do everything."

He currently has several film ideas in development, including one he calls *Insane Prank Movie.*

Green has the reputation of pushing boundaries and he did that with his Internet-based talk and variety show that ran from 2006 to this year. Green was a pioneer in using the Internet as a way to broadcast a television show, which he jokingly called *Web-o-Vision.*

He said he enjoyed the show and would do it again, despite the fact that he made just enough money on the show to cover the costs.

"It was a fairly elaborate show," he noted, which was broadcast weeknights over Livestream and then archived.

"I've always been aware of technology and curious how to apply it to make funny comedy," Green said.

He stopped the production of the show to go on tour and devote himself to stand-up. Green recently did a 12-day appearance as part of the acclaimed Edinburgh Fringe Festival, which was well received.

One unidentified reviewer wrote on www.edinburghspotlight.com, "His insanely genius 'shock humor' is what helped Tom shoot to fame and it's something he fortunately hasn't let go of. Loosely based on the story of his life, Tom doesn't hold back. He's incredibly open and honest about elements of his past making the show much more than just hilarious antics."

GABRIEL IGLESIAS

2010

Comic Gabriel Iglesias has a slightly different writing regimen than other comedians. Rather than sit down at a computer and write jokes, Iglesias said his material comes to him from just living life.

"I live it and then exaggerate it," he said.

Iglesias is one of the rising stars of comedy, with successful tours and several comedy concert DVDs to his credit.

Gabriel Inglesias

He is also one of the hardest working comics around and is on the road 45 weeks of the year.

Known for his Hawaiian shirts and expressive voices, Iglesias' routine on the six stages of being fat – *Big, Healthy, Husky, Fluffy, Damn! and Oh Hell No!* – has not only given him a comic niche unto himself but created a cottage industry.

Calling himself "fluffy," Iglesias has capitalized on his success with a host of "fluffy" products on his Web sites, www.fluffyguy.com and www.fluffyshop.com. He sells tee shirts and outerwear for men, women and babies with messages such as *Real Men Have Stretch Marks.*

Iglesias said his clothing line came out of a frustration over not finding clothes he liked – sizes on his site go up to five extra-large – and became one of the companies he set up. He also produced his first two comedy specials and has produced and set up distribution for his comedy DVDs.

"At the end of the day, I own everything [about his comedy]," he said.

He said his trademark stories, such as being pulled over by a police officer and having his friend complicate the situation, are true. The actions of his friend, comic Felipe Esparza, make up a lot of his act, he explained.

Esparza is currently one of the contestants on *Last Comic Standing,* and Iglesias said, "You can't miss this guy. He looks like a terrorist."

One might think that Iglesias is on the route to television sitcom and movie stardom, but those are not things he's pursuing.

"I got into comedy to do comedy," he explained. To do a sitcom, it would have to be the "perfect circumstances," he added.

"I wouldn't want it to fail," he said.

He has been asked to audition for movie roles as well, but passed those by due to his touring schedule.

He admitted that one of the roadblocks to making the break to other comic media is the difficulty driving around Los Angeles, where he lives.

"I hate traffic," he said. "I don't cuss, but get me in traffic and wow!"

He missed doing a guest shot on a sitcom because he didn't want to deal with the traffic.

He has done some voice acting for animation, which he does like.

"You walk in and they hand you two pages [to perform]. You're done in a day and then checks show up at your doorstep. It's beautiful!" he said.

He enjoys the freedom stand-up brings him.

While he wouldn't call his show "family friendly," Iglesias said his comedy is cleaner than most.

"At the beginning I was really, really dirty and I was told if I worked clean I'd have more opportunity. People said I have a real likable stage presence," he said.

He cautioned that some profanity might be heard, but not much.

"When I'm doing stand-up I'm the director, the producer and the writer," he explained.

JOHN KAWIE

2010

Sometimes clichés aren't trite and John Kawie has indeed made lemonade out of the lemons life has handed to him.

In 1997, the Springfield, Massachusetts, native had successfully made a difficult career transition. After almost a decade of hard work, he had left his role as a business owner and become an in-demand stand-up comedian.

A week after his wedding, Kawie faced the aftermath of something he never anticipated: a devastating stroke at age 47.

Kawie's journey through his recovery is presented in his one-man show, *Brain Freeze,* which has just been released on DVD.

Although a long time resident of New York City, Kawie, who grew up in the Hungry Hill section of Springfield, has family and friends here.

He recalled fondly going to Springfield Indians matches at the Coliseum and Giants games at Pynchon Park while growing up.

Even though he successfully headed the business founded by his father, Kawie said, "My first love was to make people laugh." When someone approached him to buy the business, Kawie saw this as his opportunity to follow his dream.

He took a course on writing humor, which culminated with a performance at a Connecticut comedy club.

"I had a great set and I loved it," he recalled. He was hooked.

"If you follow what your heart tells you to, doors will open," he asserted.

He decided to move to New York City and pursue a career as a comic. "I was broke, but I was working," he said.

Kawie explained that in the late 1980s during the boom of stand-up comedy, there were a lot of clubs in New York City, but not all of them paid. Many club owners considered giving stage time to a new comic to be enough compensation.

Kawie noted with appreciation the owner of the Improvisation as someone who would regularly give the comics at least a token payment that could pay for carfare.

To help make ends meet, Kawie landed a job at a Gap store as a clerk, while seeking time on stages at clubs. He said there is a difference between staying in New York City to work as opposed to touring. Comics watch each other in New York City and tend to write better. On the road, he explained, comics learn they can be sloppier with their performances.

Kawie was seen as an up and comer, opening for comics such as Dennis Miller and Howie Mandel. He had his own special on Comedy Central and he developed a unique niche as the country's first Arab-American comedian.

He became a writer and performer on *The David Brenner Radio Show* and wrote for Bill Maher's monologue on Comedy Central's *Politically Incorrect*. He also was a substitute host for Dick Cavett on his radio talk show and he wrote for Dennis Miller's show on HBO.

He recalled with a smile fellow comics, such as Dave Attell and Sam Kinison, who encouraged him.

"Life was good," he said.

One week after his own wedding, he and his wife Marilyn attended the wedding of a friend. The next day, Kawie didn't feel just right, but he chalked it up to a mild hangover. When he realized that his condition far exceeded his initial reaction, he was taken to a hospital.

He had had a stroke and he thought at the time he would be released the next day.

Instead, he spent months in hospitals and rehabilitation clinics regaining his abilities. He admitted, "My memory was shot."

His left arm was paralyzed and he had difficulty walking.

His outpatient therapy years were "the dark period of my life," he said.

Participating in group therapy, Kawie began to tell a joke each session as a way to work his way back. He started writing again and thought about a project.

Kawie's comic idol was Richard Pryor. He explained there are several schools of comedy. Comedians such as Jerry Seinfeld offer observations, while some such as Pryor deal in telling truths about themselves and society.

Before his stroke, Kawie had become interested in the monologues of Spalding Grey and Eric Bogosian and Kawie began to think about turning his experience into a one-man play.

His acting coach helped him for six months, writing and honing what would become *Brain Freeze.* He had trouble memorizing his work and would listen to a recording of it over and over to learn it. Memorization didn't help the comic timing he needed and he had to learn where to pause.

He said that those around him always encouraged his effort.

"I always got green lights. "I didn't get red light," he said.

Kawie started performing his show at hospitals and rehab centers to others facing the same challenges he faced. The reaction was so positive, he started performing in "off off Broadway" theaters.

He expanded his writing activities by writing a column, *Life at the Curb,* for the American Heart Association's magazine, *Stroke Connection.*

A performance in 2003 at the New York Fringe Festival led to an award, "Best Solo Show," and to glowing reviews in the New York Times and the New York Daily News.

He acquired an agent and took the show all over the nation.

In the show, Kawie speaks about dealing with the aftermath of his stroke from using a plethora of Post-it Notes to trying to button his overcoat with one hand.

While at his 40th high school reunion at Williston Academy, Kawie met a fellow alumnus who heads PARMA Recordings.

"That's how the DVD was born," he said,

Kawie said the release of the DVD will "get it out there to rehab centers I couldn't go to."

He intends to continue touring with the show, but will do far less traveling. He is now thinking about a book on his experiences. He admitted that he "sometimes" misses performing stand-up, but sometimes not.

"It's a grueling lifestyle," he said.

He wouldn't want to be a young comic starting these days. He noted that some club owners are concerned about political correctness in comedy.

"It's better when you let the comic go, let him fly," he said.

To learn more about *Brain Freeze,* visit its Facebook page or go to www.amazon.com/John-Kawie-Brain-Freeze/dp/B0040Y7EP6

BEN BAILEY

2011

Think driving a cab in New York City is a challenge? Imagine conducting a television game show while negotiating Manhattan traffic.

That's the job of Ben Bailey, the stand-up comic and actor who is the host and star of "*Cash Cab*," the Emmy-awarding winning game show.

Bailey readily admitted that driving a cab and hosting a television show was "tough at the beginning." He started the "*Cash Cab*" job in 2005.

"It's still tough," he said. He added that as he doesn't concentrate on any one of his tasks listening to the producers of the show feed him questions to ask through an earpiece, driving the cab and interacting with his guests – he does alright.

"It's sort of a Zen thing," he said.

Bailey has never had an accident, despite his multi-tasking.

In "*Cash Cab*," unsuspecting people seeking a cab get into Bailey's taxi, only to find out they are on a quiz show and their ride, if their answers are right, could pay off in hundreds of dollars.

If their answers are wrong – all it takes are three bad ones – they are back out on the street.

Bailey said the show seemed "pretty ridiculous on paper" when he auditioned for it. Originally, the producers had thought a New York cabbie would be the host, but soon realized they needed someone who could improvise and had a comic background.

He had an edge over some of the other comics, as he had already spent years as a limousine and delivery driver. To get the job, though, he had to pass the test for his taxi license, which Bailey took quite seriously.

"I was studying for a couple of weeks," he said. "I had a lot in the balance."

He was offered a pre-test, which if he passed would allow him to skip the class for the test and he had to answer the question of which bridge he would use to drive someone from 161st Street to Yankee Stadium.

The question stumped him and he was shocked to see a list of bridges in the city with names he didn't recognize.

Bailey fell into stand-up in an accidental way. He described himself as a "wise ass" in school, who enjoyed making his fellow students laugh. He aspired to be an actor and moved to California to pursue a career. He worked in hotels while trying to get a break.

He was talking to a fellow New Jersey transplant in the parking lot of the Comedy Store one night in Los Angeles where he was offered a job answering the club's phones.

Bailey watched some of the comics from the wings, thinking he could be funnier and after telling stories to other comics while they waited to perform, landed a spot on a show.

He also acted in television series such as *Law and Order Special Victim's Unit, One Life to Live* and *Hope and Faith.*

When asked which performing venue he prefers, he replied, "None of them are easy. All of them are difficult."

He added, "All are very hard, but I get a lot of enjoyment out of all of them. Stand-up is great because you get immediate feedback. The show is great because you can meet people."

Bailey has thought about starring in a sit-com and has developed several ideas. "I've been too busy to pitch them," he said.

He added the television networks really seek out reality show concepts because they are less expensive to produce and he isn't interested in doing that kind of show.

He has a busy tour schedule as a stand-up and he said with a laugh of his writing process, "For me, the jokes just fall out of the sky."

When an idea hits him, he hurriedly writes it down.

"I grab a napkin, toilet paper, a paper towel," he said.

Naturally the ideas don't spring forth finished and Bailey said that writing and perfecting new additions to his act "is as much fun as performance."

His comedic style is to tell stories with multiple punch lines along the way to the conclusion.

"I milk it," he said.

He clears the schedule for "*Cash Cab,*" though. When the producers call, Bailey sets aside eight weeks once or twice a year to shoot footage for what will become 40 new shows.

Despite the show's popularity, at first people would ask, "What on earth is this?" Bailey recalled not everybody wanting to play. He said that on one day's shooting, it took six stops before he could find someone to play the game.

CASSANDRA PETERSON

2011

In the mid 1980s when I was a radio talk show host I did a truly awful interview with Cassandra Peterson. Before the segment her publicist came on to tell me two things: I wasn't interviewing Peterson, but her fictional character and I couldn't talk about her age. Needless to say I was supposed to perform improv for 10 minutes with her since I couldn't do a real interview and I sucked.

Fast-forward more than 25 years and I'm interviewing her again, only this time I talking to the actress and not the character. The interview went so well that at the end I told her the story of our first conversation and she laughed.

She explained that she was trying to emulate her friend Paul Rubens, who as Pee-wee Herman, never broke character in interviews.

Journalistic tip: It's never fun to interview a fictional person.

***

Before *Mystery Science Theater 3000,* before *Riff Tax,* before *Cinema Titanic,* Cassandra Peterson was making fun of movies as Elvira, Mistress of the Dark.

She said in contrast to the members of those other comic groups she had "two big things working for me [dramatic pause] — my personality and my talent."

"I'm the queen of subtlety," she said with a laugh.

Peterson has brought her show *Movie Macabre* back to television in syndication and two of the new shows are now on DVD.

Each DVD has a double feature. The first is *Night of the Living Dead* with *I Eat Your Skin* – which Peterson quickly noted has nothing to do with eating someone's skin – while the second has Sir Christopher Lee's last appearance as Dracula in *The Satanic Rites of Dracula* paired with *The Werewolf of Washington.*

The new shows are funny and clever with Elvira not only poking fun at the movies – of the four only *Night of the Living Dead* is really any good – but also setting up comic bits.

Peterson, an actress who was a member of the famed Los Angeles-based improvisational troupe, The Groundlings, auditioned to be a local horror film host on a TV station in 1981. Her success in the regional market led to a syndication deal where *Movie Macabre* was seen all over the country.

Her character took on a life of its own and became a cottage industry inspiring two movies, many guest appearances on television shows and a lot of merchandise. Although she has done other roles than Elvira, Peterson is at peace with the character that took over her career.

"I was very angry," she said with a laugh. "I wanted to do Shakespeare in the Park."

She said she did have some reservations in the beginning, but realized as she landed roles on pilots for television shows she had a decision to make: work all season long in a show being paid the minimum union scale or work in October and make a year's worth of money.

Peterson owns the rights to the character and controls what she does with it.

"It's like running a company and I'm the CEO," she explained.

The down side is that because a show business corporation doesn't own her character, Elvira doesn't have the support that other characters receive.

Peterson said she "wades" through horror films in the public domain to select ones she thinks have potential for the show. Then she and her writing partner Ted Biaselli watch the film over and over – as many as four or five times – to come up with a theme for the Elvira segments and the "pop-ins" in which Elvira appears at the corner of the screen with a quip as the film is running.

She said her training in improvisational humor helps her with the writing.

She has made 20 shows for syndication and six more that will be DVD exclusives.

Peterson continues to make public appearances at various pop culture conventions and is impressed with the stories her fans tell her.

She recalled that people have come up to her teary-eyed because they watched her show as a child with a now departed parent. Many young women have told her they saw Elvira as a strong powerful woman and she was a role model.

Other fans have recalled how they had one of her posters up in their room.

"I think I helped them through puberty," she laughed.

Considering this has become a career for her, it is lucky for her own sanity that she is actually a horror movie fan.

"Totally, totally," she said. "I wouldn't have gone to the audition if I hadn't."

She quickly noted she likes "the old bad ones that are unintentionally funny," and isn't a fan of the new breed of slasher movies.

Peterson said that as a child her favorite film was the Vincent Price classic *House on Haunted Hill* and she loved the movies Price made with director Roger Corman based on the stories of Edgar Allan Poe.

She said that while other girls were interested in playing with Barbie, she was assembling plastic monster models.

"I was a pretty odd girl, but it paid off," she said.

To learn more about her show and the DVDs, log onto www.elvira.com or become her friend on her Facebook page at Elvira Mistress of the Dark (Official).

KEVIN MacDONALD & SCOTT THOMPSON

2011

It's not the easiest thing to laugh and take notes and that was the primary challenge in speaking with Kevin McDonald and Scott Thompson, two of the members of the legendary comedy troupe, *The Kids in the Hall.*

This reporter recently conducted two separate telephone interviews with the comedians and actors and that was a blessing. If they had been on the line at the same time, I would have been unable to take clear notes.

At the same time both men were refreshingly candid about a career in show business.

McDonald and Thompson have been appearing together in a stand-up act across the country.

On the show, McDonald played a number of crazy or naïve women as well as his unforgettable role as "King of Empty Promises," while Thompson broke new comedy ground with his monologues as Buddy Cole.

The Kids in the Hall television series ran from 1988 to 1995 and has been re-run since as well as collected recently on DVD. Since then, both men have been busy with a variety of projects and appearances as well as taking part in several reunion projects with fellow *Kids* Mark McKinney, Bruce McCullough and Dave Foley, the most recent being *Death Comes to Town* in 2008.

McDonald, for instance, has made a mark as a voice actor in animated productions that include *Invader Zim, Lilo and Stitch* and *Catscratch.* He likes it, even though he has no creative power.

"It's tiring," he explained. "I scream all day because my characters always fall a lot."

He noted with a little apprehension that he met a voice actor who "did me better than me."

McDonald recently made the move from Los Angeles to Winnipeg, Canada, because of a new relationship. He explained he initially made the move from Canada because "I have to go out and keep reminding people about me; reminding them about *The Kids in the Hall* and ask them for money."

Performing in the reunion tours with the rest of the group "seemed like old times," he said.

The Kids in the Hall were often noted for their performance in female roles and the steps they took to look like women. Playing in drag today means "certainly a lot more makeup," McDonald said.

One of the aspects of *The Kids in the Hall* television show that continues to impress is the edgy innovative quality of the writing. McDonald said the members used to write the television shows by bringing ideas together to McCullough's apartment and acting them out over and over. Since then with the advent of the personal computer, the team has broken up into smaller writing groups.

He said that the "hardest thing" the group ever wrote was their feature film *Brain Candy*.

"We couldn't turn a page [in the script] until everyone agreed," McDonald remembered.

He said each of the tours featured new material and that while in the writing process it seemed like "no time had passed."

McCullough was in charge of the most recent *Kids* production, the mini-series *Death Comes to Town* and McDonald said the problem the *Kids* has always had is writing longer pieces than skits.

McDonald is new to stand-up but enjoys it and is happy to be on the road with his friend.

"Kevin and I are such good friends," Thompson said. Neither man wanted to tour alone and the two decided to make a two-year commitment to a stand-up gig.

McDonald said that although part of his stand-up show is scripted, there is also room for improvisation. Thompson explained the two men do a separate set and then come together for a set.

If you're hoping to see a reprise of well-known characters or skits, you won't find them at this show, Thompson said.

He said at the beginning of the tour, they tried to do some of their well-known characters, but "we dumped them."

"It's easier [to do the tour] without a bag of wigs," he said.

Thompson was one of the first openly gay performers on television and his signature character was Buddy Cole, the acerbic barfly always holding a martini and ready with a piercing remark.

Cole was Thompson's stand-up voice for years and Thompson envisioned bringing Cole back as the star of a new show in which Buddy is undertaking a tour of Africa and the Middle East.

Thompson, along with *Kids* writer Paul Bellini, even wrote a Buddy Cole book titled *Buddy Babylon: The Autobiography of Buddy Cole.*

One can tell there is more than a little of Cole in Thompson. When I opened the interview with the admission I'm a big fan of the *Kids,* he said that would make things easier.

"The last [interviewer] was a petulant asshole and he stayed one through the interview," he said.

Thompson has also been busy since the *Kids* left the airwaves. He's had prominent roles in television series such as *The Larry Sanders Show* and *Providence,* as well as other shows.

He said he is "thrilled" to be on stage and performing stand-up, noting that much of the material is about his life.

"Stand-up is so pure," he said. "It's just you and a mic. You're like a gunslinger."

Although he improvises on stage, he sticks to the material he developed and said with a hearty laugh, "The show is filthy – really, really dirty."

Thompson is also honest about the tour and about the nature of show business and in a moment of candor, he said he needs the money from the stand-up tour.

"I've not had the most illustrious post-*Kids* career," he said. He views himself as a comic actor and writer who would be "very, very happy with different character roles."

He noted, that unlike shows such as *Saturday Night Live,* there was no "break-out" member of the troupe, with the possible exception of Foley, who landed the starring role on *News Radio.*

He said that McKinney and McCullough gravitated to "behind the camera."

Thompson had been vocal in the past about the depiction of gays on television and in film and the straight actors who get the parts. He said things have "come a million miles" since he raged against how Tom Hanks played a gay man dying of AIDS in the film *Philadelphia.*

He said he watched the sitcom *Glee* and was amazed by the gay character on it.

"I'm more philosophical about that now," he said. "I kind of forgive."

He said one observer wrote of *The Kids* that watching them performing one could tell that they loved one another.

"That's the secret," he said. *The Kids in the Hall,* that's our secret – a 'bromance.'"

THE AMAZING JOHNATHAN

2012

The Amazing Johnathan is known for his combination of comedy, interaction with audience members and magic, but according to the popular performer he is not a magician.

"I'm definitely a comedian," he said.

"I quit doing magic the night of my high school talent show," he recalled. "All six tricks went bad."

He accidentally killed a bird on stage and when his female assistant, who was in a box for another illusion, developed a leg cramp, she stood up knocking the box apart.

"It was so bad that the next day nobody teased me," Johnathan said.

But out of that terrible experience eventually came the seed for an act that he has performed for more than 20 years.

Johnathan moved to San Francisco, California, as a young man and saw street performers such as Harry Anderson, later the star of *Night Court* and *Dave's World,* and A. Whitney Brown, who was a writer on *Saturday Night Live.*

Johnathan wanted to be a street performer as well and they "taught me the ropes." He developed the persona of a slightly aggressive and definitely unpredictable magician whose tricks don't always amaze.

His performance at comedy clubs outside of Las Vegas is a relative rarity as Johnathan had essentially stopped touring for years. He said that he accepted a two-week fill-in job at the Sahara Hotel and casino while comic David Brenner was away. In 2008, he took his show to The Harmon Theater, next to Planet Hollywood. Twelve years later he is still in Las Vegas.

The job does have its advantages, he noted. It came along as he was getting tired of touring and he could drive to his job.

"I like driving to work, I leave my house at 8:45 p.m. [for a 9 p.m.] show and I get back home at 11:30 p.m.," he said.

But the experiences that can be found at smaller nightclubs across the country have been calling to Johnathan. He said that thanks to the recession the audiences at his show and others have declined significantly.

"So, I'm back on the road to get some energy from audiences," he said.

In smaller clubs, Johnathan takes the opportunity of developing new material. About half of his show is planned and the other half is ad lib – "to make it fun for myself."

Johnathan has been frequently seen on Comedy Central and that exposure is "really, really important," he said. The cable channel has repeated his comedy special.

"When I come up with new material Comedy Central gives me a special," he explained.

Normally, an hour of solid new material takes him between six and seven years to develop, but right now he is operating under a three-month deadline.

"It's really hard," he said. "You're tempted to coast on your re-runs. It really helps to have new material."

The comic has entered into a new venture: a practical joke set that will be sold by Spencer's Gifts and Toys R Us. The set has props for a number of gags to pull on friends as well as a DVD with even more suggestions.

"It's pretty cool," he said. One gag is a device that buzzes like a mosquito when the lights are off. When the unsuspecting victim turns on the lights to swat the bug the sound turns off.

He is known for his own elaborate practical jokes, one of which involved sending a friend notification of a fake job and having the person board a plane.

"My friends are very, very leery," he said.

Although other stand-up comics have used their acts as the basis of a television sit-com, Johnathan said, "I never wanted to be an actor."

Although he has done some acting, he further admitted, "It was never really appealing to me."

A game show he hosted for the late Merv Griffin was fun, but "that wasn't really acting."

"With a name like 'The Amazing Johnathan,' what am I going to do?" he asked.

JOAN RIVERS

2012

One of the most fearless caustic comics in the business, Joan Rivers was one of the most down-to-earth and nice people to whom I've spoken.

***

Joan Rivers is in a state of motion, which appears to be, looking at her schedule on her website, a typical status for her.

"We're going through a tunnel. But if we get cut off, I'll call you right back," she promised.

As I spoke to her on April 10, she told me she was in a car heading to New Jersey, where she appeared on QVC promoting her successful line of women's fashion accessories.

Then on April 11, she flew to California to prepare for the taping of her hit E! show, *Fashion Police.* She taped the show on April 12 and later that day appeared with fellow comic legend Don Rickles at a casino. Then she was back on the East Coast for a succession of appearances in New York, Pennsylvania and Vermont before heading back to the West Coast.

Whew.

One of her stops will be at Worcester's Hanover Theater for the Performing Arts on May 22 for her show *My Life in Show Business: 135 Years and Counting.*

How does she do it? At age 79, why does she do it?

Rivers said that she must have Attention Deficit Disorder.

"I get very bored. I like conquering mountains," she said. When confronted with a new project her reaction is, "OK, of course we can do it."

"Conquering mountains" has been standard operating procedure for Rivers for all of her career.

A Phi Beta Kappa graduate of Barnard College, Rivers did aspire to do something inconceivable for a woman in the early 1960s: become a comic. She worked for seven years before receiving her big break in 1968 when Johnny Carson gave her a guest shot on *The Tonight Show.*

"And it was amazing," she recalled of the experience. It came after "seven years of struggle."

Eventually, she would become Carson's permanent substitute, have her own late night show on FOX and win an Emmy for her daytime talk show *The Joan Rivers Show*.

In 1990, Rivers started her highly successful fashion business on QVC. Her business acumen was put to the test on *Celebrity Apprentice* in 2009, which she won.

She carved out another niche when she started interviewing people at red carpet events such as the Oscars and has written and performed in well-received one-woman theatrical events.

Her stints at red carpet events led to her commenting on fashion, which has in turn produced *Fashion Police*.

"I've got to say the truth," she said of the show during which she leads a discussion of the fashions celebrities have worn at recent events.

A New Yorker, Rivers said that she flies to Los Angeles every Wednesday to prepare for the show, which takes about 10 hours. Her daughter Melissa is the executive producer and assembles the photos Rivers and her co-hosts – Giuliana Rancic, George Kotsiopoulos and Kelly Osbourne – will use.

Then Rivers spends time with writers, but she added, "The best stuff comes off my head."

Viewers of the show know that Rivers adopts a take-no-prisoners attitude when discussing fashion. When asked if someone who has received a critique from her has ever confronted her, she replied, "As I always say, if you're getting $20 million a movie, what do you care if I don't like your dress?"

Rivers is involved in another television show with her daughter called *Joan and Melissa,* on WE, a reality show on their relationship, that is heading into its third season.

Does Rivers have a favorite activity or project of everything that she has done and is currently doing?

"Right now," she said. "I love being in the present tense."

She added, "I'm having a great time. What has kept me floating is every aspect [of my career], writing, performing."

Rivers is willing to laugh at herself — a comedic trademark — over the one project that didn't turn out so well, her film *Rabbit Test.*

She co-wrote and directed the 1978 comedy in which Billy Crystal becomes the world's first man to give birth. The film was not well received when it was released and Rivers said, "We finally got our first good review 30 years later."

The fact someone has called it "a classic" elicits a hearty laugh from Rivers.

A film fan, Rivers said she didn't like directing because "I don't have an eye for the camera." She is proud, though, that she was the first to bring Crystal to the big screen.

Rivers has also written a series of books, two of which include *Men Are Stupid and They Like Big Boobs: A Woman's Guide to Beauty Through Plastic Surgery* and *Murder at the Academy Awards: A Red Carpet Murder Mystery*. She has a new book coming out June 6 titled, *I Hate Everybody*.

In edgy humor typical for Rivers, she dedicated the book to O.J. Simpson.

"I just sat down and wrote about everything that annoys me," she said.

After a singular career in show business, Rivers said she doesn't compare herself to other people. "A friend of mine in the Mafia said something very smart: 'Don't look right. Don't look left. Look straight ahead.' I look at my life that way," she explained.

Would she ever retire? "I don't play cards and I hate old people," she said with a laugh.

"Life is an adventure and if you don't go through the door, you're an idiot," she added.

ROB SCHNEIDER

2012

Rob Schneider is more than a successful comedian. Speak to him for just a few minutes and you realize he is a true historian of comedy.

Among Schneider's credits are films such as *Deuce Bigalow: Male Gigolo, Deuce Bigalow: European Gigolo, The Hot Chick, The Animal, You Don't Mess With The Zohan, The Benchwarmers, 50 First Dates* and *The Longest Yard*.

Schneider explained that he has been doing more stand-up comedy in the last few years in part because the late George Carlin inspired him. Schneider started out as a stand-up comic, but said, "I never got to the place where I thought my stand-up was great. I never conquered it."

When he saw Chris Rock perform, he decided to get back on the road.

"It feels good," he said, but readily admitted that traveling was tiring.

He said the difference is now – since there has been a 20-year gap in performing live – "I feel I can take the audience further and talk about things that interest me."

Schneider also enjoys the freedom of performing live on stage, a freedom that he didn't find during his recent television series, *Rob*. A mid-season replacement series, *Rob* was based on one part of Schneider's life: his marriage to Mexican television producer Patricia Azarcoya Arce.

Although the show attracted 11 million viewers a week, it was cancelled.

Like all television shows, network execs tried to tweak the comedy.

"It's frustrating to get notes from people who don't know as much about comedy as you do," Schneider said.

He is philosophical about the cancellation, though.

"It's their money, it's their stage. You're just renting it," he said.

The show did give him the opportunity to work with one of his comedic heroes, Cheech Marin. Half of the legendary comedy team of Cheech and Chong, Schneider remembered the joy he had as a child listening to their comedy albums. Marin, he added, has "a lot of charisma and is very funny."

Marin, Schneider explained, like many successful comic performers has been typecast.

"Very few people can break [a typecast]," Schneider said. "You're stuck, but it's a good stuck. At least you're being cast."

Despite his less than pleasant experience with a television series, Schneider is looking at another potential show; this one based on a hit Australian series called *Mother and Son*. The premise is about a man who cares for his aging mother who may or may not be suffering with dementia.

Some of Schneider's film work has been in starring roles, while others have been co-starring. In *Judge Dredd*, Schneider's character did a spot-on impersonation of Sylvester Stallone to the action star's face and Schneider recalled Stallone telling him, "You better be funny or you're dead."

His association and friendship with Adam Sandler has been without any death threats.

"Adam just gives me the opportunity of playing different ethnic guys," Schneider said.

Currently Schneider is working on an animated feature, *Norm of the North*, playing a polar bear named Norm. He is enjoying the work as he said it allows him to "really create."

Ron Schneider

Since he and his wife are recent parents, he is interested in finding work such as this assignment that keeps him closer to home.

Schneider believes that there is a renaissance of comedy going on today and has a theory that when the economy has its problems, the arts flourish. He noted that after WWII, Great Britain was having problems returning to its pre-war conditions.

"There was a feeling things were not going to get better for the English," he said.

In reaction to what was happening, came the very successful comedies starring Sir Alec Guinness from the Ealing Studio, Schneider noted. Post-war Great Britain gave birth to Monty Python, which Schneider said "was the high water mark for comedy in the 20th century."

Schneider sees performers such as Louis C.K. as part of that renaissance born out of our own problems.

He said that he would like to produce a television series on the history of comedy. Considering his busy personal and professional schedule, Schneider added, "Eventually."

BILL MAHER

2013

Bill Maher is arguably one of the best known comics in this country as he and his guests on HBO's *Real Time with Bill Maher* have made headlines for their remarks.

But for Maher, performing his brand of politically-tinged stand-up is still his first love.

"It's the longest and most successful relationship in my life," he said with a laugh.

Stand-up for Maher is an insurance policy for his career. "At some point, TV puts you out to pasture," he said.

Maher explained that other comics might seek "evergreen" material for their acts but he enjoys providing commentary on current events.

"The act is always fresh to me and fresh to the audience," he said. "It's a lot of work to keep up with the act, but that's what the plane is for."

Maher's comments on *Real Time* have been known to raise the hackles of some viewers, especially conservative ones, but he doesn't worry too much about hostile audiences.

"Those people don't come to the show," he said.

Maher has played in "red" states such as Alaska, Alabama and Arkansas but said, "It doesn't matter. The more redneck, the better the audience."

He explained that liberals "are marbled into the population."

Although Maher attracts between four million and five million viewers each week to his HBO show, he wouldn't undertake a "stadium" tour as other comics have attempted.

"To play theaters of 2,000 to 3,000 [seats] – that's as good as it gets," he said. "Comedy should be intimate. It's not for arenas."

When performing live, Maher is listening to how the audience reacts and explained, "Every laugh has information attached to it."

Because of this interaction, Maher said, "No two shows are alike."

Maher became known to many people due to the success of his television show *Politically Incorrect,* which ran on Comedy Central and then ABC from 1993 to 2002. The premise of the weeknight program was to assemble four celebrities to speak about the affairs of the day.

Maher compared that show to his current one by using a sports analogy: "'Real Time' is like football – we only have one shot on Sunday and we better get it right – while 'Politically Incorrect' is more like baseball."

Politically Incorrect was not as "polished," as his current program, which started in 2003 and he said the challenge is to put together a panel of "smart people" viewers want to see.

"There are not that many [smart] celebrities," he added.

One would think that one show of *Real Time* versus producing a nightly *Politically Incorrect* would be easy, but that would be wrong.

"It's so much work," Maher admitted. "It's counter-intuitive that with a show that's once a week that you would work more, but that the nature of the beast. This show kicks my ass."

He gladly works hard as he "wants it to be so good."

Maher views *Real Time* as a "digest of what's happening [in news] in an entertaining way."

Politically Incorrect broke a key television rule about talk shows, Maher said. Due to the successful template established by Johnny Carson on *The Tonight Show,* the unwritten commandment was "never let the audience know your politics."

The reasoning, he explained, was that a host would alienate about half his or her audience.

That show worked because "the powers that be underestimated the audience," Maher said.

Speaking of the most recent news, Maher said, "The Republicans are the gift that keep on giving."

He added that he had donated to President Barack Obama's campaign, but that in hindsight perhaps he should give to the Republicans.

"I'm so grateful I found this niche," he said.

DAVID ALAN GRIER

2002

For David Alan Grier, performing stand-up is the busy comic and actor's chance to "reconnect with audiences."

Grier has a far more diverse career than many of his comedy colleagues. Fans of the star of the television series *In Living Color,* and movies such as *Jumanji, Blankman* and *Boomerang,* probably don't realize that Grier is a classically trained actor.

Grier earned his Master's Degree from the Yale School of Drama and feels equally at ease performing Shakespeare as he does stand-up.

In fact, Grier spent part of last summer in Mexico filming the up-coming TNT cable movie *The King of Texas.* The film is an adaptation of Shakespeare's *King Lear* and Grier appears with Patrick Stewart, Marcia Gay Harden and Lauren Holly.

Grier said he was happy to get back to drama, which is where he started his entertainment career. In 1981, Grier was nominated for a Tony for his performance as legendary baseball player Jackie Robinson in *The First.* He was one of three original cast members of *A Soldier's Story* who was chosen from the

David Alan Grier

Off-Broadway cast to appear in the acclaimed film adaptation.

Many of the Mexican film crew also had worked on the big screen version of *McHale's Navy* in which Grier played the well-meaning but naive Ensign Parker. On the former film, Grier would routinely break up the crew with jokes he told through a bullhorn and the crew was disappointed that Grier didn't repeat the daily gags on the set of *King of Texas.*

He explained to them that this film was serious and the gags wouldn't be appropriate.

"They'd say 'Why no joke?'" he said with a laugh.

"I've been trying to get back to drama for such a long time and I really relished it," he said. He added that the experience was great, even though the entire cast came down with dysentery.

All this bouncing from drama to comedy goes counter to the show business tendency to pigeonhole a performer, but Grier explains that having variety in one's career is fun and "the point of acting is to have fun."

He said he also enjoyed the freedom of the character parts he played in the recent films such as the romantic comedy *Return to Me* and the thriller *15 Minutes.*

"You don't have the pressure that you have when you carry the film," he said.

Although Grier enjoys appearing in films and on-stage, he doesn't have many pleasant memories of his television work, aside from the long-running comedy hit *In Living Color.* Grier starred in situation comedies *The Preston Episodes, Damon* and *DAG.*

"I haven't been successful [with sit-coms]. It's been one hellish battle after another," Grier admitted.

"You're being judged by people who can't tell a joke," he explained, referring to network executives. "Everything is hyper-managed."

The freedom offered by stand-up appearances is very appealing to Grier.

"You instantly get response of what you're doing," he explained.

BRETT BUTLER

2002

After years of struggle with addiction and depression, Butler began making a comeback with a recurring role in 2013 on the Charlie Sheen sit-com *Anger Management.*

***

It's difficult to interview comedian Brett Butler over the telephone. It's not because she isn't forthcoming or personable – which she is – it's because she's so quick and funny.

It's tough to take notes when you're laughing. Butler's mind raced from subject to subject, showing a sharp talent for observational comedy.

This isn't her first time performing locally, she recounted. About 17 or 18 years ago she performed here toward the beginning of her career in comedy. Butler is celebrating her 20th year as a stand-up comic.

Butler was working in a Houston diner as a wisecracking waitress and the owner of a comedy club urged her to perform on stage. Moving to New York City, she honed her stand-up act and eventually appeared on the premiere comic showcase of its day, *The Tonight Show with Johnny Carson.*

Butler came to national prominence in 1993 when she was picked to star in *Grace Under Fire*. Although the show was successful and ran 112 episodes, it came to an end due to Butler's problems with substance abuse.

Now, sober for four years and back working for the last two, Butler is performing around the country in comedy clubs and busy developing a new hour-long dramatic show for USA Network.

Her well-publicized problem is a subject from which she neither shies away nor exploits in her comedy. She says that while her life is the material for tabloid journalism, she turned down a guest-starring role on *Touched by an Angel* that was a "glistening eye survivor story."

She added, "This is a time of very little public grace."

In her new show, Butler will play an investigator for a law firm who is married to a disabled police officer. She is both star and producer and while she is very grateful for the chance to do the show, it's a lot of work. [The show never aired.]

"Honey, I would have rather done another sit-com," she said. Working in network television one experiences a syndrome she calls "eight white boys wearing Dockers" – the network executives who supervise a show.

Although other comics I've interviewed have expressed a certain level of bitterness over network execs interfering with the creative process on sitcoms, Butler has no such feelings.

"I'm always going to be 'Grace Under Fire' to some people," she explained. Her television stardom sells the tickets to her live appearances. Without missing a beat, Butler asks me if I had asked about her weight. I replied I hadn't and that gave her the chance to comment that she had stopped smoking and had gained some weight.

"I look like I've eaten [fellow comic] Caroline Rhea," she said with a laugh.

She's appalled by the Anna Nicole Smith reality show and likened it to watching someone fall down repeatedly. The switching of the two Miss North Carolinas, and what that might mean for beauty pageants also intrigued her.

Much of Butler's act is conceived on stage as she performs. "You have to work in clubs to get material," she explained. "Stand-up comedy is the only art form you have to have an audience even when practicing."

She keeps writing and changing her act so it remains fresh for returning audiences.

"I think I'm lazy about writing away from the stage," she said. She tries to remember the ad-libs, which were well received and then write them down. She added that she has another book in her rattling around. Her 1996 memoir *Knee Deep in Paradise* was a hit with both readers and reviewers.

Butler said that although she had been tempted to forego a return to show business and "go to Louisiana and have a horse ranch. I knew I'd be looking over my shoulder."

Making people laugh beckoned, though.

"I'm lucky to get another shot not just for a career, but for living. I'm functional, creative and employed."